An Excellent Little Bay

A History of the Gig Harbor Peninsula

Written by J. A. Eckrom

Published by the
Gig Harbor Peninsula Historical Society & Museum
2004

In an effort to simplify street names in the book, we have chosen to use the current names. Over time, Gig Harbor streets have gone through a variety of name changes. For example, Harborview Drive was mostly known as Front Street but was also called Burnham-Hunt County Road and also Highway 14. Soundview Drive has been known as Highway 14 and also as Gilbert-Wickersham County Road.

ISBN 0-9626048-2-8

First Edition: December 2004
Printed by Gorham Printing

Dedication

*This book is made possible through a
generous grant from the estate of*

Kathleen Watson

*in memory of her parents
John Houghton Watson and
Aimée Katherine Lowe Watson*

Society Acknowledgments

The Gig Harbor Peninsula Historical Society would like to thank the following individuals for helping in the publication of this book. Their advice, aid, knowledge, and insights were greatly appreciated throughout the writing and editing process.

The society thanks author J. A. Eckrom, whose research for this incredible work brought to life the peninsula's people and history; Linda McCowen for culling through the society's thousands of images to find photographs complementing Jerry's narrative and also for providing major assistance in finalizing the book for publication; Elizabeth Hurdle for her comments, suggestions, and editing of the book's text; Jean Robeson and Karen Burne for proofreading the early drafts; Rosemary Ross, Barbara Pearson, Jean Lyle-Roberton, and Don and Mary Ellen Sehmel for ideas and suggestions; Arveida Livingston for maintaining the society's photo cataloging system, allowing us to easily select and retrieve images for the book; museum assistant Kerri Rowan for helping with the last-minute additions; and to Museum Administrator Victoria Gehl-Blackwell for seeing this process through, including proofreading, book layout, cover design, photo selection, and editing.

Contents

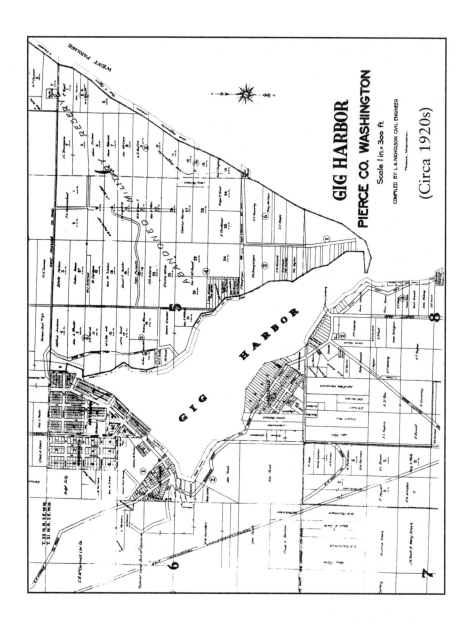

GIG HARBOR
PIERCE CO. WASHINGTON

Scale 1 in. = 300 ft.

COMPILED BY L.A. NICHOLSON CIVIL ENGINEER
Tacoma, Washington

(Circa 1920s)

Author's Acknowledgments

One of the great pleasures of this project has been meeting the many good people who contributed their time, their memories, and their talents to the telling of Gig Harbor's story.

Gig Harbor Peninsula Historical Society's former Executive Director Chris Erlich, and her successor on this project, Museum Administrator Victoria Blackwell, have been forever helpful, cheerful, and inspiring through this long process. The well-organized library and ever-changing succession of exhibits helped make this project not only possible, but downright fun.

The volunteers at the Gig Harbor Peninsula Historical Society museum are many and talented. Jean Robeson, formerly Martha Jean Insel, has been an invaluable proofreader, a remarkable source of information, and an adventurous guide. Well into her seventies, she was undaunted by swamps and huge thickets of thorny blackberries as we went in search of the remains of the home where the Watson family once lived on the hill above Gig Harbor. Linda McCowen's in-depth knowledge of the society's photograph collection was instrumental in providing the images interspersed throughout the book.

Many museums and libraries were visited in the course of the research. Tacoma Public Library's Northwest Room remains a vital source for anyone trying to write local history. Gary Reese, historical godfather to a generation of writers, recently retired, but the collection he organized and the staff he trained stand ready for whatever comes next. In addition to Mr. Reese, able assistance was provided by Bob Schuler, Brian Kamens, Glenn Storebeck, Jody Gripp, and Julie Ciccarelli.

No single source has complete back issues of *The Peninsula Gateway* and its predecessor, the *Bay Island News*. In my quest for

In the Washington State Historical Society's library in downtown Tacoma, Elaine Miller produced ledgers and correspondence from the days when Mitchell Skansie launched a fleet of fishing boats.

At the Seattle branch of the National Archive, Don Howard steered me through the murky waters of federal land sales to pinpoint many of the first property owners at Gig Harbor, Raft Island, and elsewhere.

The Washington State Archives in Olympia yielded gems and surprises, including the advent of the Gig Harbor bus service and at least a portion of Spiro Babich's arrest record for illegal fishing. He always was a defiant sort.

Randy Babich, the grandson of the legendary Spiro Babich and descendant of fishermen stretching back to founding father Sam Jerisich, took time from a busy day to help a neophyte try to understand how the fishing industry worked in the past and how it works today. As he and his crew worked to get his boat, the *Paragon*, ready for the next season in Alaska, he showed me the dock and net shed that his grandfather built in 1938 near the harbor entrance. There, laid out and explained, was equipment spanning three generations of fishing, even down to a bag of pristine cork floats, purchased by Spiro in the 1930s and overlooked until Randy cleaned out an attic corner just recently. Their size and roundness contrasted sharply with the usual battered shrunken survivors of heavy use in unforgiving seas. I work at Weyerhaeuser Company in my day job, and several of my colleagues assisted in this project. Tracey Johnson, who lives in Gig Harbor, made valuable suggestions on contacts for information. Beyond that, Tracey is unquenchably enthusiastic. In the midst of writer's block and dead-ended research, it's refreshing to turn a corner in the cafeteria and encounter someone who thinks the whole thing is exciting and wants to hear how it's going. It's a reminder that being invited to write the history of a locality is a rare privilege, and research, at its core, is downright fun.

George Sharp, a Weyerhaeuser corporate geologist, did me the favor of referring my geology questions to Kathy Troost of the University of Washington. She is enthralling in her efforts to understand

and explain why the world looks the way it does. Her direct experience with the geology of Gig Harbor, including digs in the steep bluff of Point Evans, was of immense help in making the first chapter look the way it does.

Gretchen Clauson, an executive secretary at Weyerhaeuser and resident of Horsehead Bay and Gig Harbor, contributed valuable proofreading.

No one should ever be rash enough to try and write the history of Gig Harbor without consulting the work of Gladys Para, who contributed years of fascinating historical reporting to *The Peninsula Gateway*. Likewise, no one should ever embark on the harbor's maritime heritage without studying the matchless work that Lee Makovich, Jr., local maritime historian, has done to preserve Gig Harbor's fishing history.

Among those who contributed recollections and advice were Paul and Helen Alvestad, Don Sehmel, Captain Zach the wharf rat, John Ancich, Olive Fuqua, Lee Makovich, Bert Uddenberg, Lola (Uddenberg) Kooley, Shirley (Uddenberg) Knapp, Martha Jean (Insel) Robeson, Nick Tarabochia, Leo Pierson, John Ancich, Randy Babich, Rosemary Ross, Alta Peacock, Frances (Borgen) Carlson, Jane (Shaw) Rockwell Carlson, Bud DeWalt, Adele (Larson) DeWalt, and many more. I was fortunate that my father, Alan Eckrom, was fond of Sunday drives into the hinterland from our Tacoma home. Especially after the toll was lifted from The Narrows Bridge, the Gig Harbor Peninsula was one of the many places he loved to explore, enabling a curious youngster to watch the spurt of growth that transformed a sleepy hamlet from the 1960s forward.

You never really know where vital help will come from. On the day I came out to interview as a candidate for writing this book, I discovered with a sinking feeling that I didn't know where the museum was located. Several frantic passes up and down Harborview Drive yielded no success. Time was ticking away and I was picturing a board of review closing my file with a terse, "How could this guy write a history of Gig Harbor if he can't even find our museum?" That was when an angel arrived in the form of a tall blond woman walking around the bend of the harbor walk near Donkey Creek. "Excuse me, do you know where the museum is?" I asked, and she pointed up the hill past the sewage treatment plant. The day was saved, and my destiny, at least for the ensuing four years, was sealed. Thank you, Dorothy Pryor.

My wife Sharon deserves both thanks and sympathy for cheerfully abiding endless stacks of books, papers, and files on the coffee table, living room floor, nightstand, dining room table, and pretty much any other exposed surface of our Tacoma home. For this, and for her patience and understanding while countless household chores went undone, and for being the sounding board for countless ideas and turns of phrase, Saint Sharon has my love and gratitude.

Long ago, confronting a balky soft drink vending machine, I watched my quarter repeatedly pass from the entry slot to the coin return without producing my orange drink. That was when my sister, Judy Vaver, taught me the trick of breathing heavily on the quarter. Lord knows why that works, but somehow it made the coin acceptable to the machine, and my drink was served. Many, many times that trick has served me well with coin operated copiers in the course of this project. I shudder to think how many *Peninsula Gateway* articles I might have missed without it. I recommend heavy breathing on coins to scholars everywhere.

Introduction

The mission of the Gig Harbor Peninsula Historical Society is to create opportunities to experience the heritage of the greater Gig Harbor communities. We do this by collecting, preserving, and sharing this area's history.

Since 1964, thousands of people have helped us carry out this mission by donating to the society their photographs, household items, farming and fishing implements, important documents, and a myriad of other items that were important in their lives.

Through permanent and changing museum exhibits featuring these donated artifacts and photographs, visitors young and old learn about the heritage of the harbor. History cruises along the waters of Puget Sound help invoke images of bygone days when the only form of travel was by foot, horse, or boat. Society programs and activities provide participants with a greater understanding of their community and its heritage.

Programs and exhibits are limited however, in that they can only offer a small window to the past. A book, on the other hand, deepens our understanding of our shared community heritage by providing context for our stories and individual memories. Through a generous bequest given to the society by the late Kathleen Watson, we are able to share the history of our peninsula through the pages of this book.

From pioneer hardships to a successful commercial fishing fleet to a parade celebrating one individual's trimph over nature, this narrative of the peninsula's people, places, and events brings to life the richness that created today's harbor town and surrounding areas.

Kathleen Watson understood the need to document individual and community history. She knew that the fabric of each life, when stitched together piece by piece, much like a quilt, tells the story of us all.

Through this book, we share the stories that make up our community quilt.

An Excellent Little Bay covers the history of the peninsula up to 1967, one hundred years after the first non-native settlers arrived in the harbor. Events experienced today will fill the chapters of another book tomorrow.

We hope you enjoy *An Excellent Little Bay, The History of the Gig Harbor Peninsula.*

Sincerely,

Jennifer Kilmer
Executive Director
Gig Harbor Peninsula Historical Society

Chapter 1

Twa-Wal-Kut Becomes Gig Harbor

There was a time when the harbor had no name. There was even a time when there was no harbor. On six prolonged occasions in the last 1,600,000 years, glaciers ground and scoured the earth where the harbor would one day shelter fisher's boats. Natural features were created and erased over and over again with no human witness to mark their passing. Between glacier passages, occasional layers of ash from distant volcanoes settled over the area. In cool periods near the beginning or ending of a glacial period, pine trees dotted the land. Once, an ice dam created a huge lake that drowned all the lowlands until it found an outlet far to the south.

The last of the great ice rivers, the Vashon Glacier of the continental Cordillerian Ice Sheet, smothered the land between the Cascade and Olympic Mountains for two millennia, ending about thirteen thousand years ago. It covered North America from the North Pole to a point some fifteen miles south of what is now Olympia. The future harbor site waited in frigid darkness beneath a vast sheet of ice more than two thousand feet thick. The ground itself sagged under the weight.

As the great glacier began at last to melt, rivers of chilly water surged beneath the still-formidable roof of ice, sluicing out deep channels in the helpless ground. Where the water met resistance, or where it was compelled temporarily to contest against a blocking hill, it dug deeper divots, which still dimple the land and seabed. As the earth emerged, the handiwork of the glacier was everywhere to be seen. There were hill running north and south, composed of deposits from this and past ice ages. Huge isolated blocks of ice tumbled from the main mass and dug their own graves as they melted. Geologists would call the depressions *kettles*. Many of the small lakes around the harbor, particularly those without outlets, were made in this fashion.

In random places, the glacier dropped the boulders it had wrenched from the distant mountains of Canada. They landed indiscriminately on the mud of newly exposed ground. Geologists would call them *glacial erratics*. The farmers and builders they would vex in millennia to come would offer up other names.

Released from its burden of ice, the land rose, but not sufficiently for all of it to escape the rising sea level. The glacier-carved valleys and channels filled with water and became a huge inland sea. The channel the cold river had carved beneath the ice was now a narrow place between tall bluffs of mixed sand, gravel, and silt, where the salt water surged through on the rising tide into the wide waters to the south. It was pulled back, with equal violence, into the broad north and the distant open sea when the tide fell.

On the western shore, just a bit north of this constriction, a narrow opening led into a snug little harbor. When people arrived with devices for measuring distances, they found the inner harbor to be roughly a mile long and about three-tenths of a mile across at its widest part. The shoreline totaled two and four-tenths miles when all the curves were counted. At the north end a stream emptied from a forty-seven-acre lake, some three miles up a gently sloping valley. A smaller stream contributed its might over toward the western end of the bay. It was a shallow body of water, growing shallower over thousands of years as the streams brought sediment to flatten the bottom and fill in the edges. By the time someone came to drop leaded weights on a rope, they found it not much more than six fathoms deep[1] at its deepest, with broad low-tide mudflats around its edges.

The harbor was protected on one side by a sand spit that grew over the eons, thanks to longshore currents and prevailing winds, to a length of 250 yards. This left an entrance less than two hundred feet wide and barely ten feet deep at low tide. There were hills rising up around the harbor, with terraces in places, which hinted at former lake beds from the glacial age.[2] The harbor was set in an irregularly shaped peninsula, beset with inlets and protrusions at odd angles, prone to erosion and landslides, especially around its southern extremities. In one place, on the far southwest end of the peninsula, the gradual erosion worked to build a tenuous land causeway to what had begun as an island. Geologists call such landforms *tombolos.* This former island would one day be known as Horsehead Bay.

The erosion slowed when plants took root, but present-day property owners know it has never completely stopped. A succession of plants and animals colonized the steeply rising hills above the little bay. Madrona trees especially loved the well-drained soil of the glacial outwash along the bluffs. Deer found the grazing grounds. Cougars followed the deer. Salmon found the streams, and bears and raccoons found the salmon. One day, maybe twelve thousand years ago, because everything else was there, human beings came. These Native Americans found cedar trees for the making of canoes and shelters. The sand spit and the surrounding hills provided shelter from the storms of the open waters. Above the reach of the tides, there was clear drinking water in the flowing streams. There were clams in the bay, fish in the waters, game in the woods, berries and roots in the hills. It was a good place to live.

Across the long centuries, villages must have been established and abandoned time and again. The last one, the only one to exist in the world of writing and remembrance, was on the smaller creek on the western end of the bay. The natives called this little harbor *Twa-wal-kut.* The village consisted of one longhouse roughly one hundred feet long and a half dozen other buildings about thirty feet square.[3] There was a dimly-remembered tradition among the natives that they had emigrated some time in the past from a Puyallup tribal village over on what we now know as Commencement Bay. The same hazy recollection held that some of their overflow went to establish another small village a few miles farther down the peninsula, by the bay they called Wollochet.[4]

They had their own history, their own mythology. Then, as now, young children asked endless questions about why things were the way they were. When they asked about the porpoises cavorting in open waters beyond the sand spit, the elders would tell them of the three young boys, much like themselves, who left the village in their canoes one day long ago. A whirlpool threw them into the swift currents near the point of the spit, beside the narrow chute of rushing water. This was a cautionary tale about the need for reasonable precautions in canoeing, but the elders tempered the tragedy with magic. Doquebulth the changer transformed the boys into porpoises, and they continued forever after to leap and slash across the waters they had known as children. Their mother grieved sorely for her sons. Day after day she sat on the beach, staring out toward the place where they were lost to her forever, until Doquebulth changed her into an ageless rock. Later visitors, blind to the magic of this lost world, saw only another glacial erratic boulder on the beach.[5]

The little village slumbered on, unaware of sweeping events in the lands beyond its view. It was inevitable that the world of maps and encyclopedias would one day find its way even here. White-skinned traders and explorers had been cruising up and down the outer ocean coast for a generation, and in 1792 one of their ships finally sailed in through the Strait of Juan de Fuca and down through the islands and bays of the upper sound. A party of this strange band struck out in a small boat, away from their great ship.

Puget Sound Native Americans come ashore to make a camp.

16

For a week in May of 1792, Lieutenant Peter Puget and his party of British explorers from the Vancouver Expedition made their way along the western shore. They rode the swift current through the narrow place with the steep bluffs, missing the little harbor. They swung around the south end of the peninsula and up into long, narrow Wollochet Bay. Some later said the name meant "cut throat," in memory of a young man who killed himself there when denied the hand in marriage of the woman he loved. Most held that it meant "squirting clams."

There were clam diggers on the shore when the boat slipped into the long narrow bay, but they fled to the woods with their gatherings at the first sight of these strange intruders. One old woman, perhaps too ancient to run, remained to meet them. She sat by her baskets of supplies and piles of equipment. "The former consisted chiefly of Clams," recalled a naturalist with the exploring party, "some of which were dried and smoked and strung up for the convenience of carrying them about their Necks, but a great number of them were still fresh in the shell."[6] When it became clear that the strangers meant the old woman no harm, some of the natives came back and traded clams for buttons, beads, and bits of copper.

Native canoes shadowed the explorers through much of their journey, and it was hereabouts that Puget made the acquaintance of two naked canoe parties. "In their Persons these People are slenderly made," Puget wrote. "They wear their Hair long, which is quite Black and exceeding Dirty. Both Nose and Ears are perforated, to which were affixed Copper Ornaments and Beads."[7]

A lone Puget Sound Indian glides through the water. Tall ships can be seen in the background.

At the end of a week, Lieutenant Puget was back aboard Captain George Vancouver's ship *Discovery,* prepared to sail north. The waters of the inland sea would see them no more, but the broad outlines of the shores were charted. The long island whose southern tip terminated just a few miles north of the harbor was fixed on charts as Vashon Island, named for James Vashon, a captain friend of Vancouver's. The big snowy mountain looming over the far southeastern horizon beyond the harbor entrance was identified as Mount Rainier, after another of Vancouver's naval friends. The narrow place with the swift current was on the chart now, and so was the long wooded point that formed its eastern shore, both without names. The whole of the southern reach was labeled Puget Sound, but the ink of the charts was hardly dry before that name began seeping up through the narrow place to engulf the entire expanse of the great inland sea.

Soon enough, Vancouver and his men were gone and life returned to normal. So far as we know, for a very long time the wider world knew these places only as lines on a map. A lonely fur-trading ship or two may have nosed down that way, but no record survives. In late 1824 James McMillan and John Work brought a small party of Hudson's Bay Company men up from the south. They camped for one night near a bay on the opposite shore southeast of the harbor, and for another night on Vashon Island to the north, but they were just passing through and soon vanished over the northern horizon.

Not until 1833 did men from the outside world come to stay. They erected a fortified trading post near the southeast shore of Puget Sound, calling it Fort Nisqually, after their best pronunciation of the river and tribe of the same name. They were only about fifteen straight-line miles from *Twa-wal-kut*. Natives from a hundred miles around came to trade, and it is hard to imagine that no one from *Twa-wal-kut* joined the crowd to see what these strange people had to offer. Fort Nisqually was hungry for furs, so perhaps the streams behind the harbor began to hold fewer river otters; perhaps the smoky cedar plank lodges boasted a few more steel axes or strings of beads.

The Hudson's Bay people passed by many times, bound to or from their sister forts to the north and south. Supply ships came and went. Even a steamship, the *Beaver*, had appeared by 1835. Someone, sometime, might have ventured into the little harbor, but once again they left no record. A strong tradition persists that Hudson's Bay men built cabins near what is now known as Rosedale, on the peninsula's western shore.[8] Nothing in the surviving records of the Hudson's Bay Company confirms this.

Other explanations are possible. The *Beaver* was a voracious consumer of wood to fire her boilers, and wood-cutting parties were often set ashore to produce a new supply. If one spot became a frequent timber-felling ground, it is possible that the woodcutters erected a temporary cabin for their own convenience. Another possibility is that discharged employees of the Honorable Company might have chosen to settle there and build homes. If they later abandoned those homes without staking land claims, the event might easily have drifted out of official records, while remaining in human memory. Lastly, records show that census takers found Hawaiian Islanders living in proximity to the Indians on the peninsula. The Hudson's Bay Company had many Hawaiian employees, and it could be that some of the Hawaiians were retired or discharged Hudson's Bay men.

At long last, another group of naval explorers appeared. These were Americans, known to history as the Wilkes Expedition, after their quarrelsome and gifted commander, Lieutenant Charles Wilkes. It was

the first great naval exploring expedition sent out by the United States government. They had already seen the Antarctic ice packs, the volcanoes of Hawaii, and the exotic islands of the South Pacific. They had sailed a total of eighty-seven thousand miles over many seas when in May 1841 they ventured a few miles more.

Their legacy to Puget Sound was a vast

Lieutenant Charles Wilkes

19

string of names. The wide bay where they began a small boat survey became Commencement Bay. They put a name at last on the narrow place where the tide rushed through between tall bluffs. They called it simply The Narrows, as if no other constricted passage existed anywhere on earth. The long wooded point on the eastern shore became Point Defiance, with the thought that a few big guns on its high bluff could bid defiance to any navy in the world. The rounded point at the end of the peninsula south of the harbor and east of Wollochet became Point Fosdick, for an expedition gunner's mate on Wilkes' ship, the USS *Vincennes*. Daniel Green, another gunner's mate, was immortalized with the name Green Point on the outer edge of an odd protrusion of land that folds back to make a sheltered bay at the southwest end of the peninsula.

Wilkes' charts called the bay itself Hukum Cove. Someone endowed with powerful imagination, or a powerful love of horses, later looked at its shape and made it Horsehead Bay forever after. The much wider body of water farther to the west took the name Carr Inlet from Overton Carr, the *Vincennes'* executive officer. A small island hugging the eastern shore of the Carr Inlet got the name Allshouse Island, in honor of a marine private who died in an accident the following October. The island's name was as ill-fated as the man it honored, and we know it today as Raft Island. Vanderford's Harbor, named for a pilot in the crew, eventually slipped back to the name Wollochet Bay, where clams still squirted.

The Wilkes group was observant and well-equipped. They had the time to be much more thorough than Vancouver's men had been in their brief foray. The secluded harbor behind the long sand spit could not escape their notice forever. The moment of discovery came on May 15, 1841, when Midshipman Joseph Sanford noted in his journal "a pretty little bay that is concealed from the Sound." Venturing over in a longboat, he rounded the long sand spit and found "the passage is about 10 or 15 yards wide and it gradually widenings [*sic*] until it forms a circular basin." The inhabitants must have been absent or in hiding, for he added the line, "Saw no natives today."

When he heard about the minor discovery, Lieutenant George Sinclair set out in the captain's gig, a light narrow boat built for speed, to have a look for himself. He pronounced it "an excellent little bay." Natives in or near the bay must have been watching him as well, for he added, "A number of canoes came off from which we procured an abundance of salmon." Their ship *Porpoise*, under the command of Lieutenant Cadwallader Ringgold, anchored near the western shore outside the harbor, and Sinclair went ashore again on the seventeenth to find some natives cooking on the beach. "They cook their salmon by sticking sticks into it and letting it hang over the fire," he noted, "and by way of seasoning they take up their blankets and scratch their backsides over it." It was a curious beginning for the salmon bakes and hospitality which would one day make the area famous.

That was all they had to say about the little harbor, and it was a while before they gave it a name. Puget Sound is dotted with names of Wilkes Expedition members, and this harbor could easily have been given one of them. Sanford had found it, but he was a midshipman without much pull. Or possibly his name was too close to that of Quartermaster Thomas Sandford, who already had a point up north named for him. Sinclair had ventured in, but he had a whole inlet named for him to the north. Their commander, Lieutenant Ringgold, gave his name to a channel in the San Juan Islands. Someone, perhaps in a bit of whimsy, decided to name the harbor for the boat that crossed its waters. On the maps of the world, it became Gig Harbor.[9]

Presently the explorers were gone, and once again the only non-natives were the fur traders and farmers of Fort Nisqually. All was back to normal for the inhabitants of the little harbor, who were unmindful that *Twa-wal-kut* was now Gig Harbor. Gathering clams, hunting deer, following the rhythms of a hunter-gatherer life, they knew and cared nothing for the doings of white men in cities and government halls beyond their sight and their imaginings. What could they know of the treaty of 1846, which made this American territory and not British? Did they know or care in 1853 that they were now part of Pierce County, Washington Territory?

One thing they did learn in those years was the same lesson each village and tribe would learn across the Americas – wherever a few whites appeared, more would inevitably follow. The whites were forming villages to the north and south by now. Steilacoom, settled in 1850 and incorporated in 1854, sat on the eastern shore of the south sound, a few miles north of Fort Nisqually,[10] and became the Pierce County seat. Olympia, down near the very southern end of Puget Sound, became the territorial capital.

Sometime in 1867, no one remembers the day or month, three men in a rowboat made their way down from British Columbia. They passed the growing town of Seattle and rowed past Commencement Bay, where a rude collection of settlers' cabins was not yet referred to as Tacoma. The names of the three boatmen were Samuel Jerisich, John Farrugut (or Farrago or Farrague), and Peter Goldsmith. Once past Commencement Bay and the tip of Point Defiance, they turned their boat down toward The Narrows and into Gig Harbor. Some said later that a storm had chased them, or that they sought shelter for the night. However it happened, whether they came by chance or design, they decided to stay.

Samuel Jerisich, who turned thirty-four that November, had come a long way from his birthplace in Kotor, an ancient walled city on the Adriatic Sea. It had belonged to the Illyrians, the Romans, the Medieval Serbs, the Hungarians, the Venetians, and the French.[11] In Jerisich's time it was Austrian, and that was what census takers would later write on their forms when they listed his nationality. In our time, the

The first Slavonian fishermen at the mouth of Gig Harbor, 1889. Includes Sam Jerisich, Peter Skansie, and John Jerisich

land is once again known as Montenegro, a loosely affiliated portion of Yugoslavia. It was a place calculated to turn out fishermen and sailors, and Jerisich was among them. By the time he came to Puget Sound, he had been three times around Cape Horn and had spent time in San Francisco.

Jerisich made his way back to British Columbia to retrieve his wife, Anna. She was a Canadian Indian woman, ten years his junior. Anna brought Caroline, her young daughter. Both husband and wife were illiterate, so nothing of their lives survives in their own words, but by all appearances they were savvy and tenacious. Long after Goldsmith and Farrugut (or even any memory of how to spell the latter's name) were forgotten, the name Jerisich would reside on a city dock, and people would remember Samuel and Anna as the first settlers of Gig Harbor.

The harbor and its oddly shaped peninsula had been discovered and named. Now, in the eyes of history, it had been settled.

An early photograph of Gig Harbor from the hill at the head of the bay. East Gig Harbor homes are seen at left. Millville is across the bay to the right.

Sand spit at the entrance of the harbor

23

Chapter 2

The Coming of the Slavonians

For generation on generation, salmon by the thousands carried the fate of Gig Harbor on their scaly backs. They spelled the difference between poverty and prosperity, between feast and famine. No salmon, no Indian village. No salmon, no Sam Jerisich.

As the prime movers in bringing humans to Gig Harbor, the salmon are well deserving of a place in its history. The whole of their lives is charged with peril. Even the act of conception plays out within a desperately short window of time. The male and female salmon pair up in a stream with a briskly flowing current and dig a nest, called a *redd*, in the gravelly bottom with the agitating action of their bodies. The redd can be as much as a foot deep, and in it they jointly release their eggs and sperm (called *milt* in the jargon of ichthyologists). Then every second becomes precious. After two minutes, the sperm die; after four minutes the eggs become so hard that no sperm can penetrate their outer membranes. Even once fertilized, the eggs face danger. Too much sun or too little shade can raise the water temperature fatally high. Too much water will scour the eggs out of their nests before they can hatch. Too little water will leave them stranded to bleach and dry in the hardening mud.

In her final act of motherhood, the female continues to agitate the redd with her increasingly frayed and battered tail, burying the eggs under a protective layer of sand and gravel. The salmon eggs' mortality rate is cruelly high. However, some odds work in their favor, making it likely that at least a few will survive. Because the female salmon can lay up to five thousand eggs, fifty new salmon result if just one in a hundred survives.

The adult salmon stop eating when they enter the river to spawn, and by the time the hatchlings emerge from the redds some two months later, their parents are long dead. The young orphans emerge into the world with amber sacks suspended from their stomachs. These yolk sacks provide a few days' worth of survival rations, while the salmon gain strength and master the intricacies of catching bugs and worms. They keep to the shallows at first, away from larger predatory fish, trusting the eddies and currents to bring them bits of food. Diving ducks, cormorants, and squawfish find some, but others survive.

By fall the young salmon are four to six inches long and their cumbersome yolk sacks are dim memories. Their bodies are stream-lined and ready for the next great challenge. Something, perhaps the rising water with its cargo of silt launched by the fall rains, triggers a new impulse. Moving to the center of the channel, the salmon shoot headlong out of the only world they have ever known. They become anadromous, spending part of their life in fresh water and part in saltwater. The saltwater phase may last up to four years, and carry them far from home.

Some salmon remain in Puget Sound, while others venture as far south as California. Most turn north toward British Columbia and Alaska, growing strong and fat on a diet of shrimp, sand fleas, crabs, herring, and squid. At the end of what can be a ten-thousand-mile odyssey, a mysterious impulse we call instinct tells them it is time to return home. With astounding precision, the salmon manage to find their way back across the vast ocean and across the years to the same small stream where their lives began.

Many who set out never return. Out on the open ocean, seals, sea lions, porpoises, and sea otters wait to gnash and shake and devour them in their hungry jaws. Packs of killer whales, swift and merciless, dart in to swallow them whole. Until recent decades, bears, cougars, and coyotes would line the banks to feed on those who made it back to their natal stream. Even without those predators, hazards remain. The two main streams feeding into Gig Harbor, Crescent Creek and Donkey Creek, are shorter and less challenging than many others, but the exertion of fighting their way upstream is still taxing. Some salmon weaken and die before they can complete their journey, leaving their carcasses to be picked apart by scavenging eagles. Still, enough get through to set the endless cycle in motion once again.

When humans entered the equation, the salmon became a prime target in yet another food chain. The first salmon of the season was an object of hope, pride, and ceremony. In the complex mythology by which the Indians explained the world around them, the salmon lived in villages much like their own, only smaller and hidden beneath the sea. They treated the first salmon as an emissary of his village. The flesh was opened like a book for roasting, and everyone got a chance to sample and praise the welcomed visitor. They removed the head and backbone in one piece and returned it to the water, where it could return to its own village and tell its brethren of the good treatment it received.

When the big runs of salmon came later in the season, ceremony gave way to spears, traps, and nets. In narrow places like the streams of Gig Harbor and Wollochet Bay, fishermen could build weirs, which were fences of wood and cedar boards able to trap dozens or hundreds of fish at once. This catch fed more than just the hunger of the day. Survival might hinge on taking and preserving enough salmon to feed the village through the winter. The sight and smell of long rows of salmon drying on racks over smoky fires was a defining scene of Puget Sound Indian village life.

The first white settlers fit well into this long tradition; they were fishermen. And although there were still plenty of things about this new race that baffled the Indians, they could relate to the concept of fishing for a living. The way the white people went about it was a little different, to be sure. Their ceremonies were simpler, for one thing. At most, they might offer a simple prayer to Saint Joseph, patron of fishermen, then fish until their boats were full or their strength was spent.

Once when someone asked a pioneer about the early days around Gig Harbor, he got back the answer, "You either rowed or stayed home." That summed things up pretty well. No roads connected the peninsula with anywhere else at the end of the 1860s. Except for a few deer trails and a sketchy Indian footpath or two, there was nothing but the endless beach for a person on foot to follow. As the crow flew, the nearest store was in Steilacoom. By land, this was fifty-some miles and innumerable hardships away. By water, it was an infinitely quicker and easier seven miles across – a day trip in decent weather for any good boatman.

Sam and his partners must have made the trip many times. How else could they have collected nine signatures from citizens of Steilacoom in 1889, swearing that Samuel Jerisich and John "Farrague" had "resided on land in what is known as Gig Harbor since the year 1869"? Among the signers was merchant E. R. Rogers, whose home, now a popular restaurant, still looks up The Narrows toward Gig Harbor as this book goes to press.

However well-known they were in life, the trails of these pioneers are dim in our own time. Even first settlers will come up short in a town history when the sum total of that town's records amounts to a few scratchy X marks on a handful of legal documents. Yet the sketchy documents do let us know that the founders and their descendants remained in the Gig Harbor area across the years. On September 8, 1877, John "Farragut" was recorded as conveying title to a piece of property[12] to Sam Jerisich and other parties. They were all still there

in 1880 when Brook White came through conducting the Federal census. He met fifty-four-year-old John "Ferago," a bachelor fisherman, and recorded him as having been born in Spain, as were his parents. The census recorded that Peter Goldsmith, a fifty-one-year-old fisherman, came from Slavonia, as did his twenty-year-old wife, Millie. Their two-year-old son Joseph was listed as having been born in Washington Territory.

Samuel Jerisich

27

Ages and nationalities are not always to be trusted in these accounts. The 1877 census-taker posted Sam Jerisich as a fifty-year-old Slavonian fisherman, rightly enough, but listed Anna inaccurately as a twenty-six-year-old Slavonian. To compound impossibilities, the census-taker described Anna's daughter, Caroline, as a native Slavonian as well. The civil servant even described her as ten years old, when she would have indignantly insisted that she was all of thirteen.

In July 1883, when Caroline Jerisich married, the names John "Fargo" and John Novak appeared on the wedding certificate as witnesses. The familiar names kept coming up, and so did the mysteries. In April 1886, Peter Goldsmith, referred to as "a single man," appeared in a warranty deed recording the sale of land to Alfred Burnham. In August 1887, John "Farrague" and the Jerisichs lent their names to a quit claim deed conveying twelve acres to Alfred Burnham. On October 12, 1895, John Farrague (the spelling becoming standardized at last) sold his interest in his boats, building, seine nets, and fishing equipment to Samuel Jerisich for four hundred dollars in money and labor. This had the sound of a man putting his affairs in order, and was followed all too soon by the Spaniard's last and most enduring record, a foot-high, four-inch-thick block of dark granite in the newly created Artondale Cemetery.

The stone bears a terse message and a final spelling for eternity, "John Farragut, 1825 – 1895, At Rest."[13] There were a couple of newspapers across The Narrows in Tacoma by then, but there was no obituary. We are left to wonder if anyone back in Spain ever knew that one of her native sons in a faraway land had slipped into the earth and out of history.

Peter Goldsmith showed up one last time in the 1900 census, sharing space by then with many another citizen of the Gig Harbor area. He told the census taker that he was sixty-seven years old, able to read, write, and speak English. He was a widower, and the space for occupation was left blank, suggesting that his days as a commercial fisherman were over. What had happened to Millie and the son listed as Joseph in the 1880 census? The 1900 census showed a son named

Peter, a day laborer born in June 1882. The only clue to the lost Millie was Peter Junior's statement that his mother was born in British Columbia. From that point, the Goldsmith trail grew cold.

Posterity has been kinder to Sam and Anna Jerisich. For one thing, they lived a very long time. For another, Sam got his name in the paper a few times in his old age. Most importantly, they produced eight children. Only half of them outlived their father, and only three survived to bury their ancient mother, but they left many descendants to carry the memory of the founding family forward. They were:

> Caroline Jerisich (later Dorotich), born March 12, 1867,
>   died August 30, 1937
> John J. Jerisich, born July 20, 1872, died June 24, 1935
> Michael Jerisich, born February 11, 1875,
>   died February 11, 1904
> Sam Jerisich Jr., born September 2, 1877,
>   died April 22, 1904
> Melissa Jerisich (later Skansie), born May 12, 1879,
>   died February 6, 1902
> Catherine Jerisich (later Sellen), May 24, 1881,
>   died May 23, 1902
> Julia Jerisich (later Van Waters), born 1883, died 1961
> Mary E. Jerisich, born March 15, 1890,
>   died February 25, 1909

Samuel Jerisich family – (rear, l-r) Michael, John, Sam Jr., Peter Skansie (front, l-r) Katherine, Julia, Anna, Sam Sr., Melissa Jerisich Skansie with daughter Julia, Mary. Caroline is not present.

For as long as they remained, and for as long as they were able, Jerisich, Goldsmith and Farrague were fishermen. Friendship may have held them together; necessity certainly did. They fished more with nets than hooks, and the handling of nets was beastly hard work. Purse seining was their chosen method: they floated the top of a huge net with cork or wooden floats, burdened the bottom with weights, drew it in a circle to entrap the fish, and gradually drew it shut like a clutch purse. It took at least two rowboats to manage the net, and all the strength two or three fishermen could muster to haul the nets and their harvest of fish out of the water. In later years a few fishermen developed the trick of drawing the nets ashore with horses.

Fishermen might work doubly hard when the fall salmon were running, but they pursued fish of one sort or another all year long. The cold depths of Puget Sound teemed with life. There were mottled gray ling cod, red snapper, and flounder. Wolf eels lurked in the crevices of rocky ledges. Hooks and nets might bring up red Irish lords, grunt sculpins, and cabezons, the spiny orange-tinted denizens of rocky bottoms and shallow waters. Cabezons could weigh up to twenty-five pounds and made good eating, except for their poisonous eggs. Halibut, having a weakness for hooks baited with salmon parts, was a rarity in southern Puget Sound, but could be plentiful in the outer parts of the Strait of Juan de Fuca.

Biologists in recent years have totaled up 211 species of fish in 58 families beneath the waters of western Washington.[14] As late as 1913,

Purse seining

30

Gig Harbor fisherman Frank Novak captured headlines when he landed a rare red-and-yellow-striped, white-throated, pointy-headed little fish that the paper called a kelp.[15]

The fishermen at the mid-century sold their catch in Steilacoom and Olympia, gradually expanding their reach with time as populations filled in the gaps along Puget Sound, and as canneries and salteries came into being. Since it was not always possible to get the fish fresh to market, Sam Jerisich built a smokehouse to preserve his catch for later sale.

Until the late nineteenth century, fishermen tended to throw one resident of the deep back in disgust. The fish in question was a twenty-pound shark, the *squalus acanthias*, better known as the dogfish. Swift, vicious, abundant, long-lived, and opportunistic, the dogfish is the coyote of the undersea world. It can reach two to four feet in length and carries a generous supply of oil in its body.

Yet its oil proved its undoing as the 1870s dawned. A new market for dogfish oil opened up, and Gig Harbor got an early piece of the action. In April 1871 the *Washington Standard* of Olympia told its readers, "Col. B. S. Pardee is about to engage in an enterprise which is new to this country, but which has been prosecuted with great profit on Cape Cod and Long Island Sound. It is the reduction of fish to oil, and he has selected Gig Harbor as the place to establish business. The Oregon Iron Works manufacture the machinery, consisting of a sheet-iron 'digester,' forty inches in diameter by eight feet in length, with a heater of thirty inches long. The supply of fish is abundant and easily procured."[16]

Gill netter

The white settlers used dogfish oil primarily to keep the machinery of Puget Sound's many sawmills lubricated and running smoothly. It was also good for tanning the leather drive belts and fueling lamps for night work. Those who labored beneath its glow often pronounced it superior to whale oil. One doctor even recommended it as an effective medicine for pulmonary afflictions.[17] These multiple uses demanded a lot of oil, so Sam Jerisich built the first dock on Gig Harbor, near the park that now bears his name, partially to handle the dogfish oil trade. It would be pleasing to know more about the industry and the part our fishermen played in it, but all the *Standard* had to say in follow-up at the end of April 1871 was, "The machinery for the fish oil establishment at Gig Harbor has reached its destination."[18]

Sam and his neighbors had a few things to worry about besides fish as the years went by. There were invisible lines running through the harbor. Some were benign. For instance, sailors knew that the entrance to Gig Harbor sat at 47 degrees, 19 minutes and 6 seconds north latitude, and 122 degrees, 34 minutes west longitude. It was good information for nautical charts, but nothing to lose sleep over inside the harbor.

The invisible lines that came to matter in a vital way marked townships, ranges, and sections. Many of us have a mental picture of the American West being settled by grizzled pioneers who surmounted a hill, viewed a valley, and proclaimed something on the order of, "This is where I will build my home and domesticate the wilderness." It could work that way, but at some point the pioneer was going to have to know exactly where he was, and register his location according to exacting, legally prescribed conditions. Anyone who wanted to buy or sell land needed to know that the peninsula sat mostly in Township 21 North and Range 2 East of the Willamette Meridian.

This was a system the United States government had devised early in its existence, in an effort to bring order to the settlement of its vast western lands. A township was thirty-six square miles, and within its boundaries were thirty-six numbered divisions called sections. Each section was one square mile, or 640 acres. Sections thirty-six and sixteen were set aside as public school land, but the rest were generally open for settlement.

The government owned most of the land out West at this time. In the early 1850s, with the intention of speeding settlement, it had granted parcels of 320 or 160 acres to settlers who occupied and farmed the land for at least four years. That program, known as the Donation Land Law, ended in 1855 without any takers in the Gig Harbor area. By the time Sam Jerisich and his partners arrived, the government was selling the land under the provisions of the 1862 Homestead Act. The going price was generally $1.25 per acre, and the sales were recorded in reference to particular quarter sections within the larger section. Thus the sand spit at the entrance to Gig Harbor could be identified precisely as the 4th quarter of Section 5 of Township 21, Range 2 East. That was where Sam and Anna Jerisich built their home.

The trouble was, when Sam rowed over to the land office in Olympia to file formal claim to the land, he learned that the government had other plans for this and other sections of the peninsula. Much of the area around Gig Harbor was officially military property, even if it never saw a soldier or a sailor. This state of affairs came about as a result of a proposal made to Congress in March 1864. The proposal shaped other important aspects of the region's life, as it also authorized a military road from Fort Steilacoom to Fort Bellingham, a railroad from Wallula to Walla Walla, a road from Lewiston to the Bitteroot Valley, and a mail steamer from San Francisco to Port Townsend.

In September 1866, President Andrew Johnson and Secretary of War Edwin M. Stanton finally signed the decree, setting aside some 1,200 acres around the harbor as a military reservation, along with big sections of Point Defiance, Vashon Island, and sundry other points around Puget Sound. By all signs, the government was finally paying heed to Captain Wilkes' 1841 pronouncement that fortifications on the bluffs around The Narrows could bid defiance to any navy. Evidently someone had fuzzy notions of creating a circle of fire around the constricted passage outside Gig Harbor.

Such a scheme was later given solid form on a massive scale at

Forts Worden, Flagler, and Casey, up north at the entrance to Puget Sound. The fortifications around Gig Harbor never materialized, but the undeveloped reservation lands remained officially closed to settlement, and one way or another this technicality remained a thorn in Sam Jerisich's side until almost the end of his life.

Eventually the Jerisichs gave up their struggle to homestead near the mouth of the harbor. They moved farther down the inner harbor, choosing a spot on the western shore and building homes with lumber boated up from a mill in Olympia. The Jerisich home eventually grew to seven rooms. It was a comfortable place, but Sam had to go where the fish were, and sometimes that was a long way from home. It could be lonely there for the wife of a fisherman. Many times Anna watched her husband set out on journeys that took him ever farther away on seas that might turn frightfully stormy before he returned.

Sam and his partners often camped on distant shores, leaving Anna to her own resources. When wildcats and bears nosed too close to their home, she frightened them away by beating on a tin pan with a stick. She was industrious, planting and tending a garden, mending fishing nets, cutting wood, dressing deer and bear, and making tallow candles from bear grease or mutton fat bought from the sheep flocks at Fort Nisqually. When wild berries were in season, she picked them for the family, drying the surplus for use through the winter. Living among fishermen, she was not above her own sly little fish stories. In her old age, she was fond of telling how she could walk out to the edge of the sand spit, dip a pail in the water, and bring home enough herring, trout, or smelt for dinner.[19]

As time went on, the Jerisichs gained a few more neighbors. In those days, if they were not called Austrians, most people from Sam's part of the world were known as Slavonians. (That included settlers from the coastal region of Dalmatia and a series of islands in what is now Croatia.) Word must have spread that there were Slavonians living in Gig Harbor, because the first new settlers to appear were named Guisippi Dorotich, John Novakovich, and John Jurich.

Things had only worsened along the Dalmatian coast since the day Sam Jerisich left. Fish had grown scarce in the Adriatic, and with their outmoded boats and equipment, the Dalmatians were hard-pressed to compete with their more prosperous neighbors. The region's vast expanse of limestone supported too many people and too little soil, so fishing and farming were not options for everyone. Wine was one of the viable industries, but in the 1880s an insect plague ravaged the vineyards. Add a backward economy, low wages, and an oppressive Austro-Hungarian government, and there was a formula calculated to send America and Gig Harbor a steady supply of new settlers with names ending in "ich,"[20] which is simply a patronymic suffix meaning "son of." To many of those outside the Slavonian community, they became known as the *ich* people.

Brac was one of Dalmatia's big islands, the third largest in the Adriatic Sea. Many centuries ago, gleaming white marble had been quarried from its warm pebbly beaches and exported to be fashioned into the sculptures of ancient Rome. In the harder times of the nineteenth century, the area was exporting its people. Along about 1878, two of them arrived on the shores of Gig Harbor bearing the names Dorotich and Novakovich. Over time Guisippi Americanized into Joe Dorotich, and John Novakovich shortened his name to Novak. These were the names which would appear again and again in the history of Gig Harbor.

In a strange new land with an unknown language and vast dark

Nick and Clementine Dorotich Novakovich on the front porch of their home on Harborview Drive.

forests that stretched to infinity, there was a certain comfort in living among people who spoke the language of the old country. They shared a liking for foods cooked in olive oil, followed the Roman Catholic faith, celebrated the Feast of the Three Kings every January, and missed the *Tamburzita* music of their native land.

John Novak came to Gig Harbor by way of Canada. In 1882 he met Zepina Josephine Cosgrove, the Seattle-born daughter of an Irish sailor father and a Puyallup Indian mother. The Puyallups knew her as Cheoka, the whites as Josephine. She was unhappy with the marriage her father was trying to arrange for her. Novak, a friend of her father's, offered his own hand in marriage instead.[21] Born in 1847, he was more than twenty years her senior. They were married several times over the years, by a Puyallup chief, a justice of the peace, and a priest of the Catholic Church. Perhaps their approach merits study by other couples, since the two of them remained together long enough to celebrate their golden wedding anniversary at the Silvery Glide.[22]

Despite the influx of new settlers, the majority of the population

Josephine Cosgrove Novak and John Novak, early Gig Harbor pioneers. The couple raised twelve children.

Frank Novak, left, an unknown boy, and Lukie Kimball on Harborview Drive in front of the Novak store. Joe Dorotich's home is in the background.

in the country around Gig Harbor and Wollochet Bay were Native American. The Indians around Gig Harbor seem to have identified themselves largely with the Puyallup Tribe and their numbers rose and fell with the seasons. Although most of the Indians on Puget Sound had long since moved onto officially recognized reservations, there were a few areas, Gig Harbor being one, where there was little population pressure to dislodge them from their original homes.

In 1879 a census of what was referred to as the Gig Harbor Band found forty-six men, women, and children.[23] A year later, the federal census taker trekked through the bays and islands of western Pierce County and found two Indians whom he identified by name. One was Chehalis Jim, with five children and a wife, whom the census taker called a *squaw*, in the unabashed racism of the times. George Washington, next on the list, had a wife and four children. The census finished out with the statement, "46 other Indians and 5 Sandwich Islanders (native Hawaiians) whose names could not be ascertained all living in temporary shacks and fishing for a living. Altogether 64 persons unable to speak English."

Individuals are largely lost in the irrevocable oblivion of unrecorded history, but occasionally a name and the glimmer of a story surface in some crumbling documents. In 1917 Maria Kautz, married to the Indian son of an American army officer, made a claim for a land allotment. She stated that she was born in June 1855, the daughter of a white father and "a full-blood Indian woman named Ach-ki-de-blo, who died about thirteen years ago; that the father of Ach-ki-de-blo was Wow-ti-ser, a full blood Puyallup Indian, and her mother was To-qui-a-litsa, a full blood Indian, being part D'Wamish and part Skobibish (Gig Harbor) blood."

In June 1917, a man named Mark Bridges stated that he had been married to a Mary Squallie since 1912, adding, "Her father is Dave Squallie, a full-blood Indian, still living; her mother is Annie Squallie, a full-blood Indian, still living. Both are now living at Welachet [Wollochet] Bay, Pierce County, Washington. Both belong to the Puyallup Tribe and were allotted lands with that tribe."

Later that month David Squally, himself, was heard from. The rendering of names was a tricky matter in preliterate days, and Squallie could easily morph into Squally. He said he was born on May 1, 1849, where the town of Ruston now stands, adding, "My mother was called Jane, her Indian name was not known to us. She was born in the Puyallup Valley, and died at Wollachet Bay on December 25, 1915." He said of his wife, Annie, whose Indian name was Coh-bech-ud:

> We married by Indian custom – during about 1880 and have born to us eleven children, of which six are now living.
>
> I have settled on about (8) eight acres of land on Wollochet Bay, that I have asked to home-sted [sic] on, it was formerly Military Reserve, and was just recently thrown open to home-stead entry. I have no title to this property, I owned a small tract of four and a half acres at where I have my home on Wollachet Bay. I was allotted 80 acres of land in the Puyallup Reservation, which I sold about twenty eight years ago...
>
> I am a fisherman and am also farming on my small tact [sic] of land at where we make our home near the mouth of Wollachet Bay. I ask allotments for all of our children who have not been enrolled.[24]

Annie Squally weaving one of her many prized baskets.

38

Traces of the area's long Native American history lingered on for years. In the spring of 1904, while digging out a stump on his Wollochet Bay ranch, Arda Hunt came upon an Indian grave beneath its roots. Since he estimated the tree to be three hundred years old, the body had to be at least that old.

The Goodman children, who later played such a prominent role in Gig Harbor, had an even more personal encounter with the peninsula's Native American history. Early in their Gig Harbor days, they encountered an Indian burial site about a quarter mile back from the sand spit. They collected the beads they found adorning the graves and headed for home. From this point forward, each child remembered the story differently. They all agreed that someone made them take the beads back to their rightful owners. But one version claims that Lucy's pangs of conscience turned them around before they got home, while another insists that parental prodding set them back on the path to righteousness and the burial ground.

The Indians remained a living presence in Gig Harbor, Wollochet Bay, and other points until well into the twentieth century. But change was coming, both for them and for the white settlers just beginning to dot the shores and strike off into the interior.

Chapter 3

A Growing Sense of Community

There are milestones in the evolution of a community – first school, first post office, first store, first church – actions which proclaim, "This is not a place where we are passing through. We aim to stay here, make a living, and raise our families." The order of progression gets shuffled different ways in different places, and for the Gig Harbor peninsula, the post office came first. Mail had been passing through The Narrows for a long time, to be sure. The Hudson's Bay Company ships carried company correspondence and letters from home to Fort Nisqually as early as 1833. Olympia, down at the foot of Puget Sound, had a U.S. Government post office as early as 1850, in the days when letters were still postmarked *Olympia O. T.,* for Oregon Territory. By the 1870s, post offices in Washington Territory were popping up like young alder trees. Pierce County alone had hung out sixteen post office signs by the time the area west of The Narrows got its turn.

In early 1878 the two post offices closest to the peninsula were at Steilacoom and at the new and growing city of Tacoma, around Point Defiance on Commencement Bay. In either direction, it was a long way to go to pick up or mail a letter. Then, after May 13, 1878, there was a post office operating at the head of Wollochet Bay, in the home of a battle-scarred Civil War veteran named Miles Hunt. The post office helped people feel connected to their government and to the wider world. It offered a way to reach loved ones in faraway places, and it could even supply newspapers, some of them barely a week or two old. Because there was no rural delivery in those days, everyone who wanted to send or receive a letter had to go to the post office, and the Hunt home became a de facto meeting place.

Having a post office helped bring about other changes. In order to have a post office in the first place, a community had to choose a name, which was another first for the little peninsula. The area had no recognizable town, and nothing close to one, just a few newly built homes and some more-or-less-cleared land around the muddy shores of Wollochet Bay. As of May, 1878, thanks to postal rules, the place had a name. It started as Arton, and by September of that same year the name had expanded into Artondale. The name was of English origin, translating out as "plow town dale."[25]

The Artondale Post Office was a star route from Steilacoom, which meant that mail came and went via a contracted carrier, rather than a regular postal employee. The first deliveries were handled by a man named Heitman, who came by rowboat every Saturday to pick up and deliver the community's mail.

Postmaster Miles Hunt was the first of many Civil War veterans to settle in the Gig Harbor area. He had ridden with the Second Michigan Cavalry regiment, surviving a bullet that passed into his skull above his left ear and out above his right eye. It addled his hearing and blurred his eyesight, but it never slowed his drive to make a better life for himself and his family. He had arrived a year or two ahead of them to look over the land, and in 1877 he brought his wife and five children to the claim he had staked. They had already lived in Kansas and Nebraska, and Wollochet Bay might have looked more inviting than the windowless dugout in which the family had shivered through blizzards on the Wood River in the Platte Valley country.

Miles Hunt family, 1904 – (rear, l-r) Floyd, Lloyd, Arthur, Arda, Emmett (front, l-r) Lille, Miles, Maritta, Forest

They arrived in Tacoma on the newly built railroad and found themselves crowded into an overfilled, borrowed rowboat, competing for space with trunks and boxes. Miles and oldest son Forest manned the oars, while eighteen-year-old Emmett handled the stern rudder. The only made it partway up the shoreline to the vicinity of what is now Owens Beach in Point Defiance Park before darkness fell. They built a driftwood fire, camped for the night, and scrambled into the boat in the early dawn to catch the morning tide. (Miles Hunt had lived here long enough to learn not to try to row against the tide.)

They rounded Point Defiance, swept down The Narrows at five knots an hour, and rowed around Point Fosdick into Hale Passage, with Fox Island on the left and the southern end of the Gig Harbor peninsula on the right. Finally the shoreline on the right gave way to a wide opening into the mile-and-a-half length of Wollochet Bay, which looked little different than it had in the days Vancouver and Wilkes had first committed the area to their nautical charts. It was shallow in the upper reaches, with wide mudflats in low tide. They grounded the boat at the edge of a sketchy trail and shouldered as much as they could carry for a short hike into the interior, where they saw their new home for the first time.

While they waited for their newly planted crops to grow and their trees to bear fruit, the family needed money. Father Miles opened his post office and eldest son Forest took a job in a Steilacoom store. In 1878 young Emmett achieved another family first. He took his teacher's examination, scoring a meager sixty-five, but got his certificate in a land where qualified teachers were hard to come by. He opened what was called the Artondale School, earning thirty dollars for the three-month term.

After that he was off on a vagabond teaching tour into the eastern reaches of Pierce County at Puyallup, South Prairie, and Roy. The nadir of his teaching career came at Muck Prairie, where he had five students, four books, and no blackboard. He was ready for a career change when he came back to Artondale to stay in the fall of 1881. On Halloween day he took his skiff to Steilacoom, sought out Mr. Heitman, and bought out the contract to carry mail between Steilacoom and his father's post office at Artondale.

Twenty-two-year-old Emmett Hunt was a diary keeper, and he was at the top of his form when he sat down to describe his first mail run on November 5. "Rainy and fearfully windy. Started out with the mail at 2 p.m. and, after pulling four big blisters on my hands, reached Steilacoom at just dark. Started back, then the wind rose to a terrible gale and the Sound was a seething mass of foam. As the angry billows bore me along under the silver but pitiless rays of dear Luna I was occasionally bathed with a copious supply of the briny element, which seemed to have my fate in its power. But after passing Fox Island I raised sail and the trouble was over. Got to the p.o. at 10 p.m., having completed a thrilling trip and was happy to be on terra firma."[26]

A series of grueling and dangerous crossings convinced him that he needed a better vessel. He spent the spare hours of two winter months constructing a thirteen-foot sailboat he named the *Alice*, after a girlfriend named Alice Strome. Launching in the moonlight on January 27, 1882, he made his maiden voyage with the mail the next day. Life immediately got a little easier. On February 4 he wrote, "Pulled up to Steilacoom against wind and tide. Made the trip across in five hours. Sailed the entire trip home, not making a stroke with an oar. Had the disaster to break our rudder in the worst wind while the waves were seemingly mountains high, but soon substituted an oar and came home nicely."

Hunt had taken out a land claim of his own, where he spent his twenty-third birthday putting a roof on his house. That chore finished, he wrote, "Will give the cottage a long farewell now and build a steamship."[27] The result, after three months of hard work and interminable waiting for the wood-burning engine to arrive and the boiler inspectors to grant him clearance, was the twenty-six-foot *Baby Mine*. Eight feet at the beam, with a snug little cabin, she was the first steam vessel ever launched on the Gig Harbor peninsula.

The new boat enabled Hunt to take on freight and passengers and earn a few extra dollars. When election time came around, he carried voters from their scattered shores to the polls and home again. He moved a fishing station, towed a scow, hauled bricks to Tacoma from the new kiln on Fox Island, took logs and lumber to McNeil Island for the expanding Federal Penitentiary, and on one memorable Sunday in June, he carried twenty-one passengers on a picnic party. His normal charge was fifty cents per passenger, which made the picnic excursion *Baby Mine*'s single best payday.

The going was not always easy. *Baby Mine*'s engine and boiler were cranky and prone to breakdowns. His diary entries are peppered with broken pipes, busted cylinder bolts, boiler foam, malfunctions, and makeshift repairs. Winter was a vexation as well. In January 1883 the temperature was four degrees above zero, the *Baby Mine* was frozen fast in the ice, and Emmett Hunt could walk on Wollochet Bay. That was the month when he wrote of his younger sister, "So cold Lillie put a hot brickbat into bed as a footwarmer and set the bed afire, making a hole large enough to crawl through before it was discovered. So much for experience."[28]

He found time somehow to play the fiddle a bit, teach a little spelling and singing, and canvass the region as deputy county assessor. If anyone wondered where his true priorities lay, one clue might be the woodshed he built to keep the fuel dry for his wood-burning steamer. It dwarfed his fourteen-by-twenty-foot, one-and-a-half-story cottage.

On March 28, 1884, his twenty-fifth birthday, he launched a bigger and better steamer, the thirty-one-foot, eleven-gross-ton *Gypsy Queen*. He could carry heavier loads then, and for the first time shipped regular runs to Tacoma every Tuesday with barges, passengers, or whatever the peninsula had to offer. He ended his mail contract on June 27, but found plenty of work hauling freight. He carried cattle from Anderson Island, a potato harvest from Artondale, loads of hay from McNeil Island, and his brother Forest's family from the mainland to Picnic Point on Wollochet Bay. Forest made some history of his own by opening the first store on the peninsula. It proved small and short-lived, however, burning to the ground on August 17, 1885.

There was plenty more work, success, and sorrow ahead for Emmett Hunt, but by the 1880s new people were also contributing to the building of a community. It took some of them a long time to arrive. Who could have known, when the Confederates fired on Fort Sumter in April 1861, that the Civil War would start dozens of men and women on journeys that would ultimately end at Gig Harbor?

Something on the order of two million men answered the call to arms during the years between 1861 and 1865. About 600,000 of them gave their lives for the North or the South, and many of the survivors discovered a new restlessness in themselves upon their return home. They had seen new places as they marched, and thought of new possibilities as they contemplated the future. A good many of them decided to heed the advice of New York Times publisher Horace Greeley: "Go west, young man." The aftermath of war had already sent the peninsula its first postmaster. Now, by long and twisting paths, it was sending a few more key players to fill in the story of Gig Harbor.

Some had gone into the war as soon as it began. Others waited a while. On December 12, 1864, toward the end of the war, a new regiment called the Forty-fifth Wisconsin took muster, and someone made the following routine notes on the roster:

Age: 26
Occupation: clerk
Color eyes: blue
Hair: blond
Complexion: light
Height: 5 feet, 3 inches
Name: Joseph Goodman

Recruits were hard to find by that stage of the war, and Goodman and the

Civil War veteran Joseph Goodman brought his family to Gig Harbor in 1883.

45

rest of the Forth-fifth went into the service under the inducement of a hundred-dollar bounty. Their service, as it turned out, did not give them much in the way of bragging rights. They were sent to Nashville to garrison a fort, but they were simply bystanders when General George Thomas trounced John Bell Hood's Confederates there in December 1864. The Forty-fifth never lost a man in battle, though thirty-four of their number died of disease.

The war over, Goodman took his honorable discharge in July 1865 and, like many another soldier, succumbed to wanderlust. In 1867, the same year Sam Jerisich settled in Gig Harbor, John Goodman exchanged wedding vows with a Bohemian immigrant named Rose Recht in Des Moines, Iowa. The next year the couple sailed from New York to San Francisco, speeding their passage with a railroad portage across the Isthmus of Panama. A while later, they were in the Carson Valley, where they believed the California-Nevada state line ran directly through their home. Their second daughter, Lucy, born September 25, 1869, always reported she was born in Nevada. Some of the other children, presumably born in a different room, said they hailed from California.

In 1876 a four-horse wagon took the growing family – five children by now – to Chehalis in Washington Territory. By 1881 they were in Tacoma, where a diphtheria outbreak killed several of their children. In July 1883, John, Rosie, and the survivors paid twenty

Joseph and Rose Goodman family, 1895 –
(standing, l-r) Mae, Herman, Leopold, Lillian, Cora (seated, l-r) Lucy, Joseph, Rose, Anna Goodman Wheeler with son Roy

dollars to pack everything they owned on the little steamer *Zephyr* and be dropped unceremoniously onto the sand spit at the entrance to Gig Harbor. They spent the summer, fall, and first winter in the little cabin Sam Jerisich had built when he first came to these shores. It had to be pretty dilapidated by that time, but John put in three windows and a door to make it livable, and lined the walls with newspapers to keep out the cold.

The Jerisichs came by sometimes with gifts of – what else? – fish during that first hungry winter. Rosie Goodman and Anna Jerisich, with young daughters nearly the same age, became close friends. Rosie taught Anna to sew, and Sam later bought her a sewing machine. There were some drawbacks to life on a sand spit, such as rowing across the bay for drinking water, so after a year the Goodmans relocated. Fishermen rowed them to the far end of the bay and the family carried their worldly goods a mile up Crescent Creek to their new home.

In time they would have a large house, with a roomy attic and a wide porch stretching around two sides, where they could look out on the garden and pasture. They grew yeast on the back of the stove and ground coffee in a grinder on the wall by the stairwell. Every so often, Joseph Goodman would load a cavernous valise with eggs and butter and the children would row him to Tacoma and back to sell the produce. These sales would fund more coffee, tobacco for his three pipes a day, and a copy of the *Chicago Tribune*.[29]

The little harbor had seen plenty of new things, and in January 1885 it saw one more. In an Indian cedar plank longhouse at the head of the bay, a piece of black-painted cardboard was nailed to a wall and rough board benches were pushed against the other walls. In walked Anna Goodman, and the painted cardboard became a blackboard, the benches became school desks, and seventeen-year-old Anna became a teacher.

It was a ten-student classroom, and half of the students were named Jerisich. John, Mike, Melissa, Sam Junior, and Catherine were all there. They had tired of walking all the way to Artondale to go to school. William Peterson and Peter St. Louis shared the rest of the space with

47

Anna's brother, Lee, and her younger sisters, Mae and Cora. The children scrawled their lessons on slates braced against their knees, erasing their mistakes with liberal applications of spit. The schoolroom was heated with a mud and stick fireplace, which was prone to catching fire. When that happened, their Indian neighbors came running to throw water on the blaze before Gig Harbor's seat of learning could burn to the ground.

The skid road which was used to transport timber from the nearby woods was practically next to the school, and the big logs usually thundered by twice a day on their trip to the water. At least once, a log jumped its track and smashed into a corner of the school.

Although fires and wayward logs could not close the school, a lack of funds did the trick after four months. Unemployed at the age of seventeen, Anna rowed over to Tacoma and enrolled in Tacoma High School. She supported herself by doing housework in Tacoma homes, and in 1887 she and two others comprised the high school's first graduating class.

In 1886 a new schoolhouse was built higher up the hill, and the first teacher there was Anna Goodman's younger sister, Lucy. At the time, nobody could have guessed what an amazing part of Gig Harbor's future Miss Lucy Goodman would turn out to be.

Out in Minnesota was another future immigrant named Alfred Mark Burnham. He was born in Genesee County, New York, on October 16, 1824, and by the time he migrated to Minnesota, he had picked up a medical degree from the University of Buffalo. Minnesota was still frontier country in the 1850s, and Burnham got some experience with town building there. He picked an area just northwest of the town of Albert Lea.

The new community was called Itasca, and he saw to the building of a bridge, a hotel, and a steamboat. He owned a newspaper called *The Herald* and strove mightily to build the town into the county seat. That dream died when the city of Albert Lea won convincingly in the election of November 1860. That same election put Abraham Lincoln in the White House and helped bring on the Civil War. In October

1862, Burnham enlisted for service in the Tenth Minnesota regiment. He was discharged on what was called "a people's petition" a year later and returned home.

Like Joseph Goodman, Burnham moved west in stages. He was involved in gold mining in Dakota Territory in 1866, and in 1869 had a hand in the cutting and selling of wooden ties for the new transcontinental railroad as it made its way through Wyoming Territory. He took a turn in the cattle business, and then returned to Minnesota for a time, leaving for good with his second wife Rachel and their four children in 1884. Two years later, by way of Oregon and Tacoma, he came to an obscure little backwater known as Gig Harbor, and helped change it forever.

In April 1886 Burnham bought land from Peter Goldsmith. In August of the following year, he bought an adjacent twelve acres of land, also in Lot One of Section Six, Township Twenty-one, from Sam Jerisich and John Farrague. Burnham's plan became clear on April 19, 1888, when he and his wife filed a plat map for what they called "the City of Gig Harbor." The new city lay on the same land the three founding fishermen had owned in earlier years, except that now it

The Burnhams in front of their first home, near Donkey Creek – (l-r) Nick, Alfred Bismark, Rachel, Dr. A.M. Burnham, Frank, and Mr. Young (a land promoter)

Dr. Alfred Mark Burnham. Burnham and his wife Rachel platted the town of Gig Harbor in 1888.

boasted a stone monument "marked with a cross and planted in the ground at the center of Front and Harbor Streets." For the first time, at least on paper, Gig Harbor had streets. Tacoma, Forest, and Burnham rounded out the list of street names, which the plat declared to be 60 feet wide, with 50-by-120-foot lots just waiting for new citizens to buy them and build houses.

Burnham knew how to promote a site, and he persuaded a good many citizens to come out from Albert Lea and start a new life in houses that he encouraged them to paint white. Burnham was a man of energetic and forceful ways. The people he brought in showed some initiative of their own. In 1888 one of the newcomers, Frank Hall, opened a store on the western shore of the harbor. In March of that same year, articles of incorporation were filed for a new enterprise called the Gig Harbor Mill Company. It was a joint venture of Tacomans and Minnesotans, with Francis Hall, O. B. Forbes, and Ira A. Town representing the Tacoma faction. Edward S. Prentice and James H. Parker represented the new money flowing in from Minnesota.

The new mill was an ambitious undertaking. The *Tacoma Daily Ledger* told its readers, "The company intends to lease, purchase and sell real estate, construct and operate sawmills, carry on a logging and lumber manufacturing business, maintain boats, vessels, wharves ets. buy and sell merchandise and manufacture furniture, doors, sash, blinds, moulding and all wood work used in building. The capital stock is $100,000 in $100 shares, and the general office is to be located at Tacoma. The mills are to be located at Gig Harbor and such other places as may be determined upon."[30]

George Atkinson came over from Tacoma to manage the mill, and soon a parade of ships and steamers began nosing in through the narrow harbor entrance to carry off cargoes of lumber. At its height, the mill could turn out 100,000 board-feet a day. Just one ship, the *Republic*, carried a million board-feet of lumber to Chile. The company was making good on its promises. Their sawmill was going great guns at what is now the foot of Rosedale Avenue, and they built a steamer that they named the *Albert Lea*. In 1889 they even sold a pile driver to a man in Olympia.[31] Gig Harbor still had a long way to go before it could be considered a real town, but it had turned a corner. There was a place now for people to work for a daily wage. As long as that went on, the people would keep coming.

The idea of filing a plat and starting a community must have impressed Sam Jerisich and his neighbors, because they followed suit within two months. They had purchased thirty acres of land from another Slavonian named Nikola Janovich, when he returned to Europe.[32] On June 28, 1888, Joseph Dorotich joined John and Josephine Novak and Sam Jerisich in platting a town site on a small bulge on Gig Harbor's western shore.[33] They were fishermen, not real estate boomers, and when they chose a name, they went for the practical. There was a shingle mill nearby, so they named the development Millville. They were not alone in their utilitarian approach to site naming. Developers presented with the same problem at a smelter site in Idaho around the same time came up with Smelterville.

By the time he entered into this partnership, Joseph Dorotich was more than a business partner to Sam Jerisich. He had been Sam and Anna's son-in-law since July 14, 1884. Caroline Jerisich was sixteen years old when she became his bride. That was young, even by the standards of the day, but what could her mother say? Anna had been only fifteen, by most accounts, when she entered into a country mar-

Dorotich family portrait, circa 1902, Joseph and Caroline seated; (rear, l-r) Katherine, George, Amanda, John, Clemnma, Ann; (front) Jack (left of Caroline), Mattie (right of Caroline)

riage with her Slavonian fisherman. Joe knew hard work, and Caroline knew how to read and write, thanks to the rustic little schools in Artondale and Gig Harbor. They did alright together. They built a house on one of the four lots they had kept for themselves in Millville. The house grew to accommodate a family that had reached nine children by the time the last one came into the world in 1903. The house has changed some, but it is still there as this book goes to press. A true fisherman's house, it faces the water instead of the street, which is named Dorotich.

Growth was happening all around the edges of the peninsula. There had been a post office at Artondale since 1878. And Gig Harbor had enjoyed a post office of its own at Young's Landing near the mouth of Crescent Creek since December 1885. The people over on the western shore of the peninsula were growing tired of taking turns trudging down to Artondale to see if any mail had come for them. They wanted a post office of their own, and they got up a petition to establish one. Once again, their potential post office required a name. Most of the settlers in those parts lived around the meandering bay that sat back of Raft Island, and they gathered at the home of Captain Daniel McLean to consider the question.

McLean and his first wife, Magadeline, had settled on ninety-five acres of land in late 1884. Their home had become the unofficial community center, hosting meetings, potluck dinners, and dances when a fiddler could be found. Some of the post office names nominated were

Joseph and Caroline Dorotich's home on the harbor near Millville. The house still stands today.

52

Ferndale, Rosedale, McLean's Landing, and Alpine. Brownsville was suggested, to acknowledge the two families named Brown living nearby. For a certain Mrs. White, who had helped circulate the petition, the name Brownsville conjured up images of sunbonnets and bewhiskered Texans. She wanted none of that. Ferndale finally won the day, but when the citizens learned later that Washington Territory already had a post office named Ferndale, they fell back on their second choice, and Rosedale it became forever more.[34] The official date of establishment was March 22, 1887, with James Brown as first postmaster.[35]

Rosedale had a school even before it had a name. Officially it was School District Number Twenty-six, and the first teacher, Jenny Hancock, was paid twenty-five dollars for three months of work with nine pupils. She started on July 21, 1884, and was succeeded by Sadie Bradley. Next came Fay Fuller, who taught in 1886 at the appallingly tender age of fifteen. But then, Fay always was a go-getter. In 1890 she made history by becoming the first woman to climb Mount Rainier.

The peninsula had made a good start on its educational and commercial life. It was time to address the spiritual side. Missionaries had been passing through Puget Sound country since the late 1830s, and there had been churches at Olympia, Steilacoom, and other points since the 1850s. But organized religious services were slow to make their way across The Narrows. The first attempt consisted of sending a floating church into Gig Harbor. Services were held in the cabin of the steamer *Isabel*, and the congregation rowed out and climbed a rope ladder to hear the sermon. The *Alida* was another steamer pressed into religious work. Both steamers returned to secular duties by the end of 1887, and schoolhouses served as makeshift churches for a while. In her less glorious final days, the *Alida* became a floating pest house, or quarantine station, for people afflicted with contagious diseases. Eventually she was run ashore and burned on the beach not far from Gig Harbor.

The first minister to preach on a regular schedule was Fennimore Fremont Young, whose father, Alphonzo Young, was the first postmaster in Gig Harbor. Born in Minnesota on January 23, 1857, Fennimore came naturally to the ministry. Both of his grandfathers were Presbyterian Church pastors. In his old age, he often reflected back on a miracle of his youth. "I was healed by the Lord," he said, "after I had been pronounced incurable & beyond any hope by one of the best physicians in the country & I have never taken a doce [sic] of medicine from that day to this." He began preaching in his teens. In 1878 he married Ella Mae Shaver, who followed him through dozens of moves, endured the intermittent poverty of itinerant ministry, and bore him a dozen children in fifty-eight years of marriage.

Young and his family lived for a time in Yakima, then followed his postmaster father to Gig Harbor about 1887. The Presbyterian church of Gig Harbor was officially formed on January 28, 1888, with twenty-one charter members.[36] Fennimore traveled back and forth between Gig Harbor and Yakima for a time, but he did not care for the harsh temperatures and dust storms of eastern Washington. He gave up his eastern congregation after a year, devoting his time to Gig Harbor and Rosedale. Sunday school was his strong suit, and records show that he had fifty-seven students in Gig Harbor and thirty-six in Rosedale in 1888. That had to mean he was instructing a whopping percentage of the population. He was not necessarily getting rich, however. Out in Rosedale the general practice was to pay the minister in chickens, ducks, and eggs.[37]

Alphonzo Young's house served as the first post office in the harbor. Steamboats dropped off the mail on the dock, called Young's Landing. In 1917 the Department of Natural Resources built a boat launch at the site.

In 1891, at the age of thirty-four, he was chosen to attend the General Assembly of the church in Detroit. This was a mark of success, but his return to Gig Harbor afterward marked the beginning of his decline. He distanced himself from the Presbyterian organization and began preaching nondenominational Christianity. Even if most of his congregation were not Presbyterians, strictly speaking, his new tack failed to resonate with them. In April 1893 a church investigator wrote, "We found the church at Gig Harbor greatly demoralized – the statement was also made at Rosedale where, altho, the church was not so much demoralized it had intimated its desire to dispense with Mr. Young's services and further appointments were announced for that place by the commission."[38]

The congregation might not have liked Young's stand against alcoholic beverages, but that was official church doctrine, after all. They had a harder time with his belief that he spoke in tongues and could cast out devils. His views were a shade too mystical and extreme for this matter-of-fact community, especially when it came to visions of a second coming of Christ, timed to coincide with the dawning of the twentieth century. The believers became known as Come-outers, but there were not enough to sustain a congregation, so Fennimore Young packed his bags and took his family to greener pastures around a bigger bay in California. His preaching had not been entirely in vain. In 1896 there were still six Come-outers left in Gig Harbor, waiting for a second coming that they now calculated would arrive in the spring of 1901.[39]

Fennimore and Ella Mae Young with grandchildren. Courtesy of Chapel Hill Presbyterian Church

Chapter 4

New Names, New Churches, and a Gold Rush

The first three years of the 1890s were heady days, when anything seemed possible. There were folks willing to bet enormous sums of money on the future of what had been a sleepy little harbor. In 1890 a group of investors from Tacoma and points farther afield bought up four hundred acres of Gig Harbor waterfront. They had control of almost all of the shore that was not mill property or part of the government reservation. "The harbor is bound in time to be a summer resort for Tacoma," said one of the investors. In a daring bit of prophecy, he added "Later I doubt not some plan will be evolved for bridging The Narrows."[40]

One of the early fruits borne of the investment was the Artena Land Company, incorporated on June 6, 1890, with five trustees and capital stock of $100,000. Artena was the wife of one of the investors, Mike McKay, and the development bore her name. This was a particularly ambitious development, with nearly four hundred lots available, some of them extending out into the harbor itself. Their plat map, executed by Scurry & Owens, civil engineers of Seattle, contin-

A southeastern view of Gig Harbor circa 1915. Union Dock (previously known as Young's Landing) is at left, Millville at right.

ued Front Street, which had been a Burnham creation, and added Kalama, Ash, Oak, Chehalis, Columbia, and Walnut.

In August 1890 Henry and Adaline Woodworth filed their own plat for a new development on Gig Harbor, calling it Woodworth's Addition. It added twelve blocks, divided up into lots 60 feet wide and between 120 and 147 feet long. More new street names came into being – Fennimore, Chester, White, Norton, and Florence. Three years later, when the fledgling community struggled to build some sort of a land connection to the outside world, Woodworth was named as overseer for the newly created road district in Gig Harbor and vicinity..[41]

Gradually, the blank spots on the map of the peninsula were filling in. Road and street names were arriving, at least on paper. Some would never achieve existence, and most others would change their names over time. Names along the shoreline tended to be more permanent, thanks o the Mosquito Fleet – the little steamers carrying passengers and freight into every recess of Puget Sound. In 1890 an ad for the steamer *Messenger* pledged to leave Tacoma at "8 A.M. Sunday and Thursday, returning same day, and 8 A.M. Tuesday, returning Wednesday; touching at Gig Harbor, Artondale, Potters, Fox Island, Lake Bay, Balch's Cove, Minter, Purdy and Rosedale. No freight on Sunday trip."[42]

That was just one boat. There were plenty of others, and if they were going to schedule a stop somewhere, that place had to have a name. The Wilkes Expedition had labeled most of the big features

The Messenger *makes a stop in the area. Passengers disembark by way of a ramp leading them to the beach.*

back in 1841, but there were still odd little points and inlets that stayed nameless until there was a reason to bestow one. People living in the right place at the right time could get their names onto something that might outlive them and pass down through the ages.

The native inhabitants had surely created names for many of these places, but they were largely unpronounceable to the English-speaking newcomers. The names faded away, with rare exceptions that included Wollochet Bay and Kopachuck, which means "with water" in Chinook Jargon, the trade language of the old Northwest. Toward the end of the time when the natives were a distinct and separate presence in the Gig Harbor area, an anthropologist tried to gather a few of the names. He took an old native on a journey around the shores of the peninsula and asked him to name names.

It becomes impossible, after a century or more, to sort out which were place names known to all, and which were simply features or events associated with the place in the memory of the teller. One such was a promontory near Rosedale. The native pointed it out as *Sló xElts*, which translated as "being beaten at gambling." Was he reciting a name by which every native knew this place, or was he remembering an unfortunate event from his own earlier years? At tiny Cutts Island, he said the name was *Qaqacé lts*, which had to do with crows.

Some names carried bits of mystery. Along a tiny creek at the head of Wollochet Bay, he said the name for the mouth of the creek was *Sxolo 'tsid*. As near as anyone could make out from the translation, it meant that something was missing off of something else. White settlers, who saw nothing missing, called it Artondale Creek.

Just north of Raft Island, on the eastern shore of Carr Inlet, was a long slim bay, so narrow and protected that it resembled a lake. Eleanor Lay, a Canadian-born widow, bought a piece of land in 1891 that had been part of Daniel McLean's homestead. She lived in a log house and enjoyed some success in the fruit business.

Two of her surviving children, Benjamin and Lillian, bought property nearby, and near the end of 1894 Benjamin opened a store in Rosedale. He sold everything from brooms to mustard to oar locks, lamp chimneys, and ten kinds of tobacco. He also served Rosedale as postmaster from 1895 to 1897 and was a notary public for many years. By the time Eleanor Lay died in December 1924, she and her family had made quite an impact on the area around Rosedale. Little wonder then, that the narrow bay there is known as Lay Inlet. Real estate agents likely prefer this to the native name, *Tux pE' qats*, which means "rotten logs."

Farther north, on the other side of a bulge in the shoreline, a high hill overlooks another narrow opening that cuts south toward the general direction of Lay Inlet. The point of land where the opening begins is known as Cherry Point. Families by the names of Keeney and Matthias lived nearby, but somehow or other, Joseph and Margaret J. Cherry became the point's namesakes.

Streams needed names, too, and there were two major ones flowing into Gig Harbor. The larger one, toward the northeastern shore, became Crescent Creek, presumably because someone thought the lake that it flowed from bore a crescent shape – or perhaps it was the other way around. Or, since the stream follows the somewhat crescent-shaped curve of Crescent Valley on its journey to the shore, perhaps the valley gave its name to the lake.

The other stream, on the northwest shore where the Indian village had stood, and still endured to some extent, was known for a while as

Ben Lay opened his store in 1894 at the Rosedale dock. The store sold groceries and hardware, and served as the town's post office.
Courtesy of the Tacoma Public Library

59

Burnham Creek, because Alfred Burnham lived in a house on the hill above its right bank. Somewhere along the line, the name switched to Donkey Creek, because a steam donkey, a great boiler-powered winch for hauling logs out of the woods via a cable system, was employed near its mouth at the time that official names were being bestowed.[43]

Communities were developing on the Gig Harbor peninsula in the 1890s, and each displayed its own unique character. Because they were separated by miles of woods, facing different directions on different shores, and founded by people of diverse outlooks, occupations, and nationalities, it was only natural that Arletta would differ from Cromwell, or that Rosedale would not be the same as Gig Harbor.

Some people and sights became constants in Rosedale's daily life. A black surrey with a fringe on top, driven by a man wearing a derby hat and a long black coat? A stranger might say he looked like the image on a can of Prince Albert Tobacco. Folks who lived thereabouts knew it was Albert Yates, a native of England who lived in the old Chapman log house on Hampton Road in Rosedale. The woman beside him was his wife, Sarah, and they were parents of the first

Chrissy Yates walks her dog along the railroad trestle over Whitmore Creek in south Rosedale, circa 1918.

Ladies of the Yates and Land families wait for a steamboat.

white twins born on the peninsula. It must have been a harrowing delivery, since family records insist that Daniel Gordon Yates came into the world on February 14, 1897, while his twin sister, Christina Mary, waited another two days before making her appearance.[44]

A man with a German accent, directing a road building crew? That would be Henry Sehmel. He was a native of Munden, near Hanover in Germany. Henry had been a blacksmith in his early years, and had plied the trade in Germany, New York, Chicago, and Arizona by the time he settled at north Rosedale in 1884. Here he farmed and logged, and for fifteen years supervised the country road projects in the area. His brothers Karl and Albert lived nearby, and between them the Sehmel brothers controlled more than 520 acres of land.[45]

Broken fragments of brick along the shore facing Raft Island? Dreams were in the air, and like many dreams, a few of them slid over into nightmares. The brick fragments were a monument to the hope and frustration of Francis J. Henry. He had homesteaded the site since 1882, served as Justice of the Peace from 1892 to 1894, and had watched brickworks rise up and prosper on Fox Island. Inspired, he dug what seemed to him to be good clay from a neighbor's property, and he hired a man who claimed to know the ways of making fired clay products. The venture failed. Undaunted, he borrowed money from Ross Huff, who dabbled in real estate and had a store nearby. Henry hired the same man again, with the same dismal results. The

Lay Inlet as seen from Rosedale. Cutts Island in in the center.
Courtesy of the Tacoma Public Library

venture cost him dearly, and he left Rosedale in 1897 to labor in the horse barns of the Tacoma Transit Company. Later he would grow berries in Puyallup near what became the Western Washington Fair Grounds.[46]

A rusting hulk on the shore of tiny Cutts Island? Marius Hoy, a Danish immigrant, was an inventive sort. He was a farmer and a sign painter, but his crowning achievement was the invention of a virtually unsinkable, sheet-metal, self-bailing lifeboat. Perhaps the joy went out of the project when Hoy's assistant stole the patent rights. In any case, Hoy eventually set the boat adrift in Henderson Bay. If it would not sink, it could still run aground, which it finally did on Cutts Island, where its rusting bones could still be seen in the 1930s.

Another defining institution in the life of a community, as surely as the church, school, and store, was the cemetery. A long ribbon of rowboats making their way from Gig Harbor to Tacoma on August 24, 1887, remained in memory as one of the most unusual funeral processions Puget Sound had seen. This journey of Peter St. Louis to his final resting place in the Tacoma Cemetery reminded the peninsula that it still had no formal cemetery of its own. Gradually, the need was met. Gig Harbor Cemetery, up Crescent Valley and well away from the village on the water, came first in 1891. At Rosedale, when Daniel McLean died in 1895, his widow, Sara McLean, had him buried on their home property near the graves of his first wife and infant son. Then she donated a portion of the land to the community as Greenwood Cemetery, later renamed Rosedale.

Artondale Cemetery got its start at roughly the same time on land donated by Miles Hunt, in spite of the protest of an angry neighbor who said, "I wouldn't be caught dead in your damn cemetery."[47] Many of the pioneers found rest there, including Miles Hunt when he died in 1922 at the age of eighty-nine.

In 1903, the Hales Passage Scandinavian Lutheran Cemetery Association was formed. F. W. Samuelson and Gabriel Evje donated the land, and later occupied pieces of it for eternity. Intended at first strictly for Lutherans, it later became Cromwell Cemetery and accepted anyone from the area.[48]

Logging was changing the look of the peninsula across big swathes of land. The lumber mill concentrated mostly on Douglas fir – and it had some enormous representatives of the species to choose from. As late as 1928, Julius Spadoni spent two days in the Crescent Valley felling a fir that measured twenty-nine feet in circumference.[49] When the last of the giant spar trees was cut at Point Fosdick in 1934, it was measured at 220 feet tall.[50]

The shingle mills depended on the local abundance of cedar, which had the desirable trait of splitting easily into short slabs. And cedar's durability made it well-suited for roofing and fence posts, in addition to guaranteeing that its stumps would linger like the tombstones of vanished giants for generations to come.

Every now and then, the trees took revenge. In the early fall of 1889, H. P. Hendricks, the master mechanic of the Gig Harbor Lumber Company, had just finished work on a new home in Gig Harbor. At noon on Sunday, September 29, a gigantic cedar tree crashed down on his home. He was away somewhere, and his wife was home alone. She had the good fortune to be in the kitchen, which was the only part of the house not smashed to splinters. They lost pretty much everything except their kitchenware. But nature could be capricious. Mrs.

Two loggers perch atop logs brought out by the steam donkey engine (right).

Logs are transported on rail cars from the woods to the water.

Hendricks had a caged bird. The cage was left a mass of twisted metal, and the table that had supported it was smashed beyond redemption, but the bird was found sitting on top of the wreckage, dazed but unharmed. The tree's height measured to about 180 feet tall.[51]

On October 3 of the following year, a log rolling toward a waiting saw caught twenty-three-year-old William J. Hamilton beneath its weight. With his legs broken and his internal organs crushed beyond repair, he lived just long enough to take the blame upon himself and shake hands with each of his comrades, who later crossed over to Tacoma for his funeral.[52] Yet everyone accepted that logging and lumbering were dangerous trades, and a few accidents did not stop their progress. The Gig Harbor mill had a wharf 450 ft. long and 80 ft. wide to handle the volume of lumber flowing to the ports of the world.

The first real trouble for the mills came with the beginnings of the depression of 1893. Though not as long-lasting as the Great Depression, it was quite severe. Times became hard and competition fierce. In 1890 there were 191 sawmills and 82 shingle mills in Washington.[53] When the demand for lumber declined, there was bound to be a

The Gig Harbor Sawmill Company at the foot of Rosedale Street in 1887. The mill produced logs and cedar shingles for foreign markets.

The Gig Harbor Mill Company built two tall ships, the Republic *and the* Nineva, *to deliver its lumber to customers around the world.*

shaking-out process. In November 1891 the *West Coast Lumberman* told its readers, "The Gig Harbor mill was sold under foreclosure sale to the Washington National Bank of Tacoma for approximately $23,000. The purchasers contemplate reorganizing the company as soon as the title is settled, and expect to increase the capital stock to $100,000."[54] Looking back, some folks blamed the failure on the loss of a big customer in Chile.

Every so often there would be a glimmer of hope. Two years after the mill went into receivership, there were reports that, "A Capt. Stanley, part owner of 13 vessels, is negotiating to buy the plant. It is understood the price is $30,000. In case the negotiations are successful Capt. Stanley proposes going into the cargo trade."[55] That dream was stillborn, but in April 1897 the *West Coast and Puget Sound Lumberman* enthused, "When Col. Frank Ross gets that scheme through for the building of a railroad connecting Port Townsend and Tacoma by way of Gig Harbor and that $150,000 sawmill project at the later place is under way it will make a sort of second Klondike out of Gig."

The railroad never came, and in November 1899 the *Lumberman* read the final rites for this particular dream: "The Gig Harbor mill is being moved to Clear Lake, where it will be again put to use. The mill is one of the old time cargo mills. It has been idle for a number of years. After the Gig Harbor Company failed, it was sold to the Campbell Bros., of Port Blakely. The men who now own it are C. P. Bratnober of

The E.S. Prentice Shingle Mill at the foot of Peacock Hill at the head of the bay. The mill turned out 20 million shingles in 1892.

Waterloo, Iowa and H. B. Waite, of Minneapolis, who have been running a shingle mill at Clear Lake for some time under the name of the McMaster-Waite Lumber Company. The mill has a daily capacity of 100,000 feet, and is rated as a good mill."[56] There were a number of Clear Lakes in the state. This particular one was up north a few miles south of the Skagit River on the other side of Puget Sound. The mill operated there in its new life for a few years and then burned down.

Hopes for continued employment shifted to the E. S. Prentice shingle mill, which turned out 20,400,000 shingles valued at $35,800 in 1892.[57] Shingles seemed so promising that a group in Seattle decided to open a branch factory in Gig Harbor, calling it the Teredo Proof Company. In September 1893, Milo Stewart and A. E. Atkin completed work on this new mill. It had a Perkins band machine that could turn out 50,000 shingles a day, and these would be no ordinary shingles. In an age of smoking chimneys and frequent fires, these shingles, boiled in a 108-foot-long vat, were designed to be fireproof. The mill was also capable of turning out pilings treated to resist marine wood-boring teredo worms.[58]

Yet the depression of 1893 struck this business hard, as well. When the returns for the year came in, Prentice had turned out only a million shingles, valued at $1,500. Stewart and Aker had produced a bare 400,000, valued at $700, and they had no stock on hand.[59] It was a poor start for what had been touted as a promising business, and it came at a time when the *Puget Sound Lumberman* was already warning its readers that the overall capacity for turning out shingles was now double the demand.[60]

Whatever records the mills kept seem to have been lost long ago, but there are clues that someone in Gig Harbor was still manufacturing shingles. On March 1, 1896, Emmett Hunt's steamer *Victor* lost control of the scow that it was towing in a storm, and it smashed ashore on the stretch of Commencement Bay that was already known as Old Tacoma. The 400,000 shingles that went adrift, and the 275,000 ultimately recovered, were all from Gig Harbor.[61] No one seems to remember exactly when it was that the shingle business winked out altogether. With its passing, Gig Harbor entered something of a brief dark age.

Only a few fragments of writing and documentation from these times have come down to us. Among the surviving documents is the diary of Estelle Dunham Sheldon Rust for the years 1890 and 1891. Her diary was full of cryptic references to an individual identified only as "Dr.," such as that of January 5, 1891: "Dr. sent to Mr. St. Peters last night – his wife was confined. Dr. got home between 1 and 2 o'clock p.m." A week later she wrote, "I washed today. Dr. turned the wringer and Ben brought the water."[62]

The unnamed Dr. of her diary was her husband, Dr. Hiram Rust, the first full-time practicing physician the peninsula had seen. Ben, often called Bennie in the diary, was their son, who turned fifteen on January 7, 1891. Ettie, who helped make a chocolate and coconut cake that same day, was Estelle's child by a previous marriage, as was another son named Fred. Dr. Rust did well enough with his medical practice to eventually afford the construction of a large house called Rhododendron Terrace on Gig Harbor's northeast shore. Even after his official retirement, he continued to see occasional patients until shortly before his death at the age of eighty-five, in 1922.[63]

Steamboaters and lumber fellers were not the only ones facing competition in the 1890s. Thomas J. Weekes toiled in the

Dr. Hiram and Estelle Rust (seated, left and center), with Arthur and Etta Johnston and their son Herbert (standing), at the Johnston's east Gig Harbor home.

67

vineyards of the Lord, and in 1893 was finding the ground exceedingly hard. Weekes was a Presbyterian minister, trying to rebuild the peninsula's congregation in the wake of Fennimore Young's troubled tenure. Born in Kent, England, in 1840, Weekes had started out to be a doctor. For reasons that must have made more sense then than they do across the gulf of time and distance, his father decided in 1862 to send him from England to the fledgling city of Victoria on Vancouver Island to finish his education. In an odd bit of foreshadowing, the ship that brought him was called the *Rosedale*. From Victoria he made his way to the Fraser River gold country, where it is barely possible he could have crossed paths with a young man named Sam Jerisich, both of them going their ways with no inkling of a common destiny. Sometime around 1867, Weekes began studying for the ministry in San Francisco, where he struck up a friendship and twenty-year correspondence with a newspaperman named Sam Clemens, who was transforming himself into Mark Twain.

Twenty-one years of Weekes' life were devoted to ministering in the San Juan Islands. This was a rough place, where hard-working fishermen and farmers shared the islands with smugglers, fugitives, and a range of characters who bent or broke most of the Ten Commandments with vigor. Weekes had come to Tacoma and was working for the Northern Pacific Railroad in 1893, while still making ministerial forays into Gig Harbor, Rosedale, and points west. Some credit him with being the very first to bring organized religion to the

Longbranch Peninsula, over on the far side of Carr Inlet.[64] By 1894 he had Rosedale's Presbyterian congregation back in operation, with eight members and twenty-three Sunday school

Rev. Thomas J. Weekes, minister of Gig Harbor's Memorial Presbyterian Church. The church was dedicated on September 13, 1913. Courtesy of Chapel Hill Presbyterian Church

children. Gig Harbor was a tougher proposition, but by 1897 he could report one elder, two deacons, eight members, and twenty-five Sunday school students.[65]

Unfortunately for Weekes, the Methodists had stolen a march on the Presbyterians. Their first known foothold came with a request for a baptismal christening in 1890, and soon afterward the Methodists were holding services on a barge anchored in the middle of Gig Harbor. The same barge hosted dances on Saturday night, so the faithful faced early morning cleanup chores before services could begin on Sunday. On November 18, 1892, articles of incorporation were filed for the First Methodist Episcopal Church of Gig Harbor.

By the following March they had the frame of a church building up and were getting ready to plaster the walls.[66] Dr. Alfred Burnham donated the land on a hill at the head of the bay. His sons, Bismark and Clarence, towed the building materials across from Tacoma. Robert Franklin and his wife, Sarah, donated a reed organ. Others pitched in as best they could. The family names Peacock, Johnson, Teachman, Iliss, Young, Cundiff, Carlson, Rust, Hammerlund, Rowley, and Curtiss are on the roster of the founders. The first minister was Charles W. Darrow, followed in 1894 by C. T. Jones.[67]

The donation of church land was one of the last big contributions people remembered from the town builder, Alfred Burnham. He had suffered from rheumatism since his young adulthood, and in 1896 his liver began to fail. He was

The Methodist Episcopal Church in its first location overlooking the head of the bay. It was later moved to provide a site for Union High School.

seventy-two that year, and his decades had been hard and vigorous. He was confined to bed most of the time, and toward the last his right side was paralyzed.

On July 4, Burnham stopped eating altogether. His pain was severe and his last act as a physician was to administer chloroform to himself. He inhaled the fumes of an entire pound before finding relief. The end was clearly near, and he knew it as well as his family did. At about three o'clock on the afternoon of July 11, he lapsed into unconsciousness, and at 5:15 he died. At noon the next day, funeral services were held in his home, and then the procession set out for the new Gig Harbor Cemetery, up Crescent Valley from the head of the bay.

Funerals are a time for remembering, a time for sharing stories. There were plenty of stories about Alfred Burnham, then and later. Was it true that he was so secretive about his second marriage that he carried a saw to a filer who doubled as a justice of the peace, and came away with a new wife and a sharpened saw?[68] Did he really arrive in Gig Harbor in a rowboat with a cow perched at one end, and his family balanced precariously at the other? Had he been the one who commissioned surveys for the right of way for roads to Purdy and Olalla?

Did he really string a telegraph line between his home and his son Nick's store?[69] Was he one of the three founders of Itasca, Illinois?[70] Had he saved eighty-nine patients from death in a diphtheria outbreak in Albert Lea, losing only one?[71] Was it true that he was seen to carry a grown deer for three miles over rough country to deliver it to his brother-in-law, who was rowing over from Tacoma?[72] Did he really give free land to anyone from Minnesota who agreed to come to Gig Harbor, build a house, and paint it white? Well, something sure enticed all those people to make the long journey from Albert Lea.

The town's dreamer and builder was gone, and it would take a while for the community to catch its breath and find new builders. Dreams were a different matter. Those could spring to life and fade away as easily as harbor mists on an autumn morning. The timing of the next big dream was downright remarkable. On July 16, 1897,

Emmett Hunt's little steamer *Victor* came wheezing into Tacoma with news that gold had been found in a gulch west of Gig Harbor.[73] The very next day, the big steamer *Portland* docked in Seattle and touched off screaming headlines about "A Ton of Gold" from Alaska, thereby igniting the Klondike Gold Rush.

Gig Harbor's gold rush was considerably smaller and shorter lived than the one in the Klondike. The prevailing story was that a rancher named George Barnaby was working on the county road being extended from Gig Harbor to Springfield, which later changed its name to Wauna. He was down in a gulch in the upper reaches of Donkey Creek, separated from his comrades, and came scrambling back up clutching five gold nuggets, which assayed out at $2.60 in value when he took them to Tacoma. By Monday July 19, six placer mining claims were being filed with the county auditor. Mate John Bingham left the *Victor* to try his luck with shovel and pan. Others hurried over from Tacoma. Judge Carol was spending some time at the family's summer cottage anyway, so he and his son set to digging. The objective was to get down to the bedrock, where the bulk of the gold, heavier than the ordinary gravel, would be expected to have settled.[74]

The Tacoma papers were full of Gig Harbor gold stories for a few days, and then silence descended. Evidently the miners decided in the end that the gold was a small, random gift of the long vanished glacier, and they learned that it was a long way down to the bedrock. A few folks from the peninsula tried their fortunes with the larger gold

Emmett Hunt's steamboat Victor *glides through the water loaded with passengers, livestock, and produce.*

rush in Alaska and the Yukon. Emmett Hunt's younger brother, Floyd, was one of them. He had been working on a tug and tending fish traps on the southern Sound when the news came, sending him north on the steamer *Farallon*. Over half the would-be gold seekers on his ship took one look at the rugged snow-covered mountains and returned home without ever setting foot on shore.

Floyd, who was twenty-two that year, went ashore in Dyea undaunted. Even Reverend Fennimore Young would have been hard put in the weeks ahead to discern whether the Lord was keeping Floyd Hunt safe in the palm of His hand, or whether He was just missing in repeated attempts to smite the young man dead. Rather than go straight over the mountains in search of gold, Floyd took a job working as a cook for Nelson Bennett, who was building an aerial tramway over Chilkoot Pass. (Bennett had already made a name for himself back in Washington by boring a railroad tunnel through the Cascade Mountains.)

The cookhouse was at Stone Camp, buried in snow with only the chimney protruding. One day Nelson Bennett came trundling through the snow tunnel into the kitchen with some damp dynamite that he wanted the cooks to dry out on the back of their stove. "Perfectly safe," he told them, and they must have figured that a man who dug and blasted his way through mountains would know a thing or two about explosives. Floyd and his assistant were unpacking some boxes when the dynamite blew. When the smoke cleared, they found themselves standing totally unhurt, staring up at the hole in the roof where the stove had made its exit.

On the third of April in 1898, Floyd and his assistant, Curley Bill Atwood of Tacoma, were

Floyd Hunt sought his fortune in the Alaskan gold fields in 1897.

cooking lunch. A thick wet snow fell, adding its weight to the great mass on the mountain above. At eleven o'clock it all broke loose, and a thirty-foot wall of ice, rocks, water, and snow thundered down the mountain. The avalanche missed the camp by about three hundred feet, but buried alive some seventy people, including twenty-nine of Bennett's workmen.

The next trial that came Hunt's way was typhoid fever, which finally convinced him to pack it in. He gave up on Alaska and headed back to Wollochet Bay in June 1898 to recuperate and pursue a safer life on the water.[75]

It took all sorts of folks to make a community, and there were some memorable characters in and around Gig Harbor as the century neared its end. Up from the People's Wharf and beside the GAR (Grand Army of the Republic) Hall[76] was a ten-acre picnic ground shaded by massive trees. A spring bubbled up in one corner, and there were tables and a forty-foot dance platform. The use of the hall and picnic grounds could be had for a nickel a head, and the man who took those nickels in the 1890s was W. J. Duley.

Here was a man with a strange and awful past. When the Great Sioux Uprising began in Minnesota in 1862, Duley and his wife and

children lived at Lake Shetuk. They were attacked on August 21, 1862. Duley was badly wounded, three of the children were killed, and his wife and two more of their children were carried off into

The GAR (Grand Army of the Republic) Hall was surrounded by 10 acres of picnic grounds. It was located just up from the People's Wharf (corner of Harborview and Soundview Drives).

73

three months of captivity. He became a captain of scouts in the war, and in its aftermath he was allowed a hand in an act of apocalyptic vengeance. In the largest mass execution of American history, thirty-eight Sioux warriors were hanged on a huge scaffold at Mancato, Minnesota, the day after Christmas 1862.[77]

W. J. Duley was the man who cut the rope that released the trap doors and launched the Sioux into eternity. One of the doctors who pronounced them dead was Alfred Burnham. Perhaps that was how they came to know one another, and how Duley ultimately became part of the Albert Lea migration to Gig Harbor. At any rate, he was at the picnic ground thirty-odd years later, looking on the scenes of the harbor through haunted eyes, and taking nickels from folks who wanted to eat or dance or lounge in the shade.[78]

Chapter 5

Hello and Goodbye in a New Century

On September 24, 1900, Arda Hunt, entrusted with the safety of the steamer *Crest*, chopped a hole in her hull and watched her sink to the bottom of Gig Harbor. He was proclaimed a hero.

Hunt had awakened deep in the night to the crackling sounds and the lurid red glow of a fire, and had raced to the dock in time to join the crowd watching the *Crest* burn. There was no insurance on the vessel, which was valued at $20,000,[79] and it was a loss the Hunt family could not afford. In desperation, Arda rowed out beside the burning ship and took an ax to the hull. His action scuttled the ship, but extinguished the flames. The *Crest* was later raised, and Emmett Hunt set to work rebuilding her in Tacoma. It was a rare bit of excitement for the little community in the early autumn of a new century.

A year later there was excitement of a different sort. On June 15, 1901, George Swanson was murdered and J. G. Halstrom grievously wounded by an assailant near Olalla, about a dozen miles up the west-

The Crest *loading produce and passengers at the People's Wharf. Cordwood for its boilers is stacked on the pier.*

ern shore of Puget Sound from Gig Harbor. The killer's name was believed to be Charles A. Stewart, and his aliases included James Brannan, Charles Doty, and Charley the Woodchopper. He would have had no part in this story, except that his flight took him south toward Gig Harbor. He stopped and asked for food at the home of a Mr. Bartlett about four miles south of Olalla. Bartlett spread the word, and the reconstituted steamer *Crest* brought news of the sighting to Tacoma.

By the time Deputy Sheriff J. C. F. Johnson arrived at Gig Harbor, the murderer had stalked right through the little community, and events had taken a new turn. A couple of teenagers had followed Stewart all the way from Bartlett's. They could have caught him themselves, they explained, but they felt they lacked the authority to do so. Instead, they sought out the closest thing Gig Harbor had to a law officer – Justice of the Peace L. C. Moore. Accustomed to simple civic marriages and other peaceful chores, Moore rose to the challenge. He left his hayfield and set out with the teens and a few other men to find the killer's trail.

Moore caught up with Stewart about a mile north of the Gig Harbor post office and a quarter mile up from the beach. Stewart was lying on the ground with his coat under his head, preparing to go to sleep. "Do you live around here?" the man on the ground asked Moore coolly. Yes, he did, Moore answered, and asked where his questioner lived. "Oh, I live over there," said Stewart, pointing off toward the west. At this point, Moore drew his gun and told Stewart to get up. Stewart rose slowly and casually, and was putting on his shoes when Deputy Sheriff Johnson arrived to pack him off to jail in Tacoma. When searched, he was found to be carrying a six-inch dagger. The next time someone needed a civil marriage in Gig Harbor, a man who had faced down a cold-blooded killer would perform the ceremony.[80]

Burning ships and runaway murderers were the exception to the patterns of daily life. The mundane business of living, dying, and making a way in the world was the commonplace. One day seemed much like another as the seasons wove one into another. The sights and sounds and smells were predictable. It was quieter on the harbor since the mills had closed. There were farmers living near the shores, and plenty of others who just wanted fresh eggs, so mornings might begin with the sounds of crowing roosters. The lowing of cows, the barking of dogs, the neighing of horses were familiar sounds. Roughly 155 days out of the year, on average, there was the sound of falling rain.

On Sunday, the bell of the Methodist Church called the faithful to worship. Occasional explosions echoing through the woods were a sign that one of the more affluent farmers was using gunpowder as a quick means of clearing troublesome stumps. There were steamboat whistles, which could tell the listener the time of day, give or take a few minutes, since the boats ran on a strict schedule when their machinery was working right. If you heard them enough, you could tell one boat from another without looking around.

Voices rising in song on the water were likely to belong to fishermen, bending to their heavy oars as they cleared the harbor to begin their work. The songs set a cadence, so the rowers could pull together in unison. When they came in laden with a catch of fish, their arrival was likely to be announced by the frenzied feeding calls of flocks of seagulls. Infrequently, other voices rose in a monotonous wailing chant, accompanied by the banging of pots. These songs belonged to the Indians still living around the mouth of Donkey Creek, doing their most hopeful and most desperate best to drive away the evil spirits threatening one of their sickened brethren.

The John and Lydia Carlson family and friends share a picnic on the hill above People's Wharf in west Gig Harbor.

Since anyone who wanted to cook food, boil water, or heat their home needed wood, the sounds of wood being chopped and split rang across all the settled parts of the peninsula. The scents of wood smoke floated by on every breeze. Since Gig Harbor was a fishing village, spring was heralded by the additional smell of paraffin, boiled to coat the cork fishing floats and keep them from becoming waterlogged. Black tar was also brought to an aromatic, slow-bubbling boil to coat and protect the cotton strands of the fishing nets from rot. Nets and floats were valuable, and they had to be made to last. Close to shore, there was the smell of salt air, and at low tide there was the deeper smell of broad mud flats slowly drying, fish carcasses, crabs, dead clams, and all, as they waited for the inevitable rise of the next tide.

When H. L. Fleming came through to conduct the 1900 Federal census, he counted 124 people in what was known for statistical purposes as the Rosedale Precinct. Up in Rosedale proper, he found John Carl Sehmel, better known as Charles. He was forty-eight and had been married for fifteen years to Johanna, the mother of his five children. Both of them had been in America since 1884.

The next house down belonged to his brother, Henry, who had spent nineteen of his forty-two years in the United States. He and Dora, his wife of twelve years, had four children: Carl, Adolph, Elsie and Earnest. Neighbor Eleanor Lay was sixty-three, still listing her occupation as farmer, regardless of what she and her children did with real estate.

The Charles Sehmel family on the front porch of their homestead in Rosedale.

78

Over in Gig Harbor, Sam Jerisich owned up to being sixty-seven and still listed himself as a fisherman. So did his sons, John, Michael, and Samuel Junior. His son-in-law, Joe Dorotich, was still married to Caroline, and had presented Sam and Anna with nine grandchildren, eight of whom had survived to see the new century. Joe listed his occupation as a farmer, and so did John Novak.

One of the big changes on this census was the number of Scandinavian names appearing on the forms. Erik and Martha Sandin had come from Sweden and married in Seattle. He had been in America since 1882, she for six years fewer. They had lived in Artondale on a 160-acre homestead since 1888. They planted ten different kinds of apples, and when a bear came by to sample the fruit, Martha shot it and canned the meat. The lard made excellent pie crust.

Erik and Marta Sandin with sons Arthur and baby George

Erik Sandin, left, and son, Arthur, work on the first bridge on Hunt Road, circa 1908. Marta Bjork Sandin stands in the middle of the bridge.

79

In 1898 another pair of Swedes, Frank and Marie Samuelson, set themselves up in an area known in those days as Culvert, along the tip of the peninsula east of Wollochet Bay. They called their eighty acres Sunny Hill Fruit Farm. Trees as big as ten feet in diameter had to be brought down before they could farm, and the Samuelsons sometimes planted around stumps too big and tenacious to be removed. Eventually they brought forth five acres of fruit trees, four acres of berries, and a huge vegetable garden. At one time they could count five cows and four hundred chickens, along with some hogs and a horse. Prolific was a good word for the Samuelsons, as their fourteen children might have agreed.[81]

Overlooking Gig Harbor, Nils and Mary Shyleen had a twenty-acre berry farm and a struggling laundry business that Mary had brought over from Tacoma. Nils was a carpenter, when there was work to be had. They hacked through thick brush and cut down cedar, fir, alder, and spruce trees to build their first cabin. Cougars still screamed in the trees in those days, and sometimes cut across their yard. After a visit from a bear, Nils went to town and bought a six-shooter and a better bolt for the door.[82]

Nils was from Sweden, his wife from Norway. The Shyleens had many children, and among them was a daughter named Mabel, born in October 1886. On the first day of January 1903, seventeen-year-old Mabel opened a little cloth-covered blank book, a Christmas

Frank and Marie Samuelson's family pick berries at their eighty-acres Sunny Hill Fruit Farm east of Wollochet Bay.

present, and began to write. "Well this is New Year's Day, the day to make good resolutions, one of my resolutions is that I will write down in this book, everything of interest that happens in 1903." Early on, she missed three weeks of diary keeping while she worked as a domestic servant for a wealthy woman at the Tacoma Hotel, and it was March before the diary became more of a habit. She did not quite make it all year, but she gave us a record of a long-ago spring in a little community still looking for its place in the world.

> Mon. Mar. 23 – I got up at 5:30 and washed a great big washing. In the afternoon Mrs. Jessick [Jerisich] Julia & Baby came up. The folks were looking at the garden & Julia & I sat out on the porch talking & laughing about things that happened in school, & the baby was trying to swallow all the stones she could find.

Mabel Shyleen out with her squirrel gun in 1900. Her diary reflects life in the area at the turn of the century.

Nils and Mary Shyleen with other family members at their Gig Harbor home on Soundview Drive.

81

One cryptic entry reminds us that even a small community has it rituals and mysteries:

> Wed. Mar 25 – I went to a special meeting of the lodge held at the residence of Mr. Carlson meeting for the purpose of letting Archie & Harry Lamphier ride the 'goat.' We rowed over and disembarked across the bay & then after about an hour spent in crossing ditches, climbing logs & fences & going through about one hundred and fifty gates, we finally got there. We were going through McDowell's chicken yard, when Florence warned us to 'step high' or we might step on one of the chickens & then the dog came out after us. He acted like he wanted to eat us up offely [*sic*] bad, but he didn't know which one to take & then I slipped in one of those dear little ditches & fell, & he took right after me. I thought my climax had come.

The dog did not get her, but "Mrs. Wroten discovered she had left the key at home to the trunk in which the goat was locked. But somebody got it open however & so the boys got a taste of the trunk after all. Coming home my lantern went on strike and went out. Somebody tried to fix it & got their hands covered with coal oil. I'll bet they smell like a kerosene lamp for the next ten days. I got across the bay & home without any serious fatalities." She resigned from the lodge the following month, without ever getting around to explaining what it was or why they kept a goat in a locked trunk.

The Carlson family at home in Crescent Valley. The house still stands today.

Her diary continued, "Mar. 26 – I made some floating island, but the water was so thick the islands wouldn't float." Spooning egg whites into simmering milk for a floating island dessert could be complicated for any cook. Undaunted, she went on to describe her first attempt at Irish stew.

Mabel apparently loved to read, and could get quite descriptive in her own writing:

Wed Apr. 8 – Mama came home on the 6:00 boat & brought with her the book I had so long wanted, "Little Women." I got so wrapped up in it that I almost forgot my journal."

Easter Sunday Apr. 12, 1903 – Easter morning and everything bright & fair. The flowers had all been picked yesterday. The house was filled with sweet scents of Easter Lilies, primroses, daffodils & white mountain."

Sun Apr. 19 – ...Stopped in at Atkinsons to see the lambs, that Lollie admired so much. Dan and Byde proved to be very hospitable, treating us generously to apples & butternuts. They had a joke on me. They were talking about how the wood ticks infested the sheep & were bothersome at the time. My attention was attracted by something else at the time, but however thinking they were speaking of the lambs, I remarked 'Yes it must be very difficult to raise them & take care of them & they must require a great amount of care & attention.' I could not comprehend what they were laughing so heartily at, until they informed me it was wood ticks they were talking of, not lambs."

Some things about teenage girls remain the same in any century. "Sat Apr. 18 – ...Fanny & I went over & got weighed. There was quite a difference between our weights. She weighing just 93 & I tipping the scales to 130 lbs. We were both dissatisfied, she wanting to weigh more, & I less."

83

Mabel's diary gives clues about the town's economic arrangements, as when she writes, "Wed Apr. 22 – Papa went to town to get his tool chest, as he was going to work for Arda Hunt building a scow."

She offers greater detail when she describes her ingenuity in satisfying the competing demands of household economy and entertainment:

> Friday May 1 – ...I went at ten o'clock. I was to meet Julia at the wharf. Was there on time, got the papers, and then Eddie sent a nice leg of mutton. Well, there wasn't a thing to do but go home again with the bunch of meat, for the day was quite warm, & we couldn't possibly make use of a leg of mutton, (which would surely spoil), on our May Day expedition. While I was debating, however, along came Julia, and we jumped in the cart & drove home with that leg of mutton at break neck speed, to make up for lost time. Our May Day drive seemed to start in with every thing going wrong...The road was fine going to Goodmans, & I enjoyed it immensely, as I had never been there before. When we got there we had to pass through two gates, and cross over the creek which ran through the field.

Even once they arrived safely at the Goodman's, the adventure continued, as they were confronted with an angry black dog on one side, "a saucy looking cow" on the other, and "rushing waters on either side of us...In a few minutes Mrs. Goodman came out & released us of our perilous position, & we proceeded to the house to find Lilian sick, not in bed, but unable to leave her room, So we did not stay long."

Mabel paints a vivid picture of the more commonplace hazards faced by travelers when they decided to go on up the road to visit "the famous and well renowned Crescent Lake":

> Lily had said the road was quite good, except for a short space of corduroy.[83] We went a long distance & then came the corduroy. To say it jarred us is but putting it mildly...the

farther we went, the worse the road got...No sheet of water loomed up in the distance, nothing but woods, woods, woods. Not a house or a sign of a living thing. I guess we would have been going yet, had not something dreadful happened...when we struck a mud-hole which did not appear to be any worse than the rest of them, but we found out it was a good deal worse, for horse, wagon & all sunk down to a depth which was really alarming. I told Julia to get out, and I stood up and encouraged the horse all I could; after a good deal of struggling he managed to pull us out. That settled it, I vowed I would not go another step, Lake or no Lake.

Back at home, there were endless chores in the garden. For two days in May the family worked in the garden and canned jelly, with Mabel writing and pasting 150 four-line labels on the jars and watching it be shipped off by boat for sale. Oregon grape – shockingly sour plucked from the stem, but sweet enough when canned with sugar – grew wild on their property, and Mabel tended their raspberries and strawberries, which were turning into a significant cash crop around the peninsula.

She could turn a fair phrase when something inspired her, as it did

The Goodman family enjoys a summer picnic at Crescent Lake.

85

on May 12:

> After supper went for the milk, over to Lawrences, took the lower road, Virginia's curiosity was aroused by the steep path leading to the beach, so we walked down, found the path grown over considerably; the tide was in, & what a pretty picture the scenes around presented. We were standing on the high cliff, on the trunk of a tree which projected out over the water; below us the waves were dashing & beating against the wall of clay, the thick green foliage of the trees all about us, swaying to and fro in the fresh breeze, which swept across the sound, the music of the little spring which came trickling down the rugged bank. Looking across the blue waters, in the distance, loomed up grand old Mt. Tacoma. That great white mountain of snow against the blue sky, with the soft tints of the twilight reflected against her sides, made a picture beautiful to behold.

She told her diary about the pretty flowers on the tables at a party held in Burnham's Hall, long the unofficial community center for Gig Harbor. There she met the new minister, Reverend Ball, and a few years later she added a note to the diary that he later married Miss Goodman. This would be John Rice Ball and Cora Goodman, one of the five daughters of Joseph and Rose Goodman.

She mentioned a baseball game between the Tacoma Orioles and the Gig Harbor OKs. Gig Harbor won eighteen to seventeen. She also took note of local political contests. When President Teddy Roosevelt came to Tacoma, she and her mother went over on the *Crest* to see him come down St. Helens Avenue for a cornerstone-laying ceremony. "His face was awfully tanned," she said, "and was apparently very tired with his trips as he did not stand any more than what was necessary." On Decoration Day, which was gradually evolving into Memorial Day, she went to the GAR Hall and heard Congressman Francis Cushman speak "in his usual interesting way."

From early June to late October the diary went dormant, while her mother struggled through a serious attack of measles. By the time the journal picked up again on October 21, Mabel was attending the Academy which later grew into Pacific Lutheran University, in the little suburb of Parkland, south of Tacoma. The diary sputtered to an end in 1905, but life went on, just the same.

The diarist's parents, Nils and Mary Shyleen, lived out their lives in Gig Harbor, celebrating their fiftieth anniversary and beyond. Nils outlived his wife by eight months. He served on the school board for better than thirty-five years, and helped organize and lead the Boy Scout movement around the harbor. He was up pounding shingles on his roof two days before he died at age eighty-six.

Mabel married Seburn Jerome Ellis at the Presbyterian Church in Gig Harbor in November 1912. They ultimately moved to Hollywood, where Mabel had some acting hopes for herself and their two daughters. Not uncommon for Hollywood couples, the Ellises eventually divorced. True to her genetic heritage, Mabel survived till 1973.[84]

Sam Jerisich's last years mixed triumph and tragedy. He had fought a legal battle for years to gain final and complete title to the 160 acres

he and Anna had claimed on the east side of the harbor. It turned out to be good farmland, and in the 1890s workers from the sawmill began quietly settling on the Jerisich claim and on the big military reservations adjoining it. He hired a lawyer and waited while the wheels of justice ground slowly toward a decision.

Mabel Shyleen poses for her bridal photograph, 1912. Her marriage to Seburn Jerome Ellis was the first wedding at the newly built Memorial Presbyterian Church.

Sam outwaited most of the squatters; by 1898, when the Seattle land office finally awarded him title, there were only about a dozen of them left. But they hired a lawyer of their own and took the case to the commissioner of the general land office. Legal or not, they had worked hard on their homes, and they aimed to keep them.[85]

The settlers contended that Jerisich had improved only ten acres of the land, and was entitled to no more than that. The courts finally decided that Jerisich was the only one who had resided there in good faith since 1885, which was the Interior Department's cutoff date in this case for qualifying as a homesteader, and was thus entitled to all the land.

He was a successful enough man as a fisherman and a landowner to have a new home built and to hire Nils Shyleen to undertake the work. Yet with his economic blessings, the patriarch also suffered pain. Sam and Anna knew too well the sorrow of parents who must bury their children. Melissa and Catherine died in 1902. Mike fell ill in 1904 and on January 25, a priest and a doctor came from Tacoma. Death came in February.[86] Sam Junior followed in April at the age of twenty-six.

The old man had the consolation of his surviving children, their husbands and wives, and a noisy, growing collection of grandchildren. The end came for Samuel Jerisich on December 21, 1905. Reverend Alexander came down from the Greek Orthodox Church in Seattle to conduct the services at Sam's house on the December 23, followed by burial in Artondale Cemetery.

During his lifetime, Sam Jerisich had seen a number of changes in the fishing industry. One of the biggest came toward the end, brought about in part by one of his sons-in-law. Peter Skansie left San Martin, on the Dalmation island of Brac, on July 4, 1889. He picked fruit in California for a dollar a day, and then came up to Washington, where he found he could make up to $2.50 a day at a Wollochet Bay brick-yard. When the brickworks went under, he took a job with the Gig Harbor sawmill. By the time that business failed, he was happy to make $1.50 a day at a sawmill in Tacoma. When wages fell to $1.25,

Peter was ready to go fishing with the Jerisich boys, John and Mike.[87] Along the way he married their sister Melissa, who bore a daughter, Julia Skansie, before her untimely death in 1902.

Boats in Gig Harbor were a little bigger than when Sam Jerisich and his partners first rowed in. It took a crew of six or eight, pulling on oars more than twice their height, to take the boats out of the harbor. When their fishing grounds were distant, the fishermen sometimes hired a tug or steamer to pull them along, strung one behind another in parades of boats up to thirty vessels long. They were almost exclusively purse seiners, a method of fishing the Slavonians were credited with introducing to Puget Sound sometime around the mid-1880s.

These fishermen went about their business much the same as they always had, until Peter Skansie saw a couple of Ballard fishermen take to the water in a boat powered by an engine. It was so temperamental and underpowered that the oar boats outfished it, but an idea took root in Skansie's mind. As he recalled the moment in a broken-English narrative in his old age, "around 1902 we made Power boat and inlarge 30 foot oar boat. Saw it in two and added in center 8 feet longer and installed 7 horse power Standard Gas Engine. It never failed to go and we made good season. At same time, and right after everybody made power boats, us brothers start building little cabins on our boats and others boats and little by little start build or repair small boats." Others said the year was 1905 instead of 1902, but the important thing was that a new era had begun.

Peter Skansie immigrated to Gig Harbor from the island of Brac, Dalmatia in 1889.

The "us brothers" he referred to were Mitchell, Joe, and Andrew Skansie. Peter and Andrew drifted back into fishing after a while, but Mitchell and Joe found themselves spendng more and more time at their boat-building. Mitchell had begun fishing at Gig Harbor about 1900, and had gained experience building boats during a four-year stint in Seattle. In January 1905 he married Amanda Dorotich,[88] the daughter of Joe Dorotich and the granddaughter of Sam Jerisich. Mitchell gradually became the driving force in the Skansie brothers' boat business.

At first they primarily finished hulls purchased from the Martinich yard at Dockton on Vashon Island, installing cabins and rigging the boats to seine for salmon. In 1912 Mitchell brought in a friend, Sam Kazulin, to act as foreman, and they built their first boat from the keel up. This was the *Oceania*, a sixty-two-foot seiner notable for her straight deck. Though boats normally had raised sterns, a straight deck with no step from stem to stern was simpler to build. The downside to this design became obvious when those in the crew's quarters and engine room found themselves banging their heads on the low-

The Oceania, *an early Skansie fishing boat*

(clockwise from left) Peter, Mitchell, Joe, and Andrew Skansie

ered ceiling. The Skansies never built another straight-deck purse seiner.

Their boatyard, a great roofed workshop with open ends, lay at the foot of what is now Pioneer Way, where boat after boat would slide down the ways onto the waters of Gig Harbor in the years ahead. In a big leather-bound ledger, Mitchell Skansie tracked the profits and expenses of the growing business. They were not the only boat builders in Gig Harbor's history. Robert Crawford and Conrad Anderson would establish yards of their own, and some Gig Harbor fishermen bought boats from Tacoma and elsewhere, but in a very large sense, the boats and the fishermen in Mitchell Skansie's ledger are the history of fishing in Gig Harbor in its glory days. (For a list of Skansie boats, see Appendix A.)

Robert Crawford at his boatyard at the head of the bay. He produced fishing boats and Point Defiance rowboats.

The hull of the Skansie ferry Defiance *is ready for launch in 1927. Fishing boats at left are in the yard for maintenance. Photo by Marvin Boland*

91

Skansie boats were durable. They survived dangerous waters, from California to Alaska, and many of them outlived the men they were built for. Lee Makovich, a commercial fishing historian and descendant of a prominent Gig Harbor family with ties to the fishing industry, has tirelessly pursued the story of the boats that sailed out of Gig Harbor. He knows of Skansie boats still tilling the seas in a new century.

Sometimes the boats' missions changed in startling ways. A few years ago, a 1917-vintage Skansie boat was caught by the Canadian government trying to smuggle drugs across the border. And the 1925 *Shenandoah* was donated to the Gig Harbor Peninsula Historical Society by commercial fisherman Tony Janovich in 2000. In February 2003 she left the waters of the harbor permanently when she was moved onto the society's property for restoration and preservation. The *Shenandoah* was the only Skansie-built purse seiner to live out her entire fishing career in Gig Harbor. As a museum exhibit, safe from the seas that claimed many of her sisters, she will tell the story of the fishing fleet for future generations.[89]

Conrad Anderson built boats from 1920 until 1937 at his boatyard located along the waterfront at the foot of Stinson Hill.

The Skansie-built fishing vessel Shenandoah *at its launching on March 30, 1925. Photo by Marvin Boland.* Courtesy of the Washington State Historical Society, Tacoma

Almost anyone living near the water on the Gig Harbor peninsula needed a boat of some sort. A reliable source for small boats across half a century was Harry Maloney, who lived in a home he called Camp Sleepy Hollow a hundred feet above his boat shop south of the sand spit at the harbor entrance. His boats were built of quality cedar and ranged from twelve to sixteen feet. The son of a man who built the sleek interiors of Pullman Cars, Maloney began building boats about 1910. He estimated that he turned out about six hundred in the course of his long life, in addition to wooden herring rakes and wooden spoons for attracting salmon, which became known as Maloney spoons. Some of his boats were used for years as rentals at the Point Defiance boathouse, and a few of them remained serviceable around Gig Harbor for years after Maloney's death in 1964. "He would tighten the boat ribs as tight as banjo strings," recalled the owner of a forty-year-old skiff.[90]

Harvesting the sea

Fishermen pull 800 fish from a trough, June 6, 1911, near Steilacoom, Washington.

Crews from the Skansie boats Aeroplane *and* Fairplay *pull nets by hand in 1906.*

Peter Skansie, his family, and crew onboard the Eagle, *1905, one of the first engine-powered boats in the area.*

Peter Skansie and six crewmen, including A.K. Sauness, in an oar-powred fishing boat

Fishermen used oars to propel early boats, after towing their boats to the fishing grounds.

Christy Skarponi on his sardine boat showing catch of 120 tons in one day in 1928. Fish filled the hold and covered the decks.

The Skansie's Avalon *and* Genius *moored in the harbor was a familiar sight in Gig Harbor for many years.*

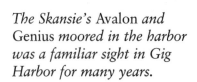

Corregidor *(Castelan)* 1942

Editor *(Castelan)* 1942

George A *(Ancich)* 1927

Glory of the Seas
(Malich) 1925

Home II *(Ross)*, A Ribich
(Ribich), Westland *(Ross)*,
Notre Dame *and* Chinook
*(Ross and Tarabochia) in
Gig Harbor*

Majestic *(Bujacich)*

Pulling in a net full of fish onboard the Majestic.

Jake Bujacich and crewmen hand-pull the fishing nets onto the Majestic.

Victory *(Gilich)*

Tony Skrivanich and Marty Bussanich use a pre-1950s turntable to pull in the net on the Elector, *built in 1914.*

Emmett Ross, skipper of the Westland *mends a net. He was considered a top purse seiner on the salmon banks.*

Welcome *(Stanich)*

Crew from Andrew Skansie's fishing vessel the Spokane *repairing a fishing net.*

Launching the Pacific Raider *in 1947 – (l-r) Nick Jerkovich, Nick Castelan, Marko Markovich, John Jerkovich, Jr., Mary Jerkovich, John Jerkovich, Sr., Mike Castelan, and Tom Jerkovich.*

Chapter 6

Merchants and Preachers and a Floating Butcher

As pieces of ground go in Gig Harbor's part of the world, the site where Donkey Creek empties into the harbor already had an eventful history. It had been the spawning ground of salmon, and the site of the Native American village of *Twa-Wal-Kut*. The United States Government claimed ownership of the whole of the Pacific Northwest as soon as the Treaty of 1846 made this American land, and eventually the government sold this one small part of its vast holdings to George and Mary Barns.

In April 1874 the Barnses did something unusual: they sold it back to the original owners. For $335, they conveyed titles to "Lot No. 2 of Section 6 and the south east ¼ of the south east ¼ of Section 6 in Township 21 North of Range 2 East containing 67.62 acres, more or less" over to "Tyee George, late of the Puyallup tribe of Indians, Tula loqua alias George of the same tribe, Tawau oola of the tribe, Old Bill, Alias Tsootsu-haimayh of the same tribe, Docter [*sic*] alias Heptchk of the same tribe, George Washington, alias Kelaratire of Gig Harbor, Swuanaghim of the same tribe and John Alias Salaghim of Gig Harbor all of Pierce County, W. T."

Indian names always suffer when white writers try to transcribe them phonetically onto paper, and these were given a second butchering in January 1881, when "Old Bill alias Tsootsa, George Washington alias Kclancatin, Tala legaa alias George Sawanaghew" conveyed ownership of the same "67.62 acres more or less" to Jackson Walla of the Puyallup Tribe. Likely this was a legal maneuver to give a single individual guardianship of the land, since the selling price this time was a symbolic dollar.

Part of the Indian village was still there in the mid-1880s, captured in the hazy background of a photograph intended to showcase the new lumber mill. The inhabitants drifted slowly away over the years, some to the Indian reservation at Puyallup, others to a less settled life on the shores of Wollochet Bay. By 1909, the land belonged to John and Josephine Novak. They leased part of it that year to a newcomer named Charles Osgood Austin, who had come to Tacoma from his native New Hampshire with his parents in 1889. Austin had gained experience with sawmills in the Washington communities of Centralia and Maltby, and his father operated a mill across Carr Inlet on the Longbranch Peninsula at Vaughn.[91] C. O. Austin brought sawmilling back to Gig Harbor, at long last.

This mill was not as big as the operations of the 1880s and early 1890s. Its capacity was only about 15,000 board-feet a day,[92] but it provided a steady payroll for as between two and thirty workers, depending on the volume of business. The mill turned out everything from moldings and fruit boxes to dock timbers and shingles.[93] Austin liked the flat tideland where logs could be floated up close to the mill. At least one of the old Indian dwellings was still standing on the site, and Austin put it to use as a tool shed. Austin's mill was an early sign of Gig Harbor's returning prosperity.

With or without a mill in operation, as long as there were big trees standing, someone would want to cut them down. In January 1910

The C.O. Austin Mill was founded in 1909 and continued until Austin's death in 1946.

99

the *West Coast Lumberman* included the Gig Harbor Timber Company on a list of operations using Shay locomotives. Another locomotive, bearing the name Storey Timber Company, operated around then or earlier, tumbling logs into a slough south of Raft Island on the Rosedale shore.[94]

Another sign of Gig Harbor's resurgence was the completion of a new wharf on the east side in the spring of 1910. The next order of business was to get some decent roads built to join the fertile farms of Rosedale and Crescent Valley with the markets of the bigger cities in Kitsap County and the waiting holds of the Gig Harbor steamboats.[95] The muddy trace where Mabel Shyleen tried and failed to drive a buggy to Crescent Lake just could not be tolerated anymore. The south end of the peninsula also cried out for a good road. This was the area that looked across to Fox Island, known variously as Hales Passage. Children down there were still walking as far as three miles over a footpath to get to school.

C.O. Austin Mill – (rear, l-r) Norman Kimball, Jesse McDaniel, John Vernhardson (front, l-r) Albert Simerson, Dexter McDaniel, C.O. Austin, and Charles Diball

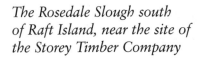

The Rosedale Slough south of Raft Island, near the site of the Storey Timber Company

The one stretch of good road seemed to be the county road from Gig Harbor to Burley, over at the head of Henderson Bay, on the way to the Longbranch Peninsula. A man who lived at Burley, L. M. Fenton, started out operating a steam launch called the *Kingston* between Burley and Tacoma, but about 1909, he started a new enterprise. He secured a contract to carry the mail, and began operating a horse-drawn stage between Gig Harbor and Burley. This went on for a dozen years, until automobiles began to make their appearance in these parts. He was known as Daddy Fenton to those who had the memorable experience of riding with him and hearing him point out the beauties of the countryside as the little stage bounced slowly along.[96]

While they waited for more and better roads, some of the people living down on the southern end of the peninsula undertook to strengthen their sea link to the greater world. They formed the Hales Pass and Wollochet Navigation Company and raised thirteen thousand dollars to purchase the steamer *Crest* from the Hunt brothers. Frank Samuelson, Elias Muri, Mark Smaby, Mrs. M. B. Bruce, and Charles Warren each invested a thousand dollars, with the other farmers of the area making up the balance through the purchase of hundred-dollar shares.

Samuelson was the first president of the organization, and Floyd Hunt stayed on as the captain of the steamer, which they renamed the *Bay Island*. Each morning at seven o'clock the little steamer left its anchorage on Fox Island for stops at Arletta, Warren, Sunny Bay, Cromwell, East Cromwell, Union, Picnic Point, Wollochet, Point

Berries from area farms are loaded on the Bay Island, *the former* Crest, *in east Wollochet at Union Dock. The Hales Pass and Wollochet Navigation Company owned the steamboat.*

Fosdick, Point Evans, Seneca, Point Defiance, Old Tacoma, and Tacoma. Passage cost twenty-five cents.

Some of the stops on the list were new names. Warren, which looked directly across toward Fox Island and little outlying Towhead Island, was the place where Charley Warren had built a store, and where the county had installed a dock with a beehive-shaped freight shed. Warren had come out from Maine sometime before the turn of the century, and his brother William joined him a while later. William and his wife bought a dozen acres of land up near Rosedale from W. B. Richards, who had purchased it from Captain Daniel McLean, an early pioneer of the area. That spot is known in our own time as Olympic View.

A post office tried to get a start at Warren in 1904, but was canceled out the following year. Not too far away, Oliver Pearson's greenhouses climbed the south-facing hillside behind his house with their burden of tomatoes and cucumbers. Pearson was a Swedish immigrant who had Americanized his name from Olaf to Oliver after he came ashore in Maine from Akaboda, Sweden. His wife Mary, the former Maria Nilsdottar/Nilson of Vanga, Sweden, was a midwife, delivering many of the babies born around the peninsula's southern shore.

Sunny Bay, which lived up to its name on any clear day, was a small dent in the mainland east of Warren, facing Fox Island and the bay that shelters Tanglewood Island. Here tiny Muri Creek made its way down to Puget Sound, and here fruit and tomatoes tended to ripen faster than

anywhere else on the peninsula. Norwegian immigrants Elias and Sarah Muri owned land on both sides of the creek and worked with neighbor Frank Samuelson to divert a portion of the water into a storage tank for irrigating their apricot trees and Samuelson's berries.

Elias and Sarah Muri of Cromwell in a family portrait with Clara (standing) and Amanda

A bit farther down the beach, in a southeasterly direction, lay Cromwell. This place, with its high eroding bluff, was named for John B. Cromwell, an Ohio native who had been a telegrapher in Nebraska, à railroad man in Montana, and then the postmaster of Tacoma. His father, Charles W. Cromwell, had died in Tacoma in 1890, and was yet another veteran of the Minnesota Sioux Uprising war of 1862. Lieutenant Charles Cromwell commanded a company of men at the Mankato execution of thirty-eight Sioux warriors – the same occasion that brought Gig Harbor's Alfred Burnham and William Duley together in time and place.[97]

East Cromwell was just inside Wollochet Bay, on the bulge of the western shore, before the bay veers off toward the northwest. Picnic Point was farther up on the eastern side of the narrowing bay. It was quite the gathering place for folks living out that way, and was also the home of an increasingly important annual fair where peninsula residents showed off their produce.

Next came Point Fosdick, east of Wollochet Bay at the southernmost tip of the peninsula. It boasted one of the older names, having been christened by the Wilkes Expedition back in 1841.

It was about this time that the whole of Pierce Country west of The Narrows – Gig Harbor, Rosedale, Arletta, Artondale, the Longbranch Peninsula, Fox, McNeil, and Anderson Islands, and sundry other points – began to be known under the collective title "Bay Island." By 1912 there were seven hundred people living in the district, and the numbers swelled well above that in summer, when the wealthy from Tacoma and Seattle came over to seek shade and relaxation in a growing number of beachfront cottages and homes.

The steamer Crest *moored at Picnic Point near the head of Wollochet Bay. The point was a popular gathering place for area residents.*

Agriculture was expanding across the peninsula. At least 3,500 crates of loganberries were coming out of the Gig Harbor area each year, and 10,000 were exported from the peninsula as a whole. E. D. Patrick, Mrs. E. M. Iliff, John Sather, J. A. Wheeler, RoyEllendorf, and JuliusWasdahl were all involved in growing the berries. A. E. Johnston concentrated on pears, apples, and cherries. Another grower, specializing in cherries, was clearing $700 per acre with his Bing, Lamperts, and Royal Annes.[98] Some of the fruit growers decided to diversify. Wheeler was also seeing some success with potatoes, and Ellendorf had started up a dairy.

Charles Ferguson lived near Wollochet Bay, and in January 1905 Mabel Shyleen paid a visit and gave her diary an uncommonly detailed view of a peninsula farm. "It was the first time I had seen their new residence, and it was even nicer than I thought it would be," she gushed. "A large yellow house, situated on a knoll, with wide verandas running around. The rooms were very large and well furnished. Wellwood is a model farm. All the cows are Jerseys, there are six or eight good horses, a lovely creek running through the barn-yard."[99]

Money being made on the peninsula meant more opportunities for merchants, and stores seemed to sprout up like mushrooms. In 1911 Harold and Gladys Forsythe opened one near Picnic Point. They were Scots, who played Gaelic songs on their victrola and inspired wonder in their visitors with the bookshelves that rose from floor to ceiling on two sides of one room of their home.[100] Their general store stayed in business into the 1970s.[101]

Early view of Crescent Valley. The Mathias and Elise Jacobson's home, barn, and berry fields are at center, Crescent Valley School is at the left.

Not far away, Mrs. Amanda Bruce started a store on her houseboat in 1910. She was bought out in 1913 by W. L. Munro, who operated the business until he sold it to a man named Harrison in 1922. Like other merchants of the time and place, Munro sold groceries on credit until his customers were able to pay, but he could be firm when necessary. Toward the end of his career, when one of his customers tried to skip out of state, leaving a debt of more than three hundred dollars, Munro attached his cow, his car, and more than one hundred dollars of his salary.[102]

Benjamin Lay continued running his store in Rosedale until 1904, when he rented it out to newcomer Charles Sumner Johnson. Lay retained ownership and the store survived for many years, into the age of refrigeration, when it earned local fame among children for its stock of cold Milky Way bars.[103]

In Gig Harbor, S. T. Strout and John Novak operated general stores near the People's Dock. This was choice real estate. People's Dock was the first landing inside the harbor, the stopping place for the steamer *Dove* and other boats, and a store there was well situated to catch everyone coming and going.

S. P. Strout General Merchandise, 1912, sold staples and "fancy" groceries.

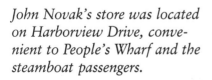

John Novak's store was located on Harborview Drive, convenient to People's Wharf and the steamboat passengers.

There were even a few merchants who did not wait for the world to come to them. Floating stores had been a fixture on southern Puget Sound for decades. Isolated communities without a store of their own depended on the visits of boats like the *Otter*, operated by the Cook brothers. The shallow waters and muddy bottom of Gig Harbor once proved too much for the stern-wheeler, until Lucien Cook resorted to filling the hold with empty barrels at low tide. "General Merchandise," a ship-length sign proclaimed, and its wares included everything from groceries to kid gloves.[104] Other store boats included the *Vaughn* and the *Bertha,* skippered by Ernie Ehricke. It was on the *Bertha* that Ehricke was caught in a storm between the mainland and Vashon Island. Realizing his boat was sinking, he dove into the chilly water and swam ashore at Gig Harbor.[105]

On Tacoma's Commencement Bay waterfront, Richard Uhlman devised a new twist on the floating store idea. Fresh meat was difficult to come by in the era before refrigeration, and from 1912 to 1918 he served as South Puget Sound's floating butcher, delivering his wares on shipboard to customers up and down the shoreline. His brother, Harry, had a chicken farm, and might have contributed eggs to go with the ham and bacon.[106] Uhlman's boat, *Butcher*, had a nine-foot beam and a fourteen-horsepower Hallin engine. It was small enough to run up on the beach and lower a gangplank for his customers to cross.[107]

Richard Uhlman provided fresh meat to area residents on his boat the Butcher, *from 1912 to 1918.*

Once, on a fogbound run along the peninsula's southern fringe, he put in close to shore and met a blind Indian known as John Skinshot, who owned seven-and-a-half acres of land along the shore. Uhlman liked the place so well that he later purchased the property,[108] and opened a nonfloating store. He also served as a clerk on the Wollochet School Board, and with his support of the Masons and the Catholic Church, became a fixture in the life of the community.[109]

Each store, afloat or ashore, was memorable. Each was unique. And each was a vital part of the community it served. But no name over the door was more durable or ultimately more important to the development of the peninsula than the name Uddenberg. Axel Uddenberg was a Swede, born in Stockholm in 1855, who went to sea in 1871 and gained his master's papers to command a merchant ship by the time he was twenty-one. He first saw Puget Sound in 1888, when he took a cargo of lumber from Tacoma to Australia. He came back to Washington to farm in 1890, first at Spanaway, and then at Roy. After a brief stint in general merchandise in Tacoma, he came to Gig Harbor about 1907 and built a home, which featured a general store on the ground floor.

Uddenberg's home was in north Gig Harbor, facing west, at what people called the head of the bay. The head of the bay was the third and last stop for steamers entering the harbor. W. P. Kendall already

Axel Uddenberg store on the pier at the head of the bay.

Axel Uddenberg arrived in Gig Harbor in 1907. The name Uddenberg became synonymous with local grocery stores.

107

had a general store nearby, but there seemed to be room for another one. It was a busy stretch, home of the post office and Frank Scott's livery stable, which catered to the farmers who brought their horse-drawn wagons down from Crescent Valley and the back country.[110]

Axel and Angelina Uddenberg had six children, with birthplaces scattered around the world. Hobert was born in Australia. Signo and Arthur hailed from the East Indies, and Bertram and Aida were born in Spanaway. The proud parents, who were distant cousins and both named Uddenberg, had been married in Hull, England.[111]

In 1910 or 1911 Axel purchased land beside People's Dock from Sam Jerisich's widow, Anna. He built a new store on pilings beside the wharf. The store was really two buildings, a hay and feed store facing the waterfront, and the West Side Grocery catering to the needs of those who came by land or sea. Axel chose his son Bert to run the operation. As a man who had commanded a ship at twenty-one, he saw nothing wrong with a turning the management of a store over to a sixteen-year-old.

The vast bulk of Pierce County's land and population lay east of The Narrows, and the few miles of the Gig Harbor peninsula did not see much of the county bureaucracy. There was not much law enforcement, and there generally was not much need of it. When Mr. and Mrs. Bernard Green departed from their ranch out toward Artondale for a year in Victoria, they saw no need to lock their door. They were right. When they came back, they found everything the way they had left it.[112]

Fred Proctor delivers groceries for Alex Uddenberg by horse and wagon.

If serious trouble came, it usually came from outside. The first time a murder took place on the peninsula proper, both the killer and the victim were visitors. In the spring of 1910 a sad little tragedy was enacted on the Gig Harbor – Artondale Road. It began on April 4, when a messenger boy carried a letter to Mrs. Frederica Schulz of Tacoma. The letter told Mrs. Schulz that her sister, Mrs. F. Haberecht, who lived on the peninsula, had been stricken with paralysis and needed assistance. Mrs. Schulz took the 9:00 A.M. passage on the *Crest*, and for days nothing more was seen or heard of her. With increasing anxiety, Frederica's husband and family investigated and discovered that Mrs. Haberecht was fine, knew nothing of her sister's coming, and had sent no note.

On April 10, bloodhounds and deputy sheriffs found Mrs. Schulz's body in the bushes along the road to Artondale. It was in a lonely place, past Floyd Hunt's ranch, about 375 feet short of the Haberecht cottage,[113] along the stretch where the road bent toward Wollochet Bay. No one heard the bullet that crashed into her left temple or the blow that inflicted blunt trauma to her scalp. Yet no one in her family had much doubt who had murdered her.

There was even less doubt when Harry Wroten looked at a photo of Charles Wezler and identified him as the sweaty, agitated man who had hired Harry and his launch to take him from the head of Gig Harbor to Point Defiance on the afternoon of the murder.[114] Before the month was out, the wild-eyed, chain-smoking Wezler was hauled from San Francisco back to Tacoma to face murder charges. In his tearful confession, he talked of his stormy nine-year marriage to Louise Schulz, their divorce, his frustrated efforts to see his two children, and his desperate plot to lure his former mother-in-law, Frederica Schulz, to Gig Harbor, where he hoped to convince her to let him see his children.

He met her on the road going up the hill from the landing, and they walked and talked for about three miles. She demanded $3,000 in alimony for her daughter, and he pleaded for one last visit with his children: "I said 'what am I going to do to see my children?' I would

109

not want to go through another year like the dreadful year I have spent. She says 'It's no use, that's all!' Just like that, 'You don't need to see the children; Louise is going to Alaska and I am going to take the children away.' That was all she said – we were still walking along and – then I shot her – I just pulled my gun out of my overcoat pocket."

He went on to confess dragging her from the road, his efforts to shoot himself in the head, the four-time failure of the gun, and then his flight and capture.[115]

If the peninsula had been given a look at the worst that men could do, it was also seeing nobler aspirations. Schools were growing and more churches were coming. Rosedale already had a congregation. In 1906, Elizabeth Lay and Nellie Mae Warren toured the community by horse and buggy, visiting every home, raising money and securing pledges of labor and material. William Warren donated a plot of ground across the road from the schoolhouse, which had served as makeshift church and Sunday school for long enough. This church was nondenominational, with the pulpit open to any qualified minister or clergyman. It became known as the Rosedale Union Church.[116]

The folks living in the Cromwell area were largely Norwegian Lutherans, and as early as 1902 they had formed a mission aid society. By 1907 a pastor was employed at an annual salary of $144 and services were held in the local schoolhouse. In 1909 the C. I. Kirkeide

Rosedale Union Church, 1940s

Cromwell Lutheran Church, built in 1909

family donated an acre of land one hundred yards up the hill from Hales Passage, and work soon commenced on a twenty-eight by forty-foot sanctuary with a fourteen-foot ceiling, a Sunday school room, and a ten-foot square bell tower. By August 1910 all was ready for the church's annual meeting.

As in many churches, furnishings and embellishment came in stages. The church's youth group undertook the task of raising funds for a bell. Anxious for the sound of a distant steeple bell, or simply excited by the prospect of a party, they attacked the challenge with gusto. They staged basket socials, tie socials, and shadow socials until there was money for a bell so large it served for decades to come.

The bell arrived even before the church got its white coat of paint, and long before it got a pulpit and steps leading up the bank from the beach. There was a choir from the beginning, but it was six years before a pump organ contributed its voice. At the start, services were in Norwegian and the males sat on the right and the females on the left, in strict Norwegian Lutheran tradition. It took a while before English-language services and unisex seating came into vogue.[117]

In Gig Harbor, the Catholics and the Presbyterians were finally catching up with the Methodists and erecting churches of their own. It had looked bad for the Presbyterians for a while. Pastor Weekes had retired in 1907. In 1908 the property where he had ministered in Vaughn was sold to the Congregationalists. In October of the same year, the minutes of the Presbytery's regional headquarters in Olympia contained the laconic note, "The church at Gig Harbor having become extinct was stricken from the roll of churches."[118]

Memorial Presbyterian Church on Pioneer Way, 1915

111

What looked like the end turned out to be a new beginning. First off, Reverend Weekes, retired or not, continued teaching Sunday school and preaching. The GAR Hall served well for such gatherings, and the de facto congregation grew. In the mean time, a mundane miracle worked its way to a climax. In 1888, a woman in New York City donated $175 in accumulated savings to an unknown source. In some unexplained way the money made its way to a bank in Tacoma and into the hands of the local Presbyterians. By 1912, interest had increased the amount to $275. Around this seed, more money was raised.

Edna Hunt, the wife of Arda Hunt, stalked the community door by door and raised another $250. Even some of the Catholics chipped in. Weekes worked his connections with Tacoma businessmen, and the general Presbyterian organization made its own contribution. When all funds were cobbled together, there was $1,400 to build a church. To crown these efforts, Oscar and Anna Gustafson donated a suitable piece of land near the foot of Pioneer Street, and construction began.

On September 13, 1913, a proud Reverend Thomas J. Weekes reported, "The people of Gig Harbor enabled us to build a neat structure with auditorium, 25x40 ft, a small vestry and tower 8x8 ft, in which is installed a fine toned bell. The interior of the church has solar lights, of 1800 C. P. [candle power] with a 1200 C. P. lamp at entrance. The building is semi-gothic in design, with a large stained glass memorial window in front."

The Lord's Supper was celebrated on September 28 for the first time with sixteen members in attendance. By October 26, James L. Snyder

Presbyterian Ladies Aid Society, circa 1900

and Roy E. Cruver were ordained as church elders. Weekes, still listed in the Presbyterian rolls under "honorable retirement," stayed on as moderator. In January 1914 he appointed Nils Shyleen, Arthur Constable, and William T. Wilkinson to the Board of Trustees. Constable was later forced to resign because his own church, the Friends, better known as Quakers, would not let him serve another church. Before his mortal life ended on April 2, 1916, Reverend Weekes had the satisfaction of seeing the Presbyterian Church well and permanently established.[119]

The Slavonians in Gig Harbor were largely Catholic, and visiting priests like Father Ignatius Vasta had been coming over from St. Leo's parish in Tacoma to conduct the Sacrament of the Mass since at least 1904. John Novak hosted them in his home, and so did Nick Novakovich and many others. As the community grew, so did the momentum to build a church. A committee was formed, consisting of Peter Skansie, Andrew Gilich, Nick Costello, Theresa Sweeney, and John Ross. Individuals, canneries, and fishing supply businesses contributed, and in 1914 the church was up in time for Easter services. Father Vasta celebrated the Mass, and Tony Stanich and John Zulyevic served as altar boys. The first baby baptized in the new church was Anna Stanich, and the first bride was Annie Ross, who married John Masnow from Hoquiam. Strictly speaking, the building was still a mission, since it had no resident pastor until the 1930s, but that stopped no one in the proud community from calling it a church.

The Methodist Church, which had risen ahead of the others, opened an "out-station" church at Artondale near Wollochet Bay in 1912. As this book

St. Nicholas Catholic Church, built in 1913

goes to press, the building is still giving service to the community as a Grange Hall. The main Methodist church building in Gig Harbor's north end, on land donated long ago by Alfred Burnham, moved to a new location in 1916. To make way for a school, the church was dismantled and moved down the hill to a spot near the water. The pitch of the hill was steeper there, enabling the church to have a daylight basement. Its Sunday dedication featured an event that could have passed for a miracle, had it not been so inconvenient. A spring of flowing water popped up in the basement's concrete floor. Until the congregation found a way to wall it off and divert it, they made the best of the gift, using the water for baptisms and coffee hours.[120]

Progress of many sorts was coming to the peninsula. It could even come sweeping down out of the sky. In 1914, only eleven years after the Wright Brothers made their first powered flight, a seaplane piloted by Tacoman Gustav Stromer landed at Nesika, a little south of the entrance to Gig Harbor. Stromer was courting Edna Coffman of

The Methodist Church ladies group gathers in front of the church at its original location. The church was moved in 1916.

Gustav Stromer lands his seaplane in Nesika, a small community outside the harbor on the west side, 1914.

114

Gig Harbor that year. She later married another, but her son became a pilot and lies today in Artondale Cemetery under a tombstone engraved with an airplane.[121]

Automobiles were common in Tacoma and other nearby big cities before they ever made their way out to the peninsula. Remembering back, people thought the first car owner might have been Frank M. Scott, helping put himself out of the livery stable business with a Dodge in 1913.[122] Fred McIntyre, who carried mail, started doing it in a Ford not long after. Merchant W. L. Munro was another early adopter, using a Model T truck for his deliveries, but then he had been a pioneer in the use of the telephone as well.[123] Soon there were others. Byron Walrath, who raised chickens in Rosedale, drove a shiny red Brush.[124] Willie Yarnell, who had moved from Rosedale to the old Burnham homestead in Gig Harbor, tooled around in a Reo. In Rosedale he left behind the first silo on the peninsula, built of concrete with the assistance of Jesse Foutch.[125]

As soon as there were enough cars, there was a need to get them across The Narrows to and from Tacoma and beyond. The steamers were fine for passengers, freight, and an occasional horse or two, but something new was needed for the automobiles. In 1918 Pierce County put the first car ferry to work on the Gig Harbor run. The 142-foot

The Lloyd Hunt family sets out on their summer vacation when traveling by automobile was still a novelty.

City of Tacoma made seven runs a day, seven days a week, between Point Defiance, Vashon Island, and the dock at the head of the bay in Gig Harbor. The location of the landing favored the Scandinavians of Crescent Valley over the Slavonians of the west side. This inequity remained a bone of contention until 1923, when the landing moved to People's Dock, beside Uddenberg's store on the western shore.[126]

Later the ferry was remodeled and lengthened to 170 feet, which increased her carrying capacity from thirty to fifty vehicles. The landing was also moved from inner Gig Harbor to a specially built ferry slip at Point Fosdick. The Tacoma landing site then became Titlow Beach at the foot of Sixth Avenue. The Skansie brothers later got into the ferry business, building the *Skansonia* and *Vashonia*. Ultimately two ferries would connect to the peninsula, one running from Point Defiance to a ferry slip just up the western shore from the Gig Harbor entrance, the other from Titlow to the Point Fosdick landing.

If the ferries supplied connections to the wider world, so did the newspapers. Since the summer of 1914, they had been filled with accounts of the conflict raging in Europe. This grew into a huge, grinding world war, unlike any that had gone before, and it must have stirred heavy feelings in immigrants with vivid memories of their homelands. As the casualties mounted into the millions, fears grew that America was drifting toward war. In 1915 there was a peace pageant in Rosedale, a rare moment when the people of the peninsula tried to influence an event beyond their own doorsteps. Anna Lay, the wife of

Ferry service to Gig Harbor began in 1917 when the City of Tacoma *docked at the head of the bay.*

storekeeper Benjamin Lay, organized it. It included many children and a woman dressed as Columbia, but it was more patriotic than pacifist. When America entered the war in 1917, Mrs. Lay gave her support, and many of the peninsula's young men marched off to war.

Dan Yates, the son of Rosedale's Albert and Sarah Yates, enlisted and was sent to France as part of the motor transport corps. He became a driver for a lieutenant colonel on General Pershing's staff and remained overseas for about a year and a half. [127] Two of Axel Uddenberg's sons went into the service. Bert, recently married, set aside his storekeeper duties at the West Side Grocery on People's Dock to go into the medical corps, working in the hospitals with the grim parade of wounded. The Yates's other son, Herman, became Gig Harbor's lone casualty, killed in action in France on October 20, 1918, as the war entered its final weeks. The First Methodist Episcopal Church installed a memorial window in his honor. Sadly, this was not the last tragedy for the Uddenbergs. In 1923 Axel would lose another son, Signo, when his ship sank in a storm at sea. [128]

On the heels of the war came a deadly outbreak of Spanish flu, known then as influenza. It was called a pandemic, because it claimed some thirty million victims across the world. Nearly half a million Americans died, and influenza's reach extended to the Gig Harbor peninsula. Near Rosedale Slough, Hattie Huff and her infant daughter Amber died of it, and were buried in one coffin in the Rosedale Cemetery.

Peace Day Celebration on May 18, 1915 at Ben Lay's store in Rosedale

In 1923 the peninsula faced another deadly disease outbreak. Old Joseph Goodman caught the bare details in his daily journal for November 21, 1923. "Wolbert's little girl died from diptheria. Shaw's girl sick. School closed." School remained closed until the danger was considered past on December 3.

Big wars always bring big changes, and one of the effects of World War I was that large numbers of women entered the work force in an official way for the first time. The very first group of women to go to work in the Bremerton navy yard, north of the Kitsap County line from Gig Harbor, included Ethel Margaret Burnham, the daughter of Biz Burnham. He did not see much of her at that time, having divorced her mother in 1908, but he was still fishing the local waters, as were some of his old competitors, the Hunt brothers.

The soldiers returned to a big homecoming in November 1919. Mrs. Arda Hunt was the organizer; Lee Makovich was the chairman, and Mitchell Skansie and Nils Shyleen lent a hand, the way they always did when something was going on in the community. Dr. Rust gave an address of welcome, and even old Anna Jerisich was prevailed upon to talk of the old days, more than forty years past, when she and

Sam first came to Gig Harbor. There had been vast changes over those years, and there were about to be more. Gig Harbor and the world were about to enter the roaring twenties.

Herman Uddenberg when he worked at the Skansie shipyard. He was Gig Harbor's lone casualty of World War I. A window at the Methodist Church was later dedicated in his memory.

118

Chapter 7

Roaring into a Depression

In 1923 Charles Edward Trombley became the owner and editor of *The Peninsula Gateway*, the successor to the *Bay Island News*. For the next thirty years he would be the voice of Gig Harbor and the peninsula. Rising each day within sight of the harbor and the sound of C. O. Austin's sawmill, he went to work on a printing press housed in a wooden building nailed together as a schoolhouse in the days when the Goodman sisters were greenhorn teachers. He was a Mason, a member of the Lion's Club, a Democrat, and a politician, serving a stint as State Representative for the Twenty-sixth District in the 1939 legislative session.[129] Each week the *Gateway* captured the large and small events of community life. Like most small community papers of the day, it was rich with the visits, birthdays, and other doings of ordinary citizens. Almost everyone was written about at one time or another, but there were some names that appeared far more often than others.

In every successful community there are always a few folks who carry more than their share of the load. These are the ones who keep

Edward Trombley, left, chats with his father, Charles E. Trombley, editor of The Peninsula Gateway. *Photo by Frank Owen Shaw, Feb. 22, 1948*

raising their hands when something needs to be done, the ones who have the vision and the influence to persuade others to follow them. They are the leaders, and communities do not go forward without them. Yet for every leader, there are many more who go about the business of making a living, of paying taxes, painting houses, trimming lawns, and just trying to get through the day while waiting for their chance to do one extraordinary thing. Leaders fill chapters in town histories; the others might show up in the background of a photo or two.

Still, it is worth remembering that the unsung many are the ones who make the gears of living turn day after day. At the end of it all, without them, leaders have no one to lead. Where would Alfred Burnham have been without someone to live in all those little white-washed houses he envisioned? Would Mitchell Skansie have built stout fishing boats without a stout crew of workers to execute his vision or hardy fishermen to crew them? Where would grocers like the Uddenbergs have been without someone to buy their coffee and cornflakes?

The Watsons were one such family, one of the many. John Houghton Watson was born the son of a schoolmaster in Penketh, England, on September 20, 1878. His future wife was born Aimée

John Houghton Watson on the Mistley Hall, *circa 1899*

Aimée Katherine Lowe, circa 1900

Katherine Lowe in Walla Walla, Washington, on July 19, 1878. Her father was a blacksmith and wagon driver. Her mother was a house-wife and boarding house owner. Aimée came with her older sister Ann to Point Evans, a rounded bluff protruding into Puget Sound a few miles south of Gig Harbor, sometime after 1909. Point Evans was the last major vestige of the old military reservation, only recently thrown open to settlement. Aimée sometimes traveled on horse-back to teach at Wollochet School.

Aimée Lowe and John Watson were married in Tacoma on May 16, 1913, and settled into a life on the shore of Point Evans. It was raw country, newly opened, and still heavily timbered. A horse-team logger named Joe Twogood hacked away at the firs and cedars, while the Watsons built a family. Their first child, John Lowe Watson, was born in February, 1914, followed on July 1, 1916, by Kathleen and in March 1919 by Alan Houghton.

The family liked the house, with the big wooden swing that John Watson built and somehow kept secret from the children until Christmas. They went away for a while, when John Watson was a strawboss in a Seattle shipyard during the First World War, but they came back and built a house closer to the harbor. They were established in the new place by 1922. They appreciated being only about a mile's walk from Lincoln School, instead of a longer ride to Wollochet School on Old Bob, the family horse.

Ann Lowe's homestead on Point Evans, circa 1912. Aimée helped her purchase the 20 acres of waterfront property, and the family helped build the cabin. John Watson homesteaded the adjoining parcel after meeting Aimée.

The other major factor behind the Watson's move was the installation on Point Evans of power lines, to bring electricity through Tacoma from Cushman Dam on the Olympic Peninsula. The line's last and greatest obstacle on the path to Gig Harbor was The Narrows, and the final set of big metal towers to hold the humming wires before they spanned the water needed to be somewhere on the high bluff at Point Evans. The spot chosen happened to belong to the Watsons. They ended up with 780 feet of waterfront and five acres of land remaining at Point Evans. For years, they returned to their old house for summer visits, until someone named Cowgill burned their buildings down.

The new Watson home was up today's Pioneer Way, well above the town. The area was known locally as Stinson Hill, after H. L. Stinson, who lived a little to the northeast of the Watsons. There was good sledding up there in the winter snow, and the family got hold of a pair of skis as well, so they were set to enjoy Gig Harbor's infrequent snows. In the rainy season there was a swampy lake, stretching brushy, thick, and mysterious into the backcountry. The soil was good enough for the loganberries that helped make ends meet.

Daughter Kathleen remembered long years later that her father, "liked the simple life. He wasn't pressured by ambition, greed or envy. He viewed people realistically, if a little cynically, and accepted his limitations. He had traveled, worked hard, supported the community demands, raised an admiring family and died uncomplaining and re-

Watsons and friends gather at a neighbor's home on Point Evans for a housewarming.

122

signed." That uncomplaining death did not occur until 1953. In the 1920s he was in the prime of life, and he admonished his children to take their share of the chores with the words, "If you don't work, you don't eat." John Junior tended the chickens. Kathleen washed dishes and worked with the cream separator. Alan, in a foreshadowing of his later life, brought in wood.[130]

Kathleen Watson, Gig Harbor Union High School Class of 1934

John Watson, Gig Harbor Union High School Class of 1931

Kathleen, seated third from right, senior class play cast photo

Alan Watson, Gig Harbor Union High School Class of 1937

(l-r) Eunice Arneson, Lola Spadoni, Kathleen Watson, and Helen Sandburg, high school tennis tournament champions, 1934

No one seemed to remember just what it was that first lured John and Aimée Watson to the peninsula, but others were coming for reasons that ran from the profound to the whimsical. In 1924, Harold Ryan, a young man studying dentistry, took a ride through Tacoma's Point Defiance Park on the city's wooded north end. He came to a viewing area near the point that gave the big park its name. Ryan got out of the car, gestured toward a little white house across the water on the Gig Harbor side, and declared, "I'm going to own that house."

That dream, and many another, came true for Ryan. The day before Valentine's Day in 1926, he carried his bride, Ruth, over the threshold of the little white house, where they would live the rest of their long lives. Gig Harbor must have been glad to have a practicing dentist in the neighborhood. As late as 1921, old Joseph Goodman had been forced to pull his own loose tooth.

Along with new arrivals, there must always be final departures. In 1922 the last great Indian ceremony remembered on the peninsula took place following the death of David Squally, who had lived on Wollochet Bay. Candles burned around the body all through the night, drums played for days, and his native brethren roamed from house to house ringing bells. Internment was in an unmarked grave in Cromwell Cemetery. Afterward, his widow Annie moved to the Puyallup Reservation.

Mayor Harold Ryan and his wife Ruth just after he was elected the first mayor of Gig Harbor in 1946

On April 12, 1926, old Anna Jerisich died in Seattle at the home of her daughter, Julia Van Waters. She came home for burial in Artondale Cemetery. The services were held in St. John's Hall, the latest incarnation of the old Grand Army of the Republic Hall, on land the Jerisichs had donated long ago. With her passing went the town's last link to the days when the first settlers nosed their boats through the narrow entrance to Gig Harbor. In October 1933, the death of Rachel Burnham at the age of eighty-eight severed another link with the past. She was buried alongside her husband in Gig Harbor Cemetery.[131]

Sam and Anna Jerisich's last surviving son, John, fished for a while on the *Emancipator* and later worked as a night watchman for the Skansie Shipyard. One night in July 1935, he fell from the gangplank of a ferry and drowned. The waters of the harbor are still and the currents are slight. Not much normally drifts in or out, but John was a Jerisich. Even in death, he could set a course seaward. His body was found days later on the shore of Vashon Island, near where generations of fishermen waited for shimmering schools of salmon.[132]

Over on the other side of the peninsula, there was an island which

(l-r) Anna Willets Jerisich, Julia Skansie, and Julia Jerisich Van Waters, 1910

Rachel Hord Burnham driving buckboard with her dog prince, 1884

125

shimmered in a string of dreams. To the Native Americans, it was *Ci'Kagwls*, meaning uplifted or elevated, which fit well with its high bluffs and rounded shores. The island had a look of timeless stability, but its bluffs watched waves of humanity's bold ventures, ambitions, and broken dreams play out their uncertain scripts.

In 1841 the Wilkes Expedition tried to name it Allshouse Island, for marine private Joseph Allshouse, who lost his life in a San Francisco accident the following October. He died without knowing that his name was fated to vanish from the map. From a distance, the island vaguely resembled a raft floating on the water, and by the time the first official land survey was done in 1857, Raft Island was the name permanently inscribed on charts and maps.

The first settlers, or at least the first landowners, on the island were Jacob Steves and Fred Steves, presumably brothers. In 1889 Fred owned thirty-three-and-one-half acres on the western shore. Two years later, Henry C. Rogers purchased an equal amount of land nearby. Jacob Steves held the lion's share, with a whopping 160 acres in the center. Jacob built a house on the south shore looking across the water toward the peninsula at Rosedale and the scene of James Henry's failed brickworks. This state of affairs lasted until 1900, when the subdividing began.

A tall traveler, fast and determined, could slosh and flounder on foot from the mainland to Raft Island's south end during extreme low tides, but most folks got there by boat. Ben Lay of Rosedale had a floating dock behind his general store, where he rented rowboats for twenty-five cents a day. In the summer of 1913, the Cruver, Wilkinson, and Smith families jostled down Rosedale Road in logger Wilkinson's two-horse flatbed wagon. They rented boats at Lay's store and passed over to Raft Island for a three-day holiday. There were eighteen of them, young and old, quite possibly the biggest crowd the island had seen in centuries.

For three magical days they dug geoducks at low tide, wandered the woods, explored as far afield as little Cutts Island, and told tall tales on the beach while bonfires held the darkness at bay. They stayed

126

in an abandoned old house that Lewis Cruver thought had belonged to Dr. Christo Balabanoff. Maybe somewhere along the line they wondered aloud about the doctor and why he had come and gone, leaving a fine home to the mercy of rats, spiders, and occasional campers.

Dr. Balabanoff had been a fixture in Tacoma for generations. No one seemed to remember exactly when it was that he and his wife Alice came and went, though he shows up in Ben Lay's store ledger in 1904, and in $650 worth of real estate transactions involving Frank Majan in 1905.[133]

Mystery loves to linger around the names and dates of the island's history. The three families of campers believed that the abandoned house they saw in 1913 had belonged to Dr. Balabanoff. Was this the same abandoned house that Amanda Henry, James' mother, moved into with another son named Tress? It had an orchard in a clearing, rightly enough, but was it an orchard of cherries? By 1915 that house had passed to E. L. Hagman. Three years later it stood abandoned again and was gaining a reputation for being haunted. It never found another occupant, and eventually the white house with the wide verandas tumbled into nothing. Not everyone could tolerate the isolation of island life.

More dreamers came and bought property on the island, nurturing vague plans of enjoying it as a home, a summer cottage, or a rustic retreat. In 1924 Metsker's *Pierce County Atlas* captured the names of the property owners. Beginning on the eastern shore facing Rosedale there was A. Higgins, followed by H. F. Strebe, William Meservey, John Flett (a National Parks naturalist), C. L. Luther, Otto Luther, C. E. McMasters, J. Keen, L. Caas, M. Bigford, and lastly A. C. Rogers, out on the west end facing Henderson Bay. The atlas-makers labeled a long narrow strip of the island "unknown."

Most of the island dreams never became reality, and the properties remained largely undeveloped. Then in 1928, wealthy California mining engineer George O. Noble tried to roll their many small, scattered dreams into his big dream of owning the whole two hundred-acre island. He bought up fourteen separate parcels and brought electricity across the water. He planned to build a fine estate on the northwest end of the island, looking out toward Henderson Bay and the Olympic Mountains, with a private wharf and a stable of riding horses. Eventually that fantasy, like those before it, vanished over the horizon and the island waited to see what someone would dream up next.

In 1942 Jess and Laura Kuhns bought the island from the long-absent Noble for $30,000. In the summer of 1946 they filed a new plat for a subdivided and domesticated island.[134] Their plat called for long, narrow properties girding what they planned to call Kuhn's Raft Island, with beaches at their front and winding roads at their back. The restrictions filed by the Kuhns and approved by the Pierce County authorities included provisions against commercial buildings, against poultry and animals (other than pets or saddle horses), and against structures closer than ten feet from property lines. There were provisions for "proper and efficient means of sewage disposal," and for the free use of the roads by all residents.

It was a rustic dream, but it was not meant for everyone. Article three of the restrictions glowered with the cold institutionalized racism of the times. "No lot or tract in said subdivision, or the building or buildings thereon shall ever be sold, leased or rented to a person not of the white or Caucasian race, nor shall any person not of such race occupy any such building or lot." There was one exception. "This restriction, however, shall not prevent occupancy by domestic servants of a different race domiciled with an owner or tenant."

The Kuhns tried a publicized auction to sell properties on the island, but found few takers. The one big sale was seventeen acres to a Catholic Youth Organization. The light slowly went out on the Kuhns' dream. They ended up selling most of what remained to Robert L. Healy and his associates.

Healy got permission to build a bridge to the island, and then sold the island and bridge rights to Archie L. Matthew, who lived at Green Point, down by Horsehead Bay. The bridge was finished in 1958, but Matthew had run out of money. On March 20, 1959, he sold the island to McDonald Realtors of Gig Harbor for $348,000. The next month a quarter-page ad appeared in the *Tacoma News Tribune* inviting all comers to, "Enjoy year 'round vacation living just 10 minutes from Narrows Bridge!" Featuring a photo of a smiling bathing beauty superimposed over an aerial view of the peninsula, the ad signaled a new page in Raft Island's history. Graham and Blodwyn McDonald had the deep pockets to make their dream a reality. They went ahead with their earthmoving equipment, developing six thousand feet of beach property and creating a water system and yacht basin.

The bridge to the island was a toll bridge, and the Catholic Youth Organization chose to rely instead on a retired army landing craft that Jess Kuhn, a former army officer, had helped them obtain. It ran for a few years, until it sank on an excursion to Cutts Island. The counselors gained high praise for their quick work in roping the children together and getting them safely ashore, and the sunken boat became a mecca for scuba divers.[135]

By 1960 there was a new and more detailed set of rules, with all references to race erased forever. The island continued to grow. By the year 2000 there were 489 residents, up sixteen percent since 1990. Money had come to the island. An average home was valued at almost $208,000. More recently, a four-bedroom, 2,500-square-foot home on two-and-a-half acres of land went on the market priced at $895,000.

Dreams and ventures still find room to grow on the island. The Greek Orthodox Church established a retreat called All Saints Camp on the east end. Children facing cancer have found a special place at Camp Agape in the spacious lodge at All Saints. Some dreams are a testament to the preciousness and tenacity of life, some endure beyond death itself. One man (whose family prefers that he remain unnamed) was born in Omaha, Nebraska, and eventually settled in Hawaii, becoming a renowned expert on the growing of pineapples and sugar cane. He became chairman of the Board of Regents of the University of Hawaii. When he died in Gig Harbor in 2001 at the age of eighty-seven, his ashes were scattered according to his wishes on Raft Island, where he became one with the island's dreams of eternity.

Reduced to its essence, history is largely the story of problems and solutions, and in the 1920s Gig Harbor began to gain some ground on the tyrannical problem of time and distance. A tally for the year 1921 recorded 107,457 passenger trips on the ferries between Tacoma and Gig Harbor. Given that most of these were the same people passing back and forth a multitude of times, it was all the more wearying to realize that passengers getting off Arda Hunt's *Florence K.* on the Tacoma side at Point Defiance still had half a mile to walk to reach the street cars. On the Gig Harbor side, which had no streetcars, the walk home was often a mile or more. If those people could get on a bus, stay on it as it crossed The Narrows by ferry, and then ride to their destination, their journeys would be made swifter and smoother.

On April 27, 1922, Hubert Secor received permission from the Washington Division of Transportation and Public Utilities to operate a motor vehicle stage service between Gig Harbor and Tacoma. Secor started with a White Motor Company bus and soon upgraded to a larger Pierce-Arrow. By December he and his partner, Henry Kaffenberger, branched out to haul freight in addition to passengers and express shipments. Additional drivers, Roscoe Savage and Roy Clark, were recruited after Secor tired of working seven days a week.

Passenger fares were twenty-five cents, which included the cost of the ferry ride. Drivers generally did not bother charging for short hops from one place to another in Gig Harbor. It became infinitely easier for people like Nellie Austin, Bertha Lund, and Erick and Ruth (the future Mrs. Harold Ryan) Erickson to attend Stadium High School in

Hubert and Dave Secor take a ticket from an unidentified man in front of the Gig Harbor Stage bus. The Sweeney Block, at the head of the bay, is behind the bus.

Tacoma. For Bertha, the trip had an added attraction. She later married the driver of her bus, and became Mrs. Roscoe Savage.[136] By or before 1928, passengers could transfer from the Tacoma bus in Gig Harbor and continue on to Bremerton in an eleven-passenger Studebaker bus. The driving by that time was split between Secor and twenty-one-year-old Orville Hemphill.

The telephone provided another tool for surmounting time and distance, and the peninsula took a great stride forward in 1931 when a phone cable was run across the bottom of The Narrows, connecting Gig Harbor with Tacoma. There had been telephone service of a sort since the advent of the Island Empire Telephone & Telegraph Company early in the century. Civil War veteran Joseph Goodman had been one of the early subscribers, paying eighteen dollars per year for what he called "telephone rent."

The town had found it convenient having Goodman's daughter, former teacher Anna Goodman Wheeler, serving as operator. She had lived in the harbor since 1883, and had been the telephone operator since December 15, 1922. She knew pretty much everyone, often to the point of being able to transfer a call to the place a person was likely to be visiting, if they were not reachable at home. From 1931 on, though, calls were handled by a Stromberg-Carlson two-participant junior multiple switchboard, capable of handling ten phones on each line, and featuring selective ringing so that each of the ten households on the party line knew when the call was for them.[137]

Anna's sister, Lucy Goodman, was still teaching school. She had attended the University of Washington and the Ellensburg Normal School,[138] then taught at Vaughn, Rosedale, Puyallup, and finally at the head of the bay in Gig Harbor. At one point she was teaching sixty-eight students in five grades, seated two at a desk, all in the same room.[139] In 1915 she came to the Crescent Valley School, where she taught grades one through four on the first floor, before the students graduated upstairs to complete grades five through eight.[140]

When she retired in 1927, Hubert Secor helped persuade her to open a private kindergarten. It was not as if Lucy had nothing else to do. She belonged to a sewing circle, attended Chautauqua programs, went for boat rides, and even went to Mount Rainier with the Iliff family. Her father was largely an invalid by now, and she spent a lot of time taking care of him, though her sisters Lillian and Anna helped a good deal.[141] Still, teaching was in her blood, and she probably was not very hard to persuade.

Miss Lucy's change of heart worked out well for Secor. He enrolled his daughter, Marian, in Lucy's school, and when Marian went on to the public school the next year, they bounced her straight up to the fourth grade.[142] Who could say how long Lucy's second career might last? Her father was still extolling the virtues of a frugal diet and three pipes a day in 1929 at the age of ninety-one. Everyone probably hoped Miss Lucy would go equally long.[143]

Pretty clearly, Lucy loved children. In just one expression of this love, the home she shared with her father became a gathering place at Halloween. In the days before trick-or-treating, it was customary to gather somewhere for a party. Lucy made popcorn balls the night before, and there were generally jelly beans, apples and peanuts on hand, along with games that might last until midnight. In 1923 there were seven visitors. By 1928 her aged father noted in his diary, "Yesterday evening sixteen wizards & witches came and had a good deal of fun and refreshments."

Lucy Goodman stands with her class in the second Gig Harbor school above the head of the bay. The building later became the offices of The Peninsula Gateway.

Halloween held another attraction for older children. Tipping over outhouses, removing gates, and performing other mischief on Halloween night had become a rite of passage for American teenagers. Up Crescent Valley, a farmer named John Wig had more than he could stand. Halloween after Halloween, he found his outhouse either lying on its side or hauled up on top of his barn. He was a nice enough man, and the youths had nothing particular against him. It was just that his big field seemed to be a magnet, come Halloween.

One Halloween, he snapped. He let fly with a load of buckshot in the dark at three or four youths. Nineteen-year-old Proc Peacock, grandson of the old Civil War veteran for whom Peacock Hill was named, lost an eye to the buckshot. No action was taken against Mr. Wig in 1930s Gig Harbor. He was deeply sorry, as were the other youths, and everyone went on with their lives. It was the end of Halloween stunts for Proc Peacock, who went on to a successful career in real estate. Sea Cliff in Eastern Gig Harbor was one of several developments he managed.[144]

Education took another stride in May 1921, when a meeting in Gig Harbor's Bay View Hall launched a drive to start a high school on the peninsula. On May 18, area residents voted 451 to 51 for the formation of a school district. Later, Stanley Starr won the five dollar prize offered by Axel Uddenberg for suggesting the best name for the school. Thanks to Starr, it would be known as Union High School.

Several sites were explored for the location. Mr. & Mrs. John Carlson even offered five acres of level, cleared ground at Midway,

Union High School was dedicated on Dec. 2, 1921. It ended the need for high school students to attend Stadium High School in Tacoma.

but it was deemed too far from the population center. The problem was solved when the Methodist church congregation agreed to move down the hill and vacate their former property.

On December 2, the high school building was dedicated, and on December 17, a party of volunteers came out with axes and saws to clear the grounds and enjoy a thirty-six-pound lamb donated by Mr. Murden, the butcher.[145] At long last, peninsula youths wanting to continue their education would not have to cross The Narrows to Tacoma. The school later developed a yearbook with the peculiar name "PERCLAWAM." Insiders know that the letters stood for the schools that sent students to Union – Purdy, Elgin, Rosedale, Crescent Valley, Lincoln, Arletta, Wauna, Artondale, and Midway.

With ferry and bus service in operation, Gig Harbor began to look like a place that could support a hotel again. In the 1920s, two rose up facing one another across today's Harborview, near the corner of Pioneer. The Novak Hotel, managed by Mrs. F. Novak, was built for $6,000 and had ten furnished rooms. It also housed W. Y. Mosher's store and meat market.

Across the street, the Peninsula Hotel was built at a cost of $20,000 and offered twelve furnished rooms to its guests. It was owned by businessman Austin Richardson and fisherman Andrew Gilich, and managed by Mrs. Richardson. It also housed the offices of A. J. Dorst, physician and surgeon; Harold Ryan, dentist; and Dr. V. P. Sorenson, chiropractor. Both buildings were among the first in those parts to have indoor plumbing and electricity.

The Gilich-Richardson Building, built in 1924, opened with the Peninsula Hotel, Sunset Pool Hall, Gig Harbor Pharmacy, plus doctor offices upstairs.

The Peninsula Hotel did so well that in April 1925, Richardson and Gilich branched out and opened a movie theater on the next block over from their hotel, on land purchased from Mitchell Skansie. The Empress Theatre could seat 450, and it usually managed to fill the seats. When it was not playing movies, the theater sometimes hosted live entertainment and high school graduations.[146]

Another sign of prosperity was the arrival of the first bank, which opened late in 1926 in a brick building on Harborview. The First National Bank, supervised by President Carl Nielson, offered four percent interest and insurance for automobile, fire, and marine property. The building was owned and built by Chris Thompson, who had started out with a farm in Rosedale back in 1908. Next door, Louis Dodge operated a barbershop billed as the "Sanitary Tonsorial and Bath Parlor."[147]

Prohibition had been the law of the land since 1919, and the injunction against the sale and consumption of alcoholic spirits became probably the most widely-broken law in the history of the United States.

Novak Hotel, A.W. McIntyre Service Station, and Steiner Shoe Repair, 1920s

The First National Bank with barbershop and baths on the right, 1926

135

In many cases, men and women who would never think of violating any other law took a certain pride in breaking this one. It was broken on the peninsula as vigorously as it was anywhere else. In January 1930, a raid on the Gig Harbor Pharmacy, located in the Peninsula Hotel, resulted in the arrest of Harry Tichacek and Lee Thrush on charges of selling liquor.[148] In late December 1932, Deputy Sheriff Northey and his officers descended on a secret distillery near Cromwell. This still was a seventy-gallon workhorse, and five hundred gallons of mash and sixty-five gallons of whiskey were found in the same raid. *The Peninsula Gateway* reported that the still was "cleverly concealed at the end of a 60-foot tunnel beneath a roadway, the entrance to the tunnel being a garage." Its operator, Bert Wynn, was arrested, and bail was set at five hundred dollars.[149]

Drinking wine mixed with water at meals was an old custom among the Slavonians. A few of them went on making their own wine in basements or other secret places, relying on a supplier from Tacoma, coming through in a van selling zinfandel grapes. One winemaker used a jack to press out the last drops of juice, but stopped when he realized the jack was raising his house.[150] Rum runners, using fast boats to carry liquor by night, found the secluded coves of the peninsula a convenient place to land their cargo, and one of the dips in the shore of nearby Fox Island became informally known as Smuggler's Cove.

There were other opportunities in Gig Harbor, and enterprising people ready to seize them. Philip H. Peyran was told that he had only a few months to live, after a complete breakdown from the shock of the San Francisco earthquake. He had already beaten that prophecy by eight years when he came to Gig Harbor as a varnish salesman in 1914.[151] A customer from Oregon made some remarks about the beauties of holly, and next thing you know, Peyran had ordered 685 holly trees, ranging in variety from Blue Stem to Golden Queen to Hedgehog.

He planted them on what had once been the Judge James Wickersham homestead, just south of the Shore Acres dock. He developed a preservative dip that kept holly clippings fresh and green for the long trip to New York or Hawaii. Soon he was known as "The Holly King," and his home was known as Hollywood Gardens. After fifteen years of trying, he came up with a cross between Golden Queen and French Holly, which he named Hollycroft Holly.[152] He sold holly tree starts for fifty cents. Soon holly trees were showing up along Crescent Valley Drive, at the intersection of Hunt and Midway, and around the peninsula. Harold and Ruth Ryan bought two hundred trees when they married and moved into their dream cottage.[153]

A helping hand could get a person a long way on this peninsula. Young Johnny Finholm was making twelve dollars a week up north at the Olalla Trading Company when Axel Uddenberg offered him twenty-five dollars a week to come to Gig Harbor and work in his store. Along about 1932, Finholm took over the running of a meat market across the street. In 1935 he crossed back over that same street and bought Axel's store when the old Swede retired at the age of eighty. Finholm's Market was born. Johnny's brother Eddie later joined him as a butcher.[154] Their frozen food lockers helped neighbors without

Philip H. Peyran's Hollycroft Farm at Shore Acres, overlooking Point Defiance to the east

Finholm's Market full of customers after a major remodel in 1955. The Finholm's Market sign is still in the same location on North Harborview Drive.

137

refrigerators survive the Depression and the rationing of World War II. And Finholm's double-wrapped meats became a mainstay for Alaska-bound fishing boats.[155]

Just across the street from Finholm's Market, a block of connected buildings stood as a reminder of what a determined woman could do. Theresa Sweeney, a native of Ireland, had arrived in Gig Harbor in 1908 with her husband, James, and four sons. By 1915 she gave up farming and dairying to become the postmistress for Gig Harbor. In February 1923 she became the harbor's first female justice of the peace.[156] In 1922 she established her business block, 40 feet deep and 113 feet wide, with its back to the waters of the harbor. Soon she was operating a department store with a $15,000 inventory and renting the rest of the space out to the post office, Harold Ryan's dental office, and a restaurant that eventually became the Home Cafe. She was also one of the prime movers in the construction of the first Catholic Church in Gig Harbor in 1913. In 1926 she stood as a Democratic candidate for the state legislature, but this was still Republican country and she lost a well fought race.[157] She remained a force in area

Theresa Sweeney's house contained a store and post office when she was postmistress, 1915.

Theresa C. Sweeney, prominent Gig Harbor businesswoman

affairs, alert to every opportunity, until her death at the age of sixty-eight, in 1941.

Opportunities? Ask Mary Jane Turner of Crawford County, Pennsylvania, what a little perseverance could accomplish. After she graduated from Pennsylvania Teacher's College in 1922, someone asked about her grade point average. "I don't know," she said, "I am just an average student—work and get what I go after." She went after teaching positions in the Northwest, first at Fairfax, before it became a ghost town in the shadow of Mount Rainier. Later she taught in Bellingham, in several spots in Oregon, and in Easton near the crest of the Cascade Mountains.

As the school year approached summer break in 1929, Turner applied to the Presbyterian National Board of Missions to teach Vacation Bible School. She was hoping for the Hoh River Valley, but that job was taken. After accepting the only spot left, she got into the old Ford she called the Galloping Goose and came clattering into a little community called Gig Harbor. She opened Bible school on June 2. By the end of the year, the church had a net gain of eighteen enrollments in Sunday school and had collected $292 in donations.

She returned to teaching in Easton in the fall, but made weekly returns to conduct Sunday school, logging 15,000 round-trip miles over the next two years. Finally in May 1931, she was brought on full-time in Gig Harbor as "Missionary-in-Charge." By the spring of 1932, she had a twelve-person Sunday school going at Horsehead Bay and

In 1922, the Sweeney block opened with a berry station, post office, cafe, barbershop, and pharmacy. Here, the Secor bus picks up passengers and mail on its daily run.

was doing a morning sermon in Gig Harbor and a two o'clock session in the old Arletta school building.

In 1933 she added Rosedale to her pastorate. On Reid Road, a woman known as Mother Little owned property overlooking The Narrows and distant Mount Rainier. She had three homes on her land and often shared them with visiting missionaries, and she invited Mary Jane Turner to live in one of them. It worked out so well that when Mother Little died in 1941, she willed her property to Mary Jane.

Mary Jane liked fresh doughnuts, music, and practical jokes. She played the banjo and ukulele, wrote poetry, and displayed a talent for promotion. If she wanted publicity in *The Peninsula Gateway*, Editor C. E. Trombley was easy to reach; Turner had him and Mrs. Lewis Kimball playing trumpet in her church every Sunday. Her efforts resulted in Sunday school attendance climbing to 103 in 1931. By 1932, it hit 170. When asked about the secret of her success, she replied, "Hard work and love of young folks." Though never officially recognized as a minister by the Presbyterian establishment, she ran the church ably and well until 1956.

In that year, as her congregation remembered it, "they discovered she was a woman," and she was abruptly dismissed by the church establishment. Undaunted, she went to Rosedale Union Church, where

she ministered until 1972. On February 7 of that year, she taught Sunday school, attended worship, helped Ray Arnold and his wife celebrate their silver anniversary, and led a Bible class. She packed her car for a vacation with her longtime assistant, Dorothy Gilmore, and then she lay down for a short nap and never woke up. She was seventy-one.[158]

Mary Jane Turner ministered to area Presbyterians as Missionary-in-Charge from 1931 to 1956.

Mary Jane Turner and Theresa Sweeney were not the only women to compete in what was still considered to be a man's world. When Herman Claussen of Sunrise Beach died in 1930, the need for his passenger boat did not die with him. The *Elsie C II* supplied the only dependable connection with Point Defiance across The Narrows, especially since no road had yet reached Sunrise Beach. Women occasionally worked as cooks or pursers on the ferries, but it was really something new to see Elsie Claussen, Herman's daughter, captaining the *Elsie C II*. Passengers may have been startled to see the pretty young blond woman behind the wheel, but they had a chance to get used to it over the next four years, on daily summer runs and weekend spring and fall trips.

Elsie Claussen had drive and ambition that carried her far beyond paths normally open to a backwater girl with an eighth-grade education. She climbed Mount Rainier, owned and operated an automobile, and worked in the office of a Tacoma lumber company. Even disaster could not end her maritime career. In the summer of 1934, while she enjoyed a rare overnight excursion to Mount Rainier,[159] a night lantern on the *Elsie C II* toppled in a windstorm, and the launch burned beyond repair at her moorings. A larger replacement boat, the fifty-six-foot launch *Elsie C III*, was christened in 1935. But what adversity and disaster could not do, death could. Elsie lived long enough to skipper the boat on its trial run, and then she was gone, a promising life ended much too soon.[160]

Elsie Claussen, able daughter of Herman Claussen, captained the "Elsie C" boats from Sunrise Beach, Tacoma, and Vashon Island in the early 1930s.

141

Another fellow looking for opportunities was a young man named Nick Tarabochia, who made his way up from the little fishing village of Skamakowa on the Columbia River in 1926. He was nineteen years old and his goal was to learn about fishing from the best fisherman he could find. In Gig Harbor there were plenty of good fishermen, but the one generally regarded, then and later, as the best of the best was Spiro Babich. Spiro was one of the Slavonians driven from the Dalmatian coast by the failure of the grape crops, arriving in Gig Harbor about 1910.

At first he fished with his brother, Andrew, who had preceded and sponsored him. By 1917 he had his own boat, the *Superior*, built by the Skansie brothers. She was sixty-five feet long, fifteen feet wide and seven-feet-six-inches deep, powered by a fifty-horsepower Frisco Standard engine. Right from the start, he aimed for the top of the line. The basic package for the boat was $5,800, and he went for the extras: $67.50 for bow chocks, $28.50 for a pump, $35.50 for wiring, $310 for a Delco engine, $45 for a searchlight, and $7.50 for extra lamp globes. The final total was $6,100, paid off in installments.[161]

In the course of his career, Spiro Babich owned or shared interest in close to a score of purse seiners. He liked to use a boat for a few years and then sell it before it needed major repairs. The names came and went – *Golden West, Vanguard, Ranger, Reliance, Dependable, Liberator,* the big ninety-six-foot *Western Queen*, and others. The one he kept the longest was the *Invincible*, built by Skansie in 1929. He pursued salmon as far north as the Bering Sea and later netted sardines off the coast of California. Spiro was one of the first to seine False Pass off Unimak Island in the Aleutian Chain.[162]

On Puget Sound, his movements can be partially traced by his arrests and fines. Fishing regulations were complex and constantly changing, and Spiro was not suited by temperament to spend much time worrying over them:

January 12, 1915 - Arrested and fined $20 for fishing south of the prohibited line in Pierce County

142

January 9, 1920 – Arrested and fined $50 for fishing within
one mile of Chamber's Creek
October 29, 1924 – Arrested and fined $100 for fishing in
the Puyallup Preserve

Reefs and storms held no terrors for Spiro Babich. He liked rough weather because it drove his more timid competitors to shelter. He was willing to work harrowingly close to the shoreline, to the point where his crew said he fished with the sheep. It paid off for him. His son Peter once watched him haul in thousands of fish with only half of his net deployed. He did take chances, but he had no tolerance for mistakes. When a fishing boat became stranded on some area rocks and friends gathered to try and get the vessel free, Babich's contribution from his homeward-bound boat was a gruff, "What are you helping him out for? The whole world knows there's rocks there."[163]

Spiro was a demanding boss. He worked fiercely hard and expected the same from his crew. It generally was not love for the old so-and-so that brought his crew back for each trip; it was the knowledge that Babich found fish and that his crews made money. Even in the Depression year of 1932, he managed to clear $33,000.[164] He was able to afford a nice brick home near the harbor entrance, with a front porch and big picture window facing the water.

Spiro rebuffed Nick Tarabochia time and again when Nick tried to join his crew, but the young man persisted. One thing may have worked in his favor. Babich was a Slavonian who liked to hire Italians for his crew. Nick was a Croatian with an Italian-sounding name. Finally Spiro said, "You run down to the market and pick up some steaks and just the two of us will have dinner. You can fix it."[165] That was how their association began, and it lasted for a dozen years.

Nick developed another ambition in his first Gig Harbor year. He spent twenty-five cents of his fisher's wages to attend a play, and there he beheld a beautiful young woman named Rose Ancich. He told a companion that he was going to make her his wife. Rose was fourteen in 1926, the daughter of fisherman Morton Ancich. She left school after the sixth grade to deliver newspapers, rowing across The Narrows to pick them up and then delivering them around the whole of the harbor. When she met Nick, she was working with her mother, Anna, selling hotdogs and hamburgers at the ferry landing.

Rose's mother did not care much for Nick at first. Rose Ancich and Clementina Skansie were considered the two prettiest girls in Gig Harbor, and Anna did not relish the idea of Rose taking up with a young man who owned nothing. Rose had other ideas. She liked his aggressiveness. He was a go-getter. And after two years, the couple eloped to San Pedro in California, where Nick fished and Rose worked in coffee shops. When they returned to Gig Harbor, they lived in a little cabin on the beach by a net shed and Nick went back to work with Spiro.

There were some marked differences between the Scandinavian farmers and the Slavonian fishermen. They pretty much split the harbor area into distinct ethnic neighborhoods. The Slavonians stayed mostly on the western shore, on either side if the site where Sam Jerisich and his partners had started Millville long ago. In the fall of 1929, *The Tacoma Daily Ledger* published a list of the Slovonian fishing boat owners headquartered in Gig Harbor: Spiro Babich, Andrew and Antone Gilich, Mato Ivanovich, Spiro and Anton Janovich, John Jerkovich, Pete Glass (the name had been Glassinovich), Anna Ancich, Sam Perovich, John Malich, Lee Makovich, John Ross, Peter Markovich, Marko Markovich, Tony Gilich, Tony Novak (in the old country the name had been Novakovich), Emmett Ross, Andrew Skansie, Peter Skansi, Nick Skansi, Mary Naterlin, Pete Skarponi, John Stanich (he was also a grocer), Anton Stanich, Martin Stanich, John Vlahovich, Mike Katich, and John Bujacich.[166]

Even in death, the ethnic communities remained apart. A Gig Harbor Slavonian's final journey was almost invariably up the hill to Artondale Cemetery. A few Scandinavians found repose among them, generally because their farms were nearby, but many more of went to their rest in Gig Harbor Cemetery, up Crescent Valley. Their "son" replaced "ich" on the tombstones: Vernhardson, Christophersen, Guttormsen, Haflidason, Hansen, Jacobson, Johnson, Nelson, Pearson,

Sigurdson, Swanson, Tollefsen, and Swendsen. One family bucked the trend. Immigrating to America, they decided the new land had enough Petersons. They changed their name to the town in Norway from which they came – Alvestad.

Their immigrants' homes revealed another difference. When Slavonians became successful, they tended to build homes resembling the stone and brick dwellings of their native land. They also became known in some circles as the brick house boys. Scandinavians tended toward the wood of their northern heritage. The Scandinavians often looked upon the Slavonians as a rough, fast crowd, but inevitably the young people from opposite sides of the harbor began to meet, and sometimes fall in love. It was the marriages of their children, more than anything else, which finally began to weld the two different nationalities into one community. This was very soon to be a community that needed all the help and unity it could get.

If the 1920s were years of opportunity, the 1930s were a decade fraught with challenges. The Watson family knew it as well as anyone. "We are so small in number," Salutatorian John Watson told the friends, teachers, and parents assembled for the Union High School graduating class of 1931, "that we might perhaps feel more humble than we do, were we not sure that at this time, everyone must realize something of what it means to us to pass out into a world of which we are unfamiliar."

The world they were joining was indeed new and unfamiliar, and a little more challenging than it had looked when they began school. The financial crash known as The Great Depression had begun in October 1929, and its effects had been felt all the way from Wall

John Watson, left, in his high school senior play, 1931

145

Street to Gig Harbor. John Watson, born at Point Evans in 1914, was a serious student. He had been able to skip several grades and still make the honor roll and excel in sports, drama and debate. He was able to go on to Business College in Seattle and get a job. [167] Others were neither as gifted nor as lucky.

The bank in Gig Harbor closed and did not reopen until 1946. So many who had thrived and prospered in the Roaring Twenties struggled just to stay alive in the Depression-era 1930s. Kathleen Watson graduated from Union High School three years after her brother John. The only money she ever received from her parents after high school was a $3.45 check to buy shoes. At one point she was working seventeen-hour days during summer break, but she ultimately managed to get through college.

If the Depression were not enough of a burden, there were other misfortunes. On the bitterly cold evening of January 11, 1930, the weather station across The Narrows in Tacoma recorded a low of seventeen degrees Fahrenheit. The water system in Gig Harbor, such as it was, froze. As the sun sank, someone set a thawer to work on the frozen pipes beneath the Novak Hotel. At about five o'clock, someone else noticed flames, and a bucket brigade of men, women, and children came tumbling out from nearby homes to try and save the building. Buckets, cans, coalscuttles, and even the coffee urn from the nearby Presbyterian Church were pressed into service, but it was a losing battle. Gene Hamilton dashed into the burning hotel to save his invalid father. Joe Weaver followed to save the old man's belongings, throwing them out the window and then crawling to safety beneath the smoke and flying embers.

The Novak Hotel, A. McIntyre's confectionery, Bill Horn's plumbing shop, the Hamlin brothers' cafe and pool room, Alvin Steiner's shoe shop, and W. Y. Mosher's meat market were all gutted. Lumber and equipment at Mitchell Skansie's shipyard had begun to burn. The breeze had carried embers across the street to the Peninsula Hotel and the theater by the time the Tacoma fireboat arrived.

This was the new boat's first real fire, and it made the fourteen-mile run in thirty-five minutes. "Throwing Gig Harbor at it," as some townsfolk said, the boat pumped 11,000 gallons of water a minute onto the fire, saving the shipyard and the buildings across the street, and finally quenching the flames in the shell of the hotel and its neighbors. Despite their efforts, though, the damage was estimated at $16,000, not all of it insured, in a community that could ill afford to lose anything.[168]

The Novak Hotel was rebuilt, but fate had not finished with it yet. Early in the predawn hours of November 15, 1937, the lunchroom next to the hotel burst into flames. The hotel, the pool hall (which by now belonged to Cal Russell), and the Stanich Brothers' Grocery were all damaged in the blaze, which again was halted by the arrival of a fire tug from Tacoma. The hotel was nearly full at the time, and Mrs. Novak reported the loss of all her furnishings.[169] Phoenix-like, the hotel rose yet again, this time in sturdy brick.

People did what they could to get through the Depression. Union High School student Paul Alvestad got up extra early to meet the ferry from Tacoma and pick up the bundle of newspapers he delivered to about forty homes scattered across Crescent Valley and up the hill on the east side. On cold days he would warm up at MacIntyre's store. The deliveries all had to be done before school, but it helped bolster the income his family derived from their twenty acres of berries on their Crescent Valley farm.[170]

Unlike many of their counterparts in the Dust Bowl Midwest, the farmers of Crescent Valley and the surrounding peninsula all managed to keep their farms. Here, the Depression was actually more brutal for the townsfolk than it was for the farmers. Nick Burnham,[171] the son of the man who had once practically owned Gig Harbor, found himself picking strawberries, pruning trees, and taking any odd job he could find to make ends meet. To try and get his battered old car rolling again, he stripped the coil off a burned tractor. His brother, Biz, who had once run his own passenger steamer against the Hunt Brothers, was considering himself lucky to work now and then on the ferry, when he was not hunting ducks or jobbing with Nick.[172]

Troubled times could lead to short tempers. The peninsula abounded in wild huckleberries. Pickers who took them to the canneries were paid three cents a pound. In 1933, pickers organized themselves into an association and began picketing, demanding five cents per pound. Reports filtering out of the woods told of threats and intimidation when non-association members tried to pick berries for sale or for their own use. Things reached a head in October 1933, when a Vaughn logger–turned-berry-picker was arrested for allegedly shooting into the car of a competitor on three occasions. It may have been something of a relief when the berry season ended that year.[173]

The federal government's Works Progress Administration (WPA) saved many. It gave men temporary employment in public works projects. One of the undertakings at Gig Harbor was the construction of a park near the mouth of Crescent Creek, which had once been school property.[174] The Arletta school was another WPA project.

The Depression era was not all bad times. With the advent of decent roads and the proliferation of automobiles, it was possible to go a little farther afield for entertainment. Horseshoe Lake, over on the Longbranch Peninsula, became the place to go from the 1930s to the 1950s. Some of the best dance bands in the region played there, and it was a good place to forget troubles for a Saturday night.

The Gig Harbor Peninsula's intricate safety net of social and benevolent organizations also helped its citizens get through the Depression. Folks on this south Puget Sound peninsula were joiners. They

Horseshoe Lake, on the Key Peninsula, opened to a large crowd in the 1930s.

joined not only the church, the Parent-Teacher Association, and the Grange, though each of those organizations added to the glue that held life and community together. There was also the Mixers Club of Rosedale, which held card parties and sponsored a strawberry festival[175] and a Christmas Bazaar.[176] And Gig Harbor had a Royal Neighbors Club, which also liked card parties, including bridge, pinochle, 500, and whist.[177] The Fortnightly Club was the oldest existing women's service club in the area. Crescent Valley formed a stamp club, the purpose of which was "to understand and promote better feeling with foreign countries." This was no small task in a world drifting toward war, and the president chosen to take the club forward into the challenging year of 1938 was Stephen Healy.[178]

Since the advent of Social Security, Gig Harbor had had an Old Age Pensioner's Union local chapter. The Waconda Chapter of the Order of the Eastern Star held regular meetings. The Gig Harbor Sportsman's Club caused fifty thousand fingerling trout to be released in Crescent Lake and launched a campaign to rid the peninsula of predatory birds and animals.[179] The Federated Clubs organization was formed to try and connect all the other clubs, and it elected *Peninsula Gateway* editor C. E. Trombley as President. A bridge across The Narrows was their main concern in 1938.[180]

There must surely have been Masons on the peninsula from nearly the beginning of white settlement, but it was June 1926 before they finally could stop traveling to Steilacoom and other distant parts to take part in their ancient and secret rites. That year they formed John

Fortnightly Club members gather on the steps of Mrs. William McLaughlin's home, 1915. The club is the oldest service club in the area, founded in 1907.

Paul Jones Lodge No. 271, with George R. McDowell as first Worshipful Master.[181] Fred Smythe was Senior Warden, and, once again, *Peninsula Gateway* editor Trombley was in the thick of things, this time as Junior Warden. The first secretary was Iceland-born John Vernhardson, who also served as president of the Peninsula Berry Growers Association and the Gig Harbor Guernsey Cattle Club. Over the years, the lodge included among its members Biz Burnham, C. O. Austin, Bert Uddenberg, Adolph Sehmel, Harold Ryan, Hubert Secor, Floyd Hunt, John Finholm, Joe Hoots, and many other names that turn up again and again in the history of the community.[182]

And even the bleak Depression years had their economic bright spots. In 1930, Gig Harbor's newspaper told its readers, "The Skansie Shipyards, under the management of Anton Cosulich, are now building three purse seine boats, each 70 feet long and equipped with 135 h.p. Diesel engines...The new boats are being constructed for Antoin Babich, Nato Evanovich and John Skansie."

As part of a national promotion for air mail, Gig Harbor joined dozens of other Washington communities in preparing letters to be mailed by air during the week of May 15–21, 1938. Each letter had a special envelope emblazoned with a drawing of a small boat setting out from a naval sailing ship, and the words "GIG HARBOR, WASH. DISCOVERED – 1841." Sign painter C. E. Shaw donated his services to erect a fourteen-by-four-foot billboard marking the spot where the plane was expected to land.

A crowd gathers on the eastern shore of the bay as the first air mail plane touches down on May 15, 1938.

When Bert R. Eckstein brought his airplane down on the beach in front of the Treutle home in east Gig Harbor on the afternoon of May 19, he found Postmaster Hopkins waiting at a temporary beachfront "branch office" with a satchel of 1,278[183] air mail letters to go out postmarked Gig Harbor.[184] He also found a big crowd of peninsula citizens, who were happy to have something to celebrate. By chance or by design, it all happened in almost the same place where Alphonzo Young had opened Gig Harbor's first post office half a century earlier. When all the counting was done, it was found that John Insel, the peninsula's rural mail carrier, had carried more air mail letters than any other rural carrier in the state.[185]

Even animals did some surprising things in the course of the peninsula's history. In April 1934, John Wheeler's six-week-old pig, perhaps with vague forebodings about the ultimate fate of fattened hogs, fled the front yard and took off down the road, with Wheeler at his heels. It was a standard chase, until the pig got to the water and just kept going, becoming the first and last pig known to have swum the half-mile-wide harbor. M. Vulevie met him on the other side and returned him to Wheeler, making him also the first Gig Harbor pig known to have made the front page of the *Tacoma Daily Ledger*.[186]

No one imagined, not even the instigator, that the first event to truly put Gig Harbor in the national spotlight would feature a few hungry roosters. It all came about because of a man whose motto was, "What can we do today to have fun?" Clarence Elven Shaw was born on a farm near Crafton, Nebraska, on November 30, 1885. He attended commercial college and studied art in Minneapolis, then spent seven years doing office work and fifteen years as a traveling salesman before settling in Gig Harbor in 1924. He shared a house at Benson and Woodworth with his wife, Vie, and children Jane, Violet, and Frank. There he phased out of selling Masonic supplies across the Northwest and into commercial printing and sign painting in the local area.

C.E. always had an idea going, and managed to bring a few of them forward into solid reality. He wrote and published a song called, *Huckleberry Picking Mary.* He invented and sold a game called

"Hoopala," with four-foot lances and a rubber ring, selling for a dollar plus ten cents' postage. The high point of his career began in the summer of 1935, when local merchants were getting together a program to try and lure a few more folks to come over and spend money. When the postmistress of Gig Harbor voiced a desire to make this community stand out from the others, Shaw's mind flashed back to the days of his youth, when the chickens and roosters had come running for their feed every time his mother had come to the front of their farmhouse and banged on a scrap pan. More as a joke than anything else, Shaw suggested a rooster race.

The first race was a little wild. One of the seven racers fled the course and was not found for days. Others bent the rules by taking short, hopping flights. Things were so chaotic that it was hard to pick a winner, but the judges settled on a black Jersey Giant belonging to Mrs. Gertrude B. Hopkins of Gig Harbor. The onlookers loved it, and there was enough press coverage to convince Shaw he had a winning idea on his hands.

He set to work on a bigger and better show for 1936. He began training his roosters when they were ten days old, using food as an incentive. "Jockey shirts" for the roosters helped spectators tell one bird from another, and restricted their wings to keep them on the ground. He experimented with different breeds and decided that white leghorns were generally the fastest, and that roosters were faster than

Clarence E. Shaw and his wife, Vie, at the Rooster Races ticket booth. Shaw trained his roosters to run at the sound of a bell, leading to food at the end of the track.

hens. He persuaded local merchants, such as the Ferry Tavern, Finholm's Market, Pastime Pool Hall, and the Hy-Iu-Hee-Hee Tavern to sponsor individual racers. On a piece of flat ground above the mouth of Burnham Creek, he built an eighty-foot horseshoe-shaped racetrack. The second annual race was held on July 26, 1936, and the event just kept getting bigger. Pathe News sent a camera crew, and national newspapers and magazines began taking notice.

Shaw's ideas just kept coming. He converted the racetrack's ordinary chicken coops into a miniature village called Roosterville. Now his racing roosters could emerge from the "Sit and Hatch Groceries," "Bill Comb Barbershop," "The Cock-Eyed Daily News," "Dr. Will Pullet's," and other fowl domiciles. For lulls between races, he taught some of the roosters to ride miniature bicycles and cars.[187] He was not the first to discover that pretty girls in skimpy costumes are good advertising, but Gig Harbor had never seen anything quite like the Roosterettes.

1938 marked the high point of the rooster years. Shaw and his roosters were flown to New York to race at Madison Square Garden, with national radio coverage sponsored by "The Hobby Lobby." Shaw

sent a telegram to C. E. Trombley, editor of *The Peninsula Gateway*. "The roosters are 'roosting high.' They are up on the 34th floor of the Shelton Hotel. This has been a wonderful trip. When one has seen New York, they can never expect

Roosterettes Doris Fraesure Bell and Helen Miller open the starting gate. Part of Roosterville, a village of chicken coops disguised as houses, stores, and a church, is visible in the background.

153

any other to equal it. Wish me luck. I need it. – Shaw."

The press conference, with its blinding flashbulbs, was too much for the birds, but when it came time to race, they sprinted like the professionals they were, with veteran sportscaster Clem McCarthy capturing the action for an estimated thirty million listeners. Even C.E. Shaw could not top that and the races gradually scaled down. His all-time champion, Dot, who did eighty yards in fifteen seconds in 1938, retired in 1940. The last race was run in 1948.

For a moment, Gig Harbor had stood tall in the national spotlight on the feathered shoulders of a few roosters. An ill-fated bridge was about to bring the peninsula one more brush with fame, this time a most unwanted one.

Sentinel *circa 1925. The Lorenz Brothers' eagle is mounted on the upper deck.*

Plying the waters

Passengers board the Elsie C III *at the Point Defiance landing, heading to Sunrise Beach.*

The crew of the Hunt steamer Atalanta, *(l-r) Arda Hunt, Lloyd Hunt, Ed Dobson, Arthur Sandin, Lee Aldrich, 1913*

Boarding a steamer sometimes meant rowing out to meet the boat.

Well-dressed passengers for the steamer ride to Arletta – (l-r) first two men unknown, Irene Baudy, Gertrude Lota, Aura Powell, Ralph Lota, Nettie Campbell, Clyde Hobart, 1911

The steamer Emrose *glides through the waters at the head of the bay with berry fields of east Gig Harbor behind.*

Upon the opening of the second Narrows Bridge on Oct. 14, 1950, three ferries return to the Skansie shipyard ending their service across Puget Sound. Photo by Frank Owen Shaw

The Skanise-built Wollochet *nears the landing, ferry riders crowd the deck*

The Gloria, *formerly* Florence K, *nears the People's Wharf, 1920s*

The steamer Bay Island *at the Arletta dock on Hales Passage.*

The Florence K *tied up at People's Wharf, then the site of Uddenberg's West Side Merchantile.*

The Arcadia *plied the waters of Hales Passage during the years between the first Narrows Bridge and the second. The steamboat was built by the Lorenz Brothers in 1928.*

Ted Finholm and Raymond Hunt load the Burro *at the Washington Co-operative dock, 1922.*

Chapter 8

The Short Life of Galloping Gertie

For years, peninsula residents had dreamed of a mighty bridge across Puget Sound.

But only an accident of geography delivered the dream in solid form to the peninsula's doorstep. The bridge was sited here because in all of Puget Sound's twenty thousand square miles, this was the only spot where the distance between eastern and western shores came down to a little less than three-quarters of a mile. That was still a breathtakingly long stretch in the 1930s, but it was close enough to be acknowledged as possible. No one was ever sure who first seriously proposed a bridge across The Narrows. Sometime around 1888 or 1889, Captain Edward Lorenz of the steamer *Meta* watched Rosedale rancher John George Schindler point to the bluffs on both sides of The Narrows and say, "Captain, some day you will see a bridge over these Narrows."[188]

Predicting was one thing; coming forward with the financial means, the political power, or the technical knowhow to actually build the

An artist's conception of a bridge spanning The Narrows

thing was quite another. Some said that honor belonged to Major Edward Bowes, the developer of Fircrest, an upscale western suburb of Tacoma, back in the early years of the twentieth century.[189] No proof seems to have survived to support the Bowes claim. He later left the area for fame as the host of radio's *Original Amateur Hour*.

Sometimes the bridge dream took other forms. At one point, Tacoma politicians and developers toyed with the idea of a railroad on each side, connected by a ferry that would take whole trains across the watery stretch.[190] As early as December 1923 the *Tacoma Times* was broaching the idea of a bridge, and *Peninsula Gateway* editor Charles Trombley condensed the article for his own readers on December 28, under the headline, *"To Bridge the Narrows"*:

> Gig Harbor is certainly getting its share of free advertising these days. Under the caption 'Bridge the Narrows' the *Tacoma Times* of this date gave a three column sixteen inch space in 12 point and some black face type to the subject of bridging the Narrows, with the idea of bringing the Gig Harbor district and the vast undeveloped district back of it in closer touch with Tacoma...
>
> The bridging of the Narrows is a mighty big proposition, but it is bound to come some day, and that day may not be so very far away, because the influences which will bring it about are numerous and of considerable importance."[191]

The bridge idea hung there for a long time, caught between a dream and a mirage, always just out of reach. Bridge engineer J. B. Straus thought it looked possible in September 1927, when he stopped by on his way to California. Straus had already designed the Montreal Bridge, and had recently submitted the winning plans for the proposed Golden Gate Bridge in San Francisco. He was confident enough of success to offer to make a comprehensive survey of the situation and submit a plan to the local Chamber of Commerce.[192] Dr. H. H. Meyers, President of the New York-San Francisco Development Company, echoed the optimism on a visit the following November. He thought it could be done for seven million dollars, and indicated his interest in taking the project on if further investigations panned out.[193]

By November 1928 the players had changed, but the optimism remained. Dr. D. B. Steinman, of the New York bridge engineering firm Robinson & Steinman, telephoned from Portland, authorizing Tacoma City Engineer C. E. Putnam to put together a crew and conduct soundings for the best place to site the bridge and its supporting towers. He knew the waters were deep, but he had been the designing engineer when piers were built in 132 feet of water for the Carquinez Bridge in California.[194] In March 1929 he was in Tacoma, outlining plans for a concrete and steel suspension bridge with a record breaking 2,400 foot suspension span. The cost, he estimated, would be $8,800,000.[195] In April, the project was further buoyed by a traffic study estimating that $700,000 could be collected in tolls each year, and by news that the state legislature had authorized funds to pave the Gig Harbor – Bremerton highway.[196]

The stock market crash came that October, and investment money was suddenly in short supply. When bridge fever returned in 1932, it was an Olympia engineer and financier named Elbert M. Chandler who sent out surveying crews to once again study the bottom of The Narrows, in desperate hope of finding shallow spots to sink his piers. Reflecting the grim financial times, the width of the roadbed in the new design was reduced to 24 feet or fewer and the center span was cut to 1,200 feet, reducing the estimated cost to three million dollars. A government agency called the Recovery Finance Corporation seemed like a natural funding source, and Chandler approached them. They responded by becoming the first of many to turn him down.[197]

In 1934, victory came in the form of House Resolution 9530: "Be it enacted by the Senate and House of Representatives of the United States of America in Congress assembled, That the consent of Congress is hereby granted to the county of Pierce, a legal subdivision of the State of Washington, to construct, maintain, and operate a bridge and approaches thereto across Puget Sound, State of Washington, at or near a point commonly known as 'The Narrows.'"[198]

Pierce County quickly joined the bridge quest, and Washington Governor Clarence D. Martin allocated $700,000 in state funds. That was the amount needed to meet the requirements of the Federal Government's Public Works Administration for participation in local projects. The program's administrator, Harold Ickes, refused the grant request on the grounds of high cost and low potential traffic volume.[199] It was remembered that Ickes had once visited Tacoma. As he gazed across The Narrows toward the Gig Harbor side and listened to bridge proposals, his first reaction had been, "What's over there?"[200]

Clark Eldridge, who worked on bridges for the Department of Highways, submitted a plan that would cost an estimated eleven million dollars. Horrified politicians selected an alternate plan from bridge designer Leon Moisseiff, with a price tag closer to seven million.[201] Eldridge went off and built the art deco-style Cowen Park Bridge over Ravenna Creek in Seattle instead. Moisseiff's new design called for a slender two-lane bridge, instead of four lanes, and had solid eight-foot girders in place of the original fifteen-foot latticework model.

There were powerful interests pushing for a bridge, and eventually they were going to overcome all objections. Populations were growing on both shores, for one thing. For another, the vast, newly created Olympic National Park was just waiting for hordes of tourists. And with war fears growing in Europe and Asia, shrinking the drive from Fort Lewis to the Naval Shipyard in Bremerton from eighty miles down to thirty was no small consideration.

Tacoma had a larger population and more wealth than Gig Harbor, which equated with political clout, so the bulk of the effective pushing for a bridge was going to come from the eastern shore of The Narrows. But the peninsula folks were no less determined. When the "Narrows Bridge Gang" was formed in a meeting at Tacoma's Winthrop Hotel, the tall man at the far left of the back row in the fifteen-member group photo was Bert Uddenberg. Their motto was, "ENLISTED UNTIL IT'S BUILT." They pledged to work in close cooperation with the Tacoma Chamber of Commerce's Narrows Bridge Committee, which included *Peninsula Gateway* editor Trombley on its 1936 roster.

Charles Wyman, at Gig Harbor's Union High School, contributed his talent for verse:

> Our school is at Gig Harbor on famed Puget Sound.
> Where good schools, fine lakes and fine beaches abound.
> Better roads and bridges can nowhere else be found.
> And a bridge across the Narrows would just
>   complete the round.[202]

Any politicians who wavered would be wise to check their mail. Cards were coming in thick and fast from the peninsula, and they all contained the Narrows Bridge Pledge:

> As a citizen of the State of Washington I earnestly favor a Bridge at the Narrows, said bridge to be built by the State with Federal aid.
>
> I am opposed to all further provisions that would tend to delay or defeat legislation to provide for building the Narrows Bridge.
>
> Therefore I hereby pledge myself to vote for no candidate for senator or member of the legislature who has not publicly declared himself ready to work actively and to vote for legislation to carry out my desires as above set forth.

This wording suggested *Peninsula Gateway* editor Trombley at his most formal. Had there been any room for doubt on the source, there was a notice in the paper advising anyone who had not signed the card to, "call at the *Gateway* office where they can be secured and sign up, and give us your moral support."[203]

There was a lot riding on the hopes for the bridge. For farmers, a bridge could mean a blessed end to the need for loading produce onto a ferry in the middle of the night to be in Tacoma by the market opening time. For merchants, it meant a steady flow of paying customers. It had been a hard pull through the Depression years, and the Peninsula Cafe – "Good Food Served With a Smile" – could use a few more customers to smile at. For an auto dealer like Bert Uddenberg, it offered another reason, the best reason yet, for his neighbors to think about buying a car. For anyone restless for a taste of the wider world, a bridge offered ready access to the resources and entertainment of the big city of Tacoma.

At last, on June 24, 1938, *The Peninsula Gateway* announced in blaring headlines, "NARROWS BRIDGE PROJECT ASSURED." Editor Trombley reported the receipt of a wire from the secretary of Senator Homer T. Bone in Washington, D. C., announcing that a Public Works Administration grant for $2,700,000 had been awarded for the construction of the long-awaited bridge. Later came a federal loan of $3,520,000 from the Reconstruction Finance Authority (RFC).

The Public Works Administration money was an outright grant and would not have to be repaid. The RFC loan would have to be paid back, but no one worried too much about it at the time. There was going to be a bridge! The Pacific General Columbia Company was contracted to start building a bridge using Leon Moisseiff's plans. The company already had the Golden Gate Bridge and the massive Bonneville Dam and Locks on their resume. Clark Eldridge, swallowing disappointment over his rejected plans, returned to act as chief engineer.

Foss tugboats bring in portions of the Narrows Bridge, 1939. The caissons withstood the collapse of the bridge in 1940 and formed the base for the second Narrows Bridge towers, opened in 1950. Photo by James Bashford

Even before the bridge got going, a service dock was built near the foot of Sixth Avenue on the Tacoma side. On the western shore, a mixer dock took shape, where the concrete for the bridge and its piers would be prepared. It would eventually be capable of turning out eighty cubic yards of concrete each hour.[204] The piers were the first big challenge. Two were needed to support the towers for the suspension cables, and the swift currents of the deep waters were a major challenge.

One of the first surprises was that a current part way down often ran in the opposite direction from its brother at the surface. Hardhat divers, working on the bottom, coordinated the lowering of forth-eight concrete anchors weighing six hundred tons apiece.[205] The anchors were formed into a circle to protect the watertight chambers, called caissons, which were built in stages down from the surface to the seabed. The western pier actually was extended fifty-five feet down into the seabed through dredging and driving. The eastern pier was even more of a challenge. The sea floor sloped there, and the penetration had to go down 105 feet before things finally evened out. Once the piers were finished and capped, great steel towers began to rise atop them.

The bridge provided work when it was desperately needed. In November 1939, 150 men labored on it daily, and many more furnished materials.[206] By December a wooden catwalk had been strung from shore to shore and across the tops of the two towers. It was not a journey for the faint of heart, but for the first time in human history, it was possible to walk across The Narrows.[207]

By February 1940 the daily employment was up to 263. They were bringing the bridge in on time and on budget. By March 1, the project was figured at 79.28% completed. The cable-spinning for the two main suspension cables, which went on around the clock five days a week, was 82.5% done by the same date. The *Gateway* told its readers that, "Four loops, or 8 wires, are successfully carried across the mile wide channel from the east shore over the top of the two 425 ft. towers at one time, at a speed of 700 feet per minute. The spinning carriage returned empty after each trip across. Sixty to 70 round trips

164

are made during the continuous 24-hour operation."[208]

There were a few accidents along the way. One of the six-hundred-ton anchor blocks toppled into The Narrows before it could reach the bridge site. A boom of logs being towed through The Narrows collided with one of the bridge piers. A derrick collapsed and injured two workmen. Parker Paint Company of Tacoma had drawn the massive job of painting the bridge, and in July 1940 one of their painters, Peter Kreiter, fell from the bridge. It was a fearfully long way down, nearly 240 feet, and few have survived such a fall. Engineers later told him he hit the water at a speed of 360 miles per hour. Kreiter came ashore with nothing worse than bruised hips.[209]

For the most part, things worked well. This was a talented group of builders, and they found innovative solutions to the occasional problem. When steel deck girders refused to fit into place, assistant engineer Andy Zori came up with the idea of packing them overnight in dry ice. The next morning the metal had contracted just enough to fit into place, like a hand in a glove.[210]

The bridge was an engineering marvel, replete with modern wonders of all kinds. Elevators installed in the towers could carry maintenance workers to any point in the 386 feet between the concrete pier and the towers' top struts. Westinghouse sodium vapor lamps illumi-

nated the new bridge, and the *Tacoma Times* praised the monochromatic character of their light.[211] To protect the toll takers from being shocked by static electricity, bronze plates were embedded in

The two main suspension cables on the Narrows Bridge are spun from wire spools unreeling onsite and afixed to an anchorage built on land at each end. Photo by James Bashford

165

the concrete roadway. The plates were grounded, and sported "whiskers" to intercept stray currents from the metal parts of cars.[212] It seemed at the time as if the builders had thought of everything.

The bridge was a vast construction by anyone's measure. The total structural length was 5,939 feet. The roadway was twenty-six feet wide, with five-foot sidewalks on both sides. The center suspension span alone was 2,800 feet long. Each of the two big suspension cables was seventeen-and-one-half inches in diameter and contained 6,308 number six wires. Between them, they weighed 3,816 tons. Their massive shore anchors weighed 52,500 tons. The two towers supporting the cables soared to 425 feet above their cement piers. Each tower weighed 1,927 tons. The west pier, closest to the peninsula, was 198 feet tall. The two piers were an inch shy of 119 feet long and almost 66 feet wide. It took 111,234 cubic yards of reinforced concrete to build them.[213]

The papers were full of gee whiz figures like that. The other things that readers on both sides of The Narrows seemed to read and argue about endlessly was the question of how much it should cost to cross. The people of the peninsula had just come off a big fight over ferry rates, and an expensive toll bridge did not sound like much of an improvement. "The bridge will not do this locality any appreciable amount of good if the tolls are kept so high that our people can not afford to use the same," cried *Gateway* editor Trombley.[214]

As the bridge neared completion, people began to notice a peculiar oscillating movement when the wind blew. The Whitestone Bridge in New York, another of Moisseiff's creations, was reported to have a similar affliction. He assured the highway department and the project's board of directors that a simple procedure had solved things back in New York.[215] The work went ahead, and so did plans for an opening celebration.

The grand opening came on July 1, 1940. C. E. Shaw ran a rooster race, with Roosterette Beverly Hemley acting as starter. The mayors of Tacoma and Bremerton joined cheering spectators to watch Fleetfoot outpace Super Shell in a field of twenty-four roosters.[216] There was "a sea of clam chowder" that featured the world's largest chowder bowl. There was a parade with floats and decorated cars. The peninsula was represented in the float department by the Lions Club, the Crescent Valley Good Roads Club, Peninsula Pamona Grange, Gig Harbor Community, and the American Legion.[217] The Gig Harbor band played a string of concerts in Tacoma, Gig Harbor, and Port Orchard.[218] Postmaster Hopkins, an old band man, composed the "Narrows Bridge March" for the occasion.[219]

Camera shops in Tacoma had been offering prizes for the best photographs of the bridge and it was announced that Gig Harbor's Lola Spadoni and Thomas E. Thompson won for the best nighttime and daytime photos, respectively.[220] Governor Clarence D. Martin paid the first toll to cross, followed by 2,052 more automobiles by eleven o'clock that night. No one even tried to count the thousands of pedestrians who flooded across that day.[221] For the Fourth of July, 5,500 cars and 5,000 pedestrians crossed the bridge.[222]

The bridge would bring changes, and some of them were already in evidence. The first sidewalks went in that year along the few Gig Harbor residential streets whose property owners were willing to pay the Works Progress Administration their materials cost of ten cents per square foot.[223] Merchants along the main routes were beginning to deal with parking problems for the first time.

The first Narrows Bridge opened on July 1, 1940. Photo by James Bashford

The people who lived at Shore Acres knew all about the downside of having a bridge. The new stream of traffic constantly roared by them, and sometimes it roared straight at them. On the early morning of September 21, two sailors in a hurry to get to Bremerton missed the curve at the bottom of Shore Acres Hill, screeched almost two hundred feet, and sheared off two gas pumps at the corner Standard gas station. Their car finally careened into the station itself, mashing in the front wall. The driver was treated for cuts and bruises – his companion was fine – and then was taken to Kitsap County jail for reckless driving.

This was the third serious accident at that corner since the bridge opened, and it had *The Peninsula Gateway* calling for a red, blinking stop light.[224] The public outcry intensified in October after another car, driven by a Mason County woman, took out Roby's last surviving gas pump. Sporting the pump as an enormous new hood ornament, the car knocked down a telephone pole, crashed over a ten-foot embankment, and slammed against the kitchen wall of the home belonging to Mr. and Mrs. H. Wenning. Again, neither the driver nor her passenger were badly hurt, but the house was knocked askew on its foundation, with a ripped wall, loose plumbing, and broken dishes.[225]

Yet even if more drivers meant more wrecks, communities on both sides of The Narrows wanted increased traffic over the bridge, and they viewed tolls as an impediment to achieving their goal. Fifty-five cents for a car and driver and fifteen cents for each passenger seemed awfully high. And resentment intensified when it was revealed that the toll was likely to stay at that rate for the next ten years. Some grumbled that it would be cheaper to continue driving to Tacoma by way of Olympia.

A move was launched to refinance and extend the repayment of the RFC loan out to fifteen years. Months of hard fighting bore fruit. By the end of October, the toll for a car and driver had dropped to fifty cents, and passengers could now ride along for a dime. Foot traffic fees also dropped to ten cents. Trucks were charged by weight, and the range ran from fifty-five cents for anything under 5,000 pounds to three dollars for a 34,000-pounder. [226] Another fight began brewing, over embarrassing questions surrounding the refinancing, but this controversy ended abruptly in a way few could have foreseen.

The Narrows Bridge was the third-largest single suspension bridge in the world, right after San Francisco's Golden Gate and New York's George Washington bridges. It took only a few blustery days to show onlookers and travelers that it had at least one trick its larger cousins never learned. This trait had suggested itself even during construction, and it became manifest after the bridge opened. When the wind was blowing right, the bridge bucked like a wild animal. At night, drivers of cars crossing the bridge would see the tail lights of cars up ahead dip out of sight and then pop up again, as if the bridge had been designed with its own set of movable hills and valleys.

Some blamed the solid steel girders encasing the roadbed, pointing out that the wind blew against them, instead of through them. Doubts also began to arise about the wisdom of being the world's most slender bridge in proportion to its length. Someone dubbed it the Bridge of San Luis Rey, after the doomed Andean footbridge of Thornton Wilder's novel.[227] That was clever enough, but it was eclipsed by the other nickname. No one remembers who first came up with "Galloping Gertie." Some thought it was suggested by the controversial girder design. Some said it was coined by the bridge construction workers. In any case, it sounded good, it was descriptive, and the name stuck, to the mounting discomfort of the bridge's designers.

Engineers and designers tried a string of remedies to stop the galloping. Hydraulic jacks were installed to act as shock absorbers beneath the roadway at the two piers.[228] Cables which had supported the catwalk before the roadbed was laid were brought out of storage to secure the deck to anchors on shore.[229] Professor F. G. "Burt" Farquharson of the University of Washington tested a model of the bridge in a wind tunnel. The model and the tests cost thousands of dollars. The model seemed to stand up all right, and Farquharson urged more study. F. S. Heffernan, whose company had supplied the sand and gravel for the project, made a bet with designing engineer Ted

Coos that the bridge would not last a year.[230] Still, it was hard to imagine something this massive and carefully planned coming down because of a little wind.

Hallett R. French, one of the agents who handled the bridge's insurance, remained unworried. As the northwest agent for Merchants' Fire Assurance Corp., he had signed his company up for an $800,000 share of the insurance on the bridge. All told, twenty-two insurance companies were involved in the coverage. Merchants' Fire Assurance did not know at the time that it was one of them. Hallett had pocketed the premium and neglected to forward the policy to headquarters. Pacific National Bank over in Tacoma was also feeling pretty optimistic about the bridge's fate. They put up a big sign with the tag line, "As secure as the Narrows Bridge."[231]

November 7, 1940, was a Thursday. Pastor Mary Jane Turner of the Gig Harbor Presbyterian Church drove across that morning. So did Aunt Ruby, a former opera singer in Reverend Turner's youth program. So did Crescent Valley's Paul Alvestad, taking his 1935 Dodge to work. (The former schoolboy newspaper carrier was now an employee of the National Soap Company in Tacoma.)[232] The winds were high, and Gertie was galloping furiously. Aunt Ruby remarked that she had crossed the Atlantic many times without being as seasick as she was that day on the bridge.[233]

Winfield Brown, a twenty-five-year-old freshman at Tacoma's College of Puget Sound, was having a better time. He paid ten cents for the experience of walking across the bouncing bridge. Cars were passing him all the way, and he could see people laughing and enjoying the unique ride. He walked all the way across to the Gig Harbor side and back to Tacoma. It was so much fun that he decided to go again. He was back near the center span when things took an ominous turn and the bridge developed a strange new motion.[234]

The workers in the tollbooth knew there was something different about this round of galloping. They were not just riding up and down. This time the roadway was also twisting from side to side. Drivers on the world's most expensive roller coaster found themselves looking

170

down at the water on one side and then the other. Elbert Keith Swinney and his screaming wife, Hazel, crossed over to the peninsula on a Golden Rule Bakery truck. E.K., as he was known, had experienced the galloping many times, and he wanted to share the experience with his wife and five-year-old son, Richard. In later years, Richard clearly remembered watching a workman walk toward them. One moment he was at the top of a hill. The next moment the hill became a valley and the workman dropped out of sight.

The Swinneys made it across. So did Tacoma's Mel Monson, with a load of school supplies for Kingston, up in Kitsap County.[235] At about 9:30 that morning, Mrs. Frances Carlson crossed in her two-door Model A Ford, carrying mail from the Gig Harbor post office to the big post office in downtown Tacoma. She noticed the regular up and down motion that she had come to regard as fun, but the twisting from side to side was new and frightening. She believed herself the last driver from the Gig Harbor side to pay a toll on the bridge.

Five minutes behind her, the driver of the Bremerton-Tacoma stage decided to park and wait for the wind to settle down.[236] Dr. Jesse W.

When Galloping Gertie began to twist as well as gallop, the bridge could not withstand the strong winds on November 7, 1940. Photo by Howard Clifford

Read and Wilbur Raleigh drove across to the Gig Harbor side to take some pictures of the writhing bridge. They believed they were in the last vehicle to successfully cross. From a bluff, they watched a less fortunate truck come to grief.[237] That delivery truck ended up overturned in the roadway, after Ruby Jacox and Arthur Hagen of Tacoma, partners in the Rapid Transfer Company, realized they would have to abandon it. It took them nearly half an hour of crawling on the undulating bridge to reach safety. Workmen met them at the western pier and took them to Gig Harbor Hospital, where they were treated for bruises.[238]

Leonard Coatsworth, a *Tacoma News Tribune* reporter, was headed home to Tacoma with belongings from his beach house in Arletta. With him in the car was his daughter's cocker spaniel. Poor Tubby was apparently not a particularly lucky dog, as he had only three legs and was partially paralyzed.[239] Coatsworth was part way across when the violent swaying of the bridge threw his car from curb to curb. He slammed on his brakes and tried to scramble out, but the doors were jammed. He was something of a fanatic about driving with his window down, winter or summer. It was down that day, even in a forty-mile-an-hour wind, and he climbed out that way. He tried to rescue Tubby, but the dog was not cooperative, and the car continued to slide from side to side as the roadway twisted. Coatsworth had to set off on foot without him.

A few steps made it clear that no one could stand on this snake-dancing ribbon of concrete and steel. He crawled most of the way on bleeding knees and bruised hands, desperately clawing his way toward shore and safety. At one point his strength gave out and all he could do was lie clutching the curb and gasping for breath. He was aware of someone up ahead of him, sometimes crawling, sometimes able to walk. It was college student Winfield Brown, now feeling scared and seasick, but fortunate enough to be younger and a bit more agile than a veteran reporter.[240] The sound of cracking concrete spurred Coatsworth, and he finally made it to the first tower, where the going was a little easier.

One of the toll takers phoned Barney Elliott, who worked in a Tacoma camera shop with his partner, Harbine Monroe. They raced down with their cameras and found Leonard Coatsworth already safe on the Tacoma side. True to his reporter's instincts, he had called his newspaper as soon as he was safe, and the *News Tribune* sent out backup photographer Howard Clifford and a part-timer named James Bashford. There seemed to be a lull in the wind, and Clifford, Bashford, and Professor Farquharson, the wind tunnel man, went out to see if they could rescue the dog.

They got part way there when the gyrations worsened. Farquharson had driven down from Seattle to take pictures, in case they might provide a clue to stop the swaying, and he got close enough to reach into the car. It had been a bad day for Tubby. He had been tossed around in the car by forces he could not comprehend, his owner nowhere to be seen, and now some stranger was trying to abduct him. Bared fangs and a punctured finger told Farquharson that Tubby was not going to be moved.

"Let's leave, the bridge is going down!" warned Elliott. "It can't fall down," Farquharson protested, "we tested the model in worse winds than this." Maybe so, but cracking concrete, twisting steel, and snapping cables suggested otherwise. Some of the loose pieces of concrete were sliding across the roadbed like icebergs in a stormy sea. Clifford started running, which was not easy. His legs would flail in the air one moment, and in the next instant the bridge would come up to meet him with a hard smack.[241]

Down below, the trains along the Tacoma side of The Narrows were stopped, fearful of passing under the writhing bridge. On the water, Bud Brown and his five companions on a drilling barge watched light poles snap off and tumble into the water. Their barge was stranded until their foreman brought the workboat back from its inspection trip to check the damage on the west end.

There was plenty of irony for this crew, if they wanted to consider it while they waited. They were down here because their task was to drill holes for a future support intended to stop the swaying, and here they were with the bridge coming apart above them. All sorts of things were raining down, some of them hitting the barge, others plunging into the water with a roar like a clap of thunder. They took cover in a little house on the barge, not that it would have helped much if a big piece of iron or steel had hurtled down from that height. Their luck held.[242]

Finally the last human was off the bridge, staggering shoreward to be captured on Barney Elliott's sixteen-millimeter Bell & Howell movie film. Growing knots of people watched from the Tacoma and peninsula sides. Then, at 11:08 a.m., the roadway between them, six million dollars worth of hopes and dreams, ripped apart like a piece of cheap cloth and fell into The Narrows: vehicle, dog, solid girders, and all. A bridge of amazing statistics contributed one last superlative. It produced the largest splash anyone on Puget Sound ever saw.

By the time the wind had finished its work, some two thousand feet of the center span were gone. The towers had flexed like fishing rods with a big one on the line, but they remained standing, for all the good that did anyone at the time. Among those watching from the Gig Harbor side was Bill Skansie, the son of boat builder and ferry operator Mitchell Skansie. "What are you crying for?" he beamed to his wife, Evelyn. "We're back in business."[243]

The roadbed of the bridge splashes into the waters below, snapping the cables and bending the towers. Only the caissons were left intact. Photo by James Bashford

And so they were. The first order of business, shock and dismay not withstanding, was to get the ferries back up and running until someone could figure out what to do about the bridge. Pilings at the Point Fosdick landing had been removed to allow barges to tie up alongside, so traffic would have to run on the Point Defiance – Gig Harbor route for the time being.

An agreement was reached by midnight, and by 7:15 on Friday morning the *Skansonia* was departing on her first run from Point Defiance to Gig Harbor. The *Defiance* was being treated for dry rot, and until that was finished the smaller *Vashonia* served as the second boat. Together they ran from six in the morning until midnight.[244] Ultimately the state bought the boats, but retained Bill Skansie to run them, and sold tickets out of a side room of the red brick house where Mitchell Skansie had watched the boats take shape.

That Christmas, Mary Ruddy, a member of the Chapel Hill Presbyterian congregation, got a card from Professor Farquharson. It read "A Bridge Of Steel May Fall, For Winds Blow Strong—And Tides Run Hard—Christmas Is A Bridge...Between A World Of Hate And a World of Love. Its Foundations Are Stronger Than Steel...And The Winds And Tides Will Not Destroy."[245]

The fallen bridge had a long post mortem. Everyone wanted to know why it had fallen. "Too slender" was an obvious culprit. So were the closed girders. Congressman John Coffee was shrill in his cry for an investigation and retribution. "The federal government is determined to find out persons and firms to blame for the tragedy and expose them, regardless of prominence," he warned. Clark Eldridge, the first designer and chief engineer, turned the blame back on the federal agencies which had forced the penny-wise design compromises that ultimately cost the life of the bridge. In the end, the only one who went to prison was Hallet French, the apparently otherwise-decent insurance agent who now fervently wished he had sent the premium to headquarters.

Experts pointed out the one benefit of the disaster: It taught the world a lesson in how not to build a bridge. They were likely to get it right next time, and there seemed little doubt that next time would be coming soon. Only something huge would prevent or delay the construction of another bridge.

Two bridge workers walk along the broken cables on the first Narrows Bridge, February, 23, 1943. Photo by James Bashford

Chapter 9

The Peninsula Goes to War

Readers must have been startled and then mildly amused by *The Peninsula Gateway*'s front page on December 5, 1941. "Local Hospital Bombed During Peninsula Black-out," screamed the headline. "While the entire peninsula lay blacked out early Sunday morning, two giant 'war birds' slipped past the outer observation posts undetected, and as they soared over the Gig Harbor hospital, let go their cargoes. Two pairs of tiny lungs rent the air with shrieks and wails, and when the pandemonium had subsided it was learned that two baby boys had been born, one to Mr. and Mrs. Harold Roby, the other to Mr. and Mrs. Oscar Berntsen of Cromwell."

People could chuckle and say, "Oh, of course, the 'war birds' were storks." This bit of gallows humor came in the context of one war raging in Asia between the Japanese and Chinese, and another in Europe, pitting the British and Russians against the invading Germans and Italians. Two days later, bombs of a very real sort rained down on Pearl Harbor in Hawaii, and life in Gig Harbor and the rest of America was changed forever.

December 7, 1941 started out as an ordinary Sunday on the Gig Harbor Peninsula. It was warm for late fall, in the low fifties with clouds and just a scattering of rain. The wind blew out of the southwest at about twenty miles an hour that morning. Sunrise came at 7:42 and sunset at 4:21.[246] The Wollochet-Midway Good Roads and Improvement Club had met the night before and heard state representative and *Peninsula Gateway* editor C. E. Trombley speak on old age pensions. Keith Uddenberg had opened a second grocery store that week in what had been the Safeway building, and was advertising large cans of milk at three cans for a quarter. Big boxes of Kellogg's Corn Flakes were going two for nineteen cents, and Emperor grapes were fifteen cents for two pounds. Anyone who telephoned 2230 got free delivery.

Finholm's 20th Century Food Store, not to be outdone, was offering "Spry" dog food, six cans for twenty-five cents, a twelve-ounce package of Sno-White fresh fluffy marshmallows for ten cents, and a dozen large Sunkist oranges for twenty-nine cents.

Next door to Bert Uddenberg's Motors, Luters Electric and Plumbing was renting vacuum cleaners for a dollar a day, or fifty cents for a half day. Mrs. H. W. Forsythe was advertising to buy two day-old calves. In the same want ad column, J. B. Borgert was advertising fresh rock cod, true cod, and sole, suitable for canning or salting.

The Peninsula Dry Goods Company in the Gilich block was presenting itself as "The Store with the Christmas Spirit." One dollar could buy twenty-one "Exquisite" boxed Christmas cards; a mere thirty-five cents could purchase twenty-one "Fascinating" ones. "Buy early" was the theme of the quarter-page ad, which closed with a pledge to "make this Christmas the best and brightest and merriest for you in our history. A small deposit will hold till Christmas."

Anyone inclined to take the ferry over to Tacoma had a good choice of movies upon arrival. William Holden was starring in *Texas*, while William Powell and Myrna Loy shared billing with Aster the dog in *Shadow of the Thin Man*; it was their eleventh picture together. Rosalind Russell and Don Ameche could be seen in *The Feminine Touch*, and Spencer Tracy chilled audiences in *Dr. Jekyll and Mr. Hyde*. Jimmy Stewart drawled through *Navy Blue and Gold*, while Errol Flynn's latest picture, *Dive Bomber*, was about to become a much more memorable title. Starring in *Nine Lives Are Not Enough* and *International Squadron* was a busy actor who had visited Puget Sound a few years before, to film *Tugboat Annie Sails Again*. His name was Ronald Reagan.

Residents had been following news of the war, especially the fighting in Europe, with deep concern. The peninsula was peopled with immigrant families, and many had close relations living in war-ravaged lands. When the Russians attacked Finland in the Winter War of 1939-40, how could it help but stir memories and worries for merchant John Finholm in Gig Harbor? John Watson had to wonder how his family in England was faring when he read of the blitz.

Especially in the fishing fleet, there had to be worry and dismay when the Germans overran Yugoslavia in April 1941. The force of the community's fear and sorrow hit home for Martha Jean Insel when a newsreel of the fighting and destruction in Yugoslavia flashed across the screen at the Roxy Theater and she heard members of the audience break into sobs.[247]

Whatever Peter Land might think of Hitler and the Nazis, it would have been hard not to worry about friends and family back in the Leipzig-area town of Deutzen, where he had been born in 1902. He had come to America as a stowaway on a foreign vessel in 1923.[248] When Albert Yates died in 1925, his widow Sarah had hired Land to maintain their property at Rosedale. A year later, he married Sarah's daughter, Christina. In 1933 their only child, Rosemary Alice Land, was born. Little did anyone in the family imagine what the war had in store for them.

The Scandinavians in Cromwell and Crescent Valley had already seen Norway and Denmark overrun by the Nazis. There were growing concerns that America might be pulled into the widening conflict, but until the seventh day of December, the conflict seemed remote.

Sunday meant religious services around the peninsula. St. Nicholas Catholic Church in Gig Harbor had early mass at eight o'clock and late mass at ten. Anyone feeling the weight of sin could attend a confessional half an hour before first mass. Mary Jane Turner delivered her inspirational message at the Rosedale Union Church at ten that morning, and an hour later she was at the altar of the Gig Harbor Memorial Presbyterian Church. Most of the churches, including Gig Harbor Methodist Episcopal, the Gospel Lighthouse of Artondale, and Immanuel Lutheran of Cromwell, held morning services.

Bethel Lutheran Church of Wollochet bucked the tide with divine worship scheduled for seven (the newspaper did not specify a.m. or p.m.) with a text from Luke 12:30-35. "God the Only Cause and Creator" was the subject of the lesson-sermon at the Christian Science Church. Several churches also had evening services scheduled, and Dorothy Gilmore planned to direct choir practice at Gig Harbor Presbyterian at eight that evening.

News of the devastating surprise attack on Pearl Harbor began crackling in over the radio about the time Sunday morning services ended. Word of mouth passed it along swiftly. Most people remembered for the rest of their lives what they were doing when they heard the news. John and Trillium Insel, up on Stinson Hill, were generally lenient with their three children, not minding if the kids often chattered through a radio program. Martha Jean Insel, who was eight years old that year, does not remember why her parents turned on the radio that day. She guesses it must have been a phone call, but she always remembers how seriously her parents listened, and how startled she was when they admonished the children to be quiet.

Lee Makovich, Jr., one of Martha Jean's first-grade classmates, was playing in the yard of his neighbors, Mr. and Mrs. Andrew Skansie. It was Mrs. Skansie who came out and told him, "You better go home and talk to your mamma." That was unusual, since he played there all the time and never got sent home. His parents, looking shocked and upset, told him that Pearl Harbor had been bombed. He had no idea where Pearl Harbor was, and he was too young to be afraid, but he understood that something very important had happened.[249]

Bert Uddenberg's daughter, Shirley, was in her early teens. She liked geography and she already knew that Pearl Harbor was in Hawaii. She told people about it as they drifted into the Uddenberg's dairy store after church. Their reaction was often one of disbelief.[250] Her much younger brother, Bert Junior, was riding his bicycle in the street when some adults told him what had happened.[251]

On Wollochet Bay, teenager Bud DeWalt heard the shocking news crackling from the loudspeaker on one of the boats at the newly created Tacoma Yacht Club outstation.[252] Sixteen-year-old Don Sehmel and his friend Carl Grieb rowed ashore at Rosedale after a morning of duck hunting to find their nation at war. Don was not altogether surprised. He followed current events, and knew about President Roosevelt's recent ultimatum to the Japanese. His one big fear was that the war would end before he had a chance to join in, and he soon lied about his age in order to join the marines. Carl, for his part, went into the navy.[253]

Paul Alvestad, Union High class of 1935, was already in service. He had been in the naval reserve, and had been called to active duty as the foreign crisis deepened in the spring of 1941. He was home on leave that Sunday, but he set out immediately for the naval base at Bremerton.[254]

A car breakdown had stranded Joe Hoots in Tacoma that morning. He was on Sixth Avenue, trying to find a ride to the ferry landing, when someone told him that Pearl Harbor had been attacked. When he wondered aloud if they could be joking or mistaken, he was told it was all over the radio.[255]

Brothers John and Peter Ancich and their crew were in San Francisco, unloading their herring catch from their boat, *Invader*, when the news came in over the radio. They were sent home and it was the end of fishing until further notice.[256]

Life was going to change. The first visible sign came when the few lights glowing in the peninsula nights went suddenly dark. Indoor lights could still burn, provided the curtains were heavy enough, but porch lights and outdoor lights of any sort were forbidden. Night travel became more difficult. Car headlights had to be covered except for a horizontal strip a half-inch wide and three inches long. Any taillight shining upward had to be covered, as well. William Skansie announced that night-time ferry service would cease, to comply with blackout orders. The boats would tie up at Point Fosdick on the peninsula and at Sixth Avenue in Tacoma, ready for emergencies. Come what may, they would be back in service by 6 A.M. to carry the Bremerton navy yard traffic.

There were dozens of organizations on the peninsula, and each took in the news and adapted to the realities as best they could. The

Crescent Valley PTA called off the Penny Carnival it had scheduled for December twelfth, but went ahead with a quilt raffle, moving the venue to Finholm's Market on the thirteenth. The American Legion Post Number Ninety-Nine met in Glen Cove over on the Longbranch Peninsula as scheduled on December tenth, and they surprised no one by pledging themselves "as individuals and as an organization to co-operate 100 percent with the National Defense program." Dances and Christmas programs largely went on as scheduled, subject to black-out restrictions.[257] Local sports continued, with the Gig Harbor Union High School Bulldogs basketball team battling back from behind to defeat Silverdale High by a bare margin of 34 to 33 on January 27.[258]

Recruiting began for civil defense workers, but in the early going Deputy Sheriff R. C. Paulson had his hands full trying to enforce the new regulations. Chicken ranchers quickly found themselves at odds with the United States government. They might obey the blackout commands like good citizens in their own home, but they were accustomed to turning on the lights in their chicken coops early in the morning to stimulate egg production. Paulson was compelled to remind them that the blackout applied to everyone, including chickens. Eventually the local authorities produced a brochure detailing alternative lighting methods for the poultry producers.[259]

Chicken farmers faced another dilemma as the war progressed, in the form of a chronic shortage of the petroleum briquettes many of them used to heat their brooder stoves.[260] The lack of heat was no small consideration, since the United States had pledged to supply its allies with seventeen million cases of eggs in 1942.[261] A little later, there was another casualty on the feathered front. *The Peninsula Gateway* announced that the rooster races scheduled for the July Fourth holidays would be the last such competition held until the war's end.[262]

Local merchants were prepared to muster equal measures of patriotism and profit by the time the first war-time issue of *The Peninsula Gateway* came out on Friday, December 12. The Gig Harbor Hardware & Grocery was following up descriptions of fifteen-cent Sally May soap flakes and twenty-nine-cent boxes of chocolate cherries with a closing line about the availability of black-out paper at two-and-one-half cents per square foot or $1.25 for a roll of 250 square feet.

Gateway editor Trombley added his own voice to the war effort with an editorial headlined, "Our Country's War." He sounded as dazed and rattled as the rest of his readers:

> War, the thing we have been talking about, possibly dreaming of, and anticipating, for a period of many months, has finally come upon us. No matter how unbelievable it may all seem, nevertheless, we are faced with an unrelenting, must do task, no matter what the price may be and that task demands the defeat of Japan, Germany and Italy.
>
> We must throw every ounce of strength and resource into the battle, because it will take just that to defeat the above mentioned countries, whose dominant desire at this time is to crush, conquer and destroy us, economically and internationally, that we as a world power and all we stand for may be driven from the earth.

He finished by bringing it all closer to home. "Locally we are in a 'hot spot,' and for that reason we have a double duty to perform, for it is our duty to consider, not only local obligations, but also those obligations that have to do with the country as a whole. All orders should be carefully carried out, and we should be ever on the alert for whatever work may be in store for us."

There was plenty to do. Even with a careful black-out, no one knew for sure that Japanese bombers might not come roaring out of the western sky. The Puget Sound Naval Shipyard in Bremerton, the Boeing Aircraft Plant near Seattle, the McChord Airfield, and the big army base at Fort Lewis were all close by, as the crow and bomber flew, and they were all prime targets if the enemy came. Out at Arletta, Mr. and Mrs. Oscar Dulin made their property available for the local air raid watch, with the Lions Club volunteering to take the midnight to 4 a.m. graveyard shift. By January, the Dulins had a volunteer force of 125 men and women, each taking a four hour shift at least once every three weeks or so.

A cabin with heating, plumbing, electricity, and telephone connections had been raised for their use. John D. Edwin worked up a listening device with microphones and horns sensitive enough for a listener with earphones to hear the drone of a plane's engines and detect its direction six or seven miles out. That kind of technology might save many lives, but it did have its drawbacks. One observer was stunned and partially deafened for a time when someone drove up to the listening station and carelessly blew their car horn.[263]

Later, a thirty-foot spotting tower was erected much closer to Gig Harbor on Stinson Hill, at the north end of mail carrier John Insel's land, along the property line he shared with Ed Kimball. At the top of four flights of zigzagging stairs there was a cabin with glass windows all around. Furnishings consisted of a counter, a logbook, a telephone, and a chair or two. There was an electric heater for cold weather and a privy at the bottom of the steps for calls of nature.

Flash cards helped volunteers learn to recognize aircraft head-on, in profile, and from the ground looking up. Any plane the observers saw was logged, and its direction, speed, and type reported by phone to the control center in Seattle. They became good at what they did. In February 1944 the Aircraft warning service conducted drills to test the readiness of the observation posts. The average amount of time for a post to become operational was twelve minutes. Trillium Insel, the post's Chief Observer, did it in two minutes. She received a medal from the Army Air Corps for superior performance.[264]

Aircraft spotted from the tower were almost always Boeing B-17 bombers and P-38 fighter planes, but no one could be sure the next one would not be a Japanese zero. On one occasion, a spotter, perhaps out of boredom or an inflamed imagination, phoned in a graphic account of an aerial dogfight. Alarmed, the Seattle Control Center called Mrs. Insel for confirmation. She reported all quiet on the Gig Harbor front.[265]

A good cross-section of the community took turns in the tower. Sometimes young Bert Uddenberg Junior accompanied his father on his shifts. When the regular volunteers failed to report, young Martha Jean Insel and her sister, Trillium, sometimes stood watch. Once a spotter brought along a pet and left it alone in the tower when the next shift failed to appear. Barking and whining from the tower alerted the Insel family that the safety of this corner of the free world was in the custody of an unhappy dog.

First aid training became a priority, with the Fortnightly Club lending the use of their hall for a major session on January 7, 1942. [266] Nationwide, the Red Cross First Aid Manual became the best seller of 1942, with eight million copies passing into American hands.[267] By September 1942 the area was ready with three fully equipped casualty stations, 135 graduates of first aid training and ten trucks equipped for ambulance service.[268]

Lincoln School began air raid drills, with older students appointed to shepherd younger ones in groups of ten to the respective girls' and boys' basements, where they were to huddle as far from the windows as they could get. [269] If the school should be evacuated, local homes were designated as shelters for the children.

If the bombers did come, air raid wardens were a vital part of the community's hopes for survival. Bert Uddenberg Senior, chairman of the local defense committee, named Harold Rucker as air raid warden for Gig Harbor precinct one and Lee Thrash for precinct two. John Finholm and Judge H. R. Thurston were fire wardens for the same respective precincts.

These were not honorary positions; there was plenty to do. One of the first orders of business was to get a complete listing of the homes under their watch, the number of adults and children living in them, the light, water, and fuel facilities, and the readiness of each to face an emergency. The canvassing began with Harold Rucker's junior warden, Bud Conan, working his way through Crescent Valley. Adolph Sehmel was soon at work in East Gig Harbor, while Rucker and Finholm began knocking on doors at the head of the harbor. At the first Defense Council meeting at Gig Harbor on the evening of January 30, a sobered populace listened to State Defense Council officials tell them how to extinguish incendiary bombs and deal with poison gas.[270]

The Red Cross was another popular cause. Clarice Skansie, local chair of the first big drive, appointed representatives for the districts under her care. She chose Vera Eide for Rosedale and Artondale; Betty Johnson for Wollochet Bay; Mary Kennan for Horsehead Bay and Arletta; Katherine Pearson for Warren; Lillian Graham for Cromwell; Ethel Treutle for the head of the bay, east Gig Harbor and Crescent Valley; Angeline Gilich for east Gig Harbor; Tony Gilich for east Gig Harbor, Delores Cosulich for Shore Acres; and other folks for the areas farther afield. Their combined efforts raised $1,371.80 in the first two weeks. [271]

There was work for everyone. Senior citizens were called upon to help harvest the crops. In August all the boys of the peninsula who owned bicycles were asked to meet at the top of Ford's hill to be enlisted in the messenger corps.[272] Within a month there were twenty messenger boys reporting to John Insel. Mrs. Ruth Ryan pressed ahead with the sale of Christmas seals, helping things along by pointing out that the coming of war only added more work to the fight against tuberculosis. *The Peninsula Gateway* was pleased to report that returns were good.[273]

Wars eat up raw materials at a furious rate, and the Ladies Fortnightly Club and Lincoln School's Boy Scout Troop Forty-four set to work scouring the area for paper and scrap metal to be recycled for the war effort. Ed-

Saving scrap metal was one way for the home front to contribute in World War II.

ward New was their Scoutmaster, and the Lions Club helped sponsor the effort. Frequently young Martha Jean Insel got out of class to sort newspapers from glossy magazines in the school basement and tie them into bundles of set sizes. Much of the string she used was donated and sometimes had to be untangled by her class while they memorized spelling words.[274]

Lee Makovich Sr. donated the use of the vacant lot next to his home as a collection point for a growing mountain of scrap metal.[275] By April, a room in the Sweeney Block, north of the Gig Harbor Post Office became home for the scrap until it could be trucked off to Tacoma.[276] It became clear soon enough that with most iron and steel channeled into vital war industries, there was not going to be a new bridge across The Narrows until peace returned.

Rubber was another vital commodity, and by July the Peninsula District had contributed an astounding 104,000 pounds of scrap rubber. "The committee in charge, Erick Erickson, chairman, Harold Rehn and Clarence Allison, are to be congratulated on the fine showing made and the efforts of all who assisted are to be appreciated," proclaimed *The Peninsula Gateway*.[277]

There were constant reminders that war meant fighting and killing. Before December 1941 was half gone, word of casualties began to filter back from the distant fighting front. Gordon B. Secor, who was in the service "somewhere in the Pacific," sent word that he was alive and well. Not everyone was as fortunate. Only that October, William Edward Reeder had stood before his family and friends and exchanged wedding vows with Gladys DeWalt. Now the newspaper, in the vague language of military censorship, was reporting him "killed in action in the Pacific since the outbreak of the war." [278]

Then the story took an unexpectedly happy turn. Gladys, a bride of barely two months, was officially a widow. Yet even as the peninsula mourned its first to fall, Gladys knew the report could not be true. She had already heard from her husband. In time, details of the story sifted back from the Pacific. Reeder had been at Pearl Harbor, a First Fire Controller on the battleship *California*, the day the bombs had fallen. Ordered to make a report of the men saved from his ship, he forgot to include his own name. He survived the war, stayed in the navy, and retired with the rank of commander.[279]

Many times war meant long days waiting – hand-wringing, floor-pacing, nervous-making waiting – for word to come back from some distant place where a local son or husband might be standing in harm's way. On the first of March, 1942, a Japanese dive bomber sent the 476-foot U.S. Navy oiler *Pecos* to the bottom of the Java Sea. One of the hundreds of men on board when the *Pecos* ended her death throes was Machinists' Mate W. P. Mason of Gig Harbor. Word of the sinking got back quickly enough, but it was close to a month before his wife, Charlotte, found out he was one of the 231 plucked safely from the water by the destroyer *Whipple*.

News from the fighting fronts was still largely bad in the spring of 1942, and the May 1 issue of the *Gateway* spoke to local fears of a U.S. invasion with a front page headline reading, "First Steps Taken for Guerilla Band." Perhaps the idea was fueled by accounts of the exploits of such bands operating behind enemy lines in the Philippines and the steppes of Russia. On the evening of April 29, the *Gateway* reported, Roy Cheeseman of Crescent Valley rose in the Improvement Hall to pass out sign-up sheets and explain how a guerrilla band could play a role in home defense. Cheeseman was filling in for a more knowledgeable speaker who could not make it down from the Bremerton navy yard. Another meeting was scheduled for May 13, but from there the whole idea just seemed to fade away.[280] Perhaps the big victory at Midway in the Pacific that June persuaded doubters that there was no longer a danger of invasion.

Even with tire rationing, and later gasoline rationing, traffic in the area mushroomed. In February 1942, 33,610 vehicles crossed The Narrows on the overworked ferries. Fewer than 25,000 had come across in the same period a year before. The number of bus passengers more than doubled to 14,487. Truck traffic rose to 4,765 from February 1941's 3,312, and things were just getting warmed up.[281]

The war brought military convoys and all sorts of traffic through town, and on September 22, 1942, the Commander in Chief himself passed through. President Franklin Roosevelt was on a tour of military bases and defense plants. Wartime security kept details of his travels under wraps, but it was hard to miss an escort of guards on motorcycles coming off the ferry *Defiance* from Tacoma, followed by the presidential limousine, which was a convertible Packard decorated with flags on its front fenders. [282] The little parade passed up Burnham Drive and took the Gig Harbor-Bremerton Highway to the Bremerton navy yard, where Roosevelt addressed the workers. The peninsula had experienced its first presidential visit, such as it was.

The war did not come to Gig Harbor, but an ever growing number of peninsula sons and daughters were going off to find it. John and Aimée Watson watched their children leave one by one. John Junior stayed the closest to home, working for the Civil Service at Seattle's Harbor Island and managing a boat building plant [283] at Winslow on Bainbridge Island. His wife, Jeanice, became head of personnel at Fort Lawton.

Alan, the Watsons' youngest son, had been knocking about at various Gig Harbor area jobs since graduating from high school. He was attending the University of Washington at the age of twenty-two when Pearl Harbor was bombed. He joined the Coast Guard, serving at a string of stations up and down the west coast. For a time he was assigned to patrol long stretches of ocean beach on horseback. It was lonely work, and he sometimes took his dog along on the saddle.[284] Later he found himself caught up in the flaming battles around the Philippines at Leyte, Lingayon, Gulf of Manila, Palu, and elsewhere.

The Watsons' daughter Kathleen left her teaching job at Snoqualmie Falls to work in the Quartermaster's office at Fort Lawton. The young woman who had been charmed a decade before by the wonders of Seattle next found herself in wartime Washington, D.C., training at the American University for overseas duty with the recreational branch of the Red Cross. She was stationed first at Norfolk, England operating a big bus-like clubmobile catering to the U.S. Eighth Air Force, sometimes meeting the bomber crews as they returned from their missions. Kathleen and her crew made an average of 1,200 doughnuts a day for hungry and homesick fly boys, handing them out through the side window of the bus. To wash the doughnuts down, they served coffee in winter and lemonade in summer.

Kathleen got to see London, and it came near being the last stop of her life. Someone was teaching her to drive a truck when an odd-looking aircraft swept across the British sky. Suddenly its odd buzzing engine stopped and it plunged swiftly and silently toward the earth. "Duck," yelled her companion, and they dove for some shrubbery beside the street. About a hundred yards away there was a jarring explosion, and the houses near the aircraft's landing site collapsed in a smoldering mass of shattered walls and broken glass. This was her rude introduction to the V-1 buzz bomb, a pilotless flying bomb hurled against London in one of Hitler's secret weapons programs.[285]

Family names that stretched back to the early days of settlement were showing up on distant battlefields. In March 1944, *Peninsula Gateway* readers learned that Marine Private Don Sehmel, son of Adolph Sehmel, had received a commendation for bravery under fire in the far Pacific. The commendation explained how, "Private Donald Adolph Sehmel, performed meritorious service while serving with a forward observer team, at Cape Gloucester, New Britain, when a jeep with a radio, which was the sole remaining means of communication for the forward observer party, became mired in a stream during critical point in the attack on the airport at Cape Gloucester, Private Sehmel, without regard for his own safety, worked for 20 minutes under fire from enemy mortars, machine guns and snipers to free the jeep. As a result of fearless devotion to duty, the jeep reached the assault units and restored communications, which made possible effective artillery support for the advance."[286]

Although he charged everyone else $1.50 a year, Editor Trombley made every effort to get free copies of *The Peninsula Gateway* out to local citizens in the armed forces. By October 1943 the special mailing list was up to ninety-five, and he and his readers received grateful letters from the far corners of the war-ravaged world. Warren McColley,

U.S. Navy, sent thanks from the Admiralty Islands in the southwest Pacific. Johnnie Lysell sent his thanks in the fall of '44 from "Somewhere in England." Sometimes the writers had been away a very long time. "It has been sixteen years since I lived in Gig Harbor," wrote Captain Ralph W. Welch from England, "but in spite of the many unfamiliar names in the paper, it's good to read news of my old friends. I enjoy too, the '20 Years ago' column and its report of the big news of the time when I was a kid there. I'm really beginning to feel quite ancient."

Sergeant Albert O. Northey, from "Somewhere Overseas," wrote in September 1944, "The war looks pretty good these days, and I hope it won't be long 'till all of us can return to the Harbor and our homes. Take it from me, I have seen lots of country, but the Northwest ranks top with me."

Sergeant Steve Strittmatter was a frequent contributor. From "Somewhere in France," he wrote in July 1944, "I remember while training in the states, digging foxholes was one of the most hated jobs for us soldiers and then they were only shallow ones, just good enough to get by. Now the minute we stop everyone grabs a shovel and the dirt really flies. As for myself, I am an expert digger. The only thing that can stop me is 'water.'"

"Last night," Strittmatter continued, "a guard was very much alert and saw what he calculated to be the luminous dial of a wrist watch moving up through the undergrowth of a hedgerow. He challenged and upon no response he emptied his Tommy gun into the hedgerow. After the din and roar had died away and the smoke had lifted, out came a firefly."[287]

In October 1944, Sergeant Strittmatter was in a fine mood. "When I went through France," he wrote, "a sweet little French girl threw a kiss at me. In Belgium a girl kissed me on the cheek. When I entered Holland a very pretty Dutch girl threw her arms around me and kissed me right on the mouth. Gosh, I can hardly wait till I get to Germany."[288]

In the same issue, Dave Mitts, who had already lost a brother in the war, reported he had been getting the *Gateway* at intervals for fifteen months. "A few days ago at 'mail call' I received a couple of copies. They were about two months old but as it was all the mail I received I was surely glad to see them. I read them through entirely – including what my old boss Keith had to sell in his store."

Later in the war, Mitts received the Silver Star for gallantry in Germany. On January 3, 1945, according to the report, "Tech. Mitts, a radio operator, accompanied a cavalry force in an assault upon a heavily defended enemy strong point near Berg. Shortly after he had established contact with his artillery batteries, the advancing troops met such an intense concentration of hostile fire that they were forced to withdraw. Determined to procure artillery support, Tech. Mitts, disregarding the danger, remained at his post and relayed adjustments which brought effective fire upon many German gun positions. His actions so reduced the enemy's fire power that the cavalry attack was resumed and the position taken."[289]

While his former hired help battled the Nazis across Europe, Keith Uddenberg and his customers fought one of the most vexing battles of the home front. Rationing was one of the ways the reality of war came home to people thousands of miles from the battle front. Local citizens had begun to feel its tightening grasp as early as January 1942, even before it hit the grocery stores.

Tires were the first commodity to become restricted. Word went out that there would be 111 local tire-rationing boards in Washington State, and that the statewide January quota was to be 4,919 tires. This meant that only government vehicles and those used in civilian defense were likely to get new tires. Recapping and retreading were still an option for the rest of the country's vehicles, and folks could still buy as many new bicycle tires as they could find.[290]

Vast forces were in motion, and their consequences could be felt as far away as Rosedale and Gig Harbor. The ships that used to carry coffee from South America in time of peace were being diverted to more pressing service in Europe and the Pacific. That meant the supply of coffee was shorter, and to insure that it was shared fairly, the government capped prices and imposed rationing. Prices stayed about the same. IGA Coffee was twenty-nine cents for a one-pound tin at Gig Harbor Hardware and Grocery the week Pearl Harbor was bombed, and Shurfine Coffee was still only twenty-nine cents at Keith Uddenberg's Shurfine Market and Grocery when Dave Mitts, Steve Strittmatter, and their buddies stormed across Western Europe in September 1944.

Coffee and sugar marched onto the rationed foods list first, joined in time by a score of items including canned juices, meat, fish, dairy products, vegetables, and soups. Elastic also disappeared. Women could not purchase corsets or girdles. Draw strings were pressed into service to hold up underpants. When nylons disappeared from the shelves, some women painted seams up the back of their legs.[291]

Before they could transact business, merchants and customers needed to know more than just the price of an item. They also needed to know how many ration stamps, or points, that item would cost. Each month every American received one ration book filled with forty-eight small blue ration stamps for canned goods, and another book of sixty-four red stamps for everything else that was on the ration list. Anyone who ran out of ration stamps before the end of the month would have to wait until the next month to buy more goods, unless they could secretly buy or borrow stamps from someone else.

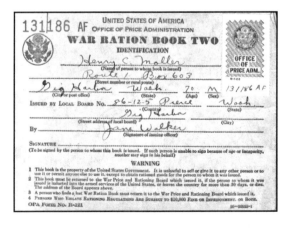

War Ration Book Two provided stamps needed to buy rationed items, like canned food and sugar. It was issued in February 1943.

To make the game more interesting, the number of stamps needed to acquire an item went up and down, depending on the available supply. In March 1943 merchants like Keith Uddenberg and John Finholm would tear ten blue ration stamps out of the book of anyone buying applesauce, but by the same month a year later, they took twenty-five.[292] Anyone needing additional stamps for medical or other reasons could appeal to the local rationing board, located by Anderson's Shipyard on Harborview Drive. Mary Secor was one of those who could be found working in that office.[293]

The experience moved the owner of Finholm's Market and Grocery to run poetry in place of an advertisement in *The Peninsula Gateway*:

"The Village Grocer"
(With Apologies to Longfellow)

Under a spreading web of rules
The Village Grocer stands;
His brow is all tied up in knots
His head is in his hands
There hardly is from day to day
A rule he understands!

His hair is thin, bloodshot his eyes,
His face is gray or blue;

His brow is wet with honest sweat
His business all askew
His customers are dizzy, but
The grocer's dizzy too.

Day in, day out, from morn 'til night,
You hear the loud disputes
As women fight for sauerkraut
And beans and processed fruits,
All grocers get are loud Bronx cheers
And most discordant boos.[294]

As early as February 1942, *Gateway* editor Trombley was promoting Victory Gardens. "Everyone who can should prepare a garden this season," he warned, "because foods of all kinds will be high in price. The long afternoons which the war saving time provides will give us an opportunity to work in our gardens which will be time well spent. The Victory Garden idea is a good one. Let us all encourage it."[295] On a national scale, the gardens were a marked success. In 1943, at least a third of all the vegetables consumed in America came out of the country's 20.5 million Victory Gardens.[296]

As the expense of fighting a world war mounted, citizens were encouraged to dig deeper into their pocketbooks to help defray the costs. The government sold war bonds, and $135 billion worth were purchased during the war. If buying bonds could help keep their loved ones safe and bring them back sooner, the citizens of the peninsula were more than willing to do their part. In April 1943 alone, the Gig Harbor Post Office reported the sale of 274 war bonds, worth a total of $11,500.[297] The next month, the children of the Arletta School completed their own months-long "jeep drive." They raised $954.20

to purchase another jeep for the war effort. Invited to name the vehicle, the children dubbed it "Tojo's Headache."[298] In August of the following year, Mrs. Bertha Moshir of Gig Harbor was awarded an Otto green lapel watch for selling $15,537.50 cash value "E" bonds.[299]

"This is no year to raise peacocks and kumquats, only essential foods!" the Washington Co-op warned in 1942. This unknown woman proudly posed in her impressive Victory Garden for Frank Owen Shaw.

195

Reminders of the war were everywhere. On a reader board in front of the Presbyterian Church, Dorothy Gilmore undertook the task of entering the expanding list of names of local citizens in the armed forces. She faced the sad duty of painting gold stars beside the names of those who made the supreme sacrifice. People going to worship could look at the reader board and know that Harold Mitts, George Nelson, and others would never join them again.[300]

Sometimes the dangers hit closer to home. Many peninsula men and women went to work in the Bremerton navy yard, where huge fighting ships were repaired and sent back into the battle. Huge machines moved vast tons of steel with round-the-clock urgency, and there could be dire consequences if things went wrong. In a reversal of the normal flow of wartime events, Charles Edwards was sent home to Gig Harbor from the air force in October 1944 to attend the funeral of his brother, Sylvester, a First Class Rigger killed in an accident at Bremerton.[301]

In the zeal to help, even good intentions could take a wrong turn. On May 8, 1942, a Gig Harbor realtor pointed an accusing finger in a letter to the editor of *The Peninsula Gateway*. "Will you be so kind as to explain, not only to me, but to many others," he asked, "why so many young men of draft age in Gig Harbor are exempt from army and navy service? These young men flaunt their brand new cars and what goes with them before the eyes of a wondering people. Is it possible this material for our army and navy has been overlooked or misunderstood? Cannot older men go out into the waters of Puget Sound and elsewhere and do the work of these young men who are so badly needed in the cause of Democracy?"

Angry responses arrived in the next issue. Among those speaking for the fishermen was young Nick Ancich. "For the sake of accuracy, let's consult the record," he began. "NONE of the men who do the fishing are exempt. They have all registered for the draft, except 15 who are still under draft age. The 15, together with 35 of draft age who have registered have signed up with the government to be ready at a moment's notice to follow emergency orders. They have been assigned to different boats, subject to government orders. Their present orders are to fish this season. Fish is regarded by the government as essential defense food."

He pointed out that six of the fishermen had been deferred from direct military service until the end of the season, and that all of them were giving volunteer time to defense tasks, such as acting as air raid wardens. Fishing was hard work, best suited to the young and physically fit, he reminded readers. In conclusion, he asked, "How much time are those who so carelessly make insinuations against the fishermen giving to defense service or even to work classed as essential?..."[302]

He was a well spoken young man, with a promising future, lost much too soon. In less than a year, Nick Ancich, Gig Harbor Union High graduate and frat boy at the College of Puget Sound, was dead of gland trouble at the age of twenty-one. Among his surviving family members was his sister Rose, who had become the wife of fisherman Nick Tarabochia.[303]

It was on August 27, 1942, that Nick Tarabochia experienced his best and his worst day as a fisherman all in one. The San Juan Islands had long been a favored fishing ground for Gig Harbor fishermen. In the early days, some had even maintained semipermanent camps on the islands' shores. Several Gig Harbor boats were there that day off Cattle Point on San Juan Island, including the *Veteran* and Antone Skansie's *Avalon*. The going rate just then was $1.07 per salmon, and the fish were running in vast numbers. Dreaming of riches, Nick Tarabochia's crew on the fifty-six-foot *Phyllis T.* pulled in an estimated eight thousand salmon before they realized something was dreadfully wrong. The weight of the fish was too much for the boat. Water poured in the hatches, which were open to accept the stream of fish, and the *Phyllis T.* went to the bottom with just her mast light remaining above water. The *Phyllis T.* was eventually raised and repaired, but fishermen never forgot about the boat that sank under the weight of her own success.[304]

Willing or otherwise, some fishermen found their boats commandeered by the government. They were generally well compensated. In

1937 John Skansi had launched his seventy-six-foot herring and pilchard seiner, *Challenger*. In 1943 he saw the craft hauled over to Tacoma's Western Boat Building Company, painted navy gray, and sent back to sea as the navy's District Patrol Craft YP-89. Perhaps the navy liked the boat's 260-horsepower Superior diesel engine.[305] Fishermen were offered the option of buying their boats back at a discount price after the war. John Skansi got his boat back in good condition. Not everyone was as fortunate. Some of the boats returned much the worse for wear.[306]

In the spring of 1943, Spiro Babich's boat, *Crusader*, transporting mechanics and carpenters from Astoria to a cannery at Nakvek in Alaska, foundered on the rugged Alaskan coast in a blinding fog. All eleven men, including Paul Babich, survived the ordeal of sea and cold and hunger, but *Crusader* and all her equipment were lost in two hundred feet of water.

In September 1944 the *Gateway* reported that the Bujacich boat *Majestic* was sunk without loss of life in a collision with a government transport in Alaska. The boat was salvaged and lived to sink and experience resurrection at least one time more.

If the war took things away, and it most surely did, it also brought opportunities. The Gig Harbor Shipbuilding Company had to set aside the building of fishing boats for the duration, but Company boatwrights found plenty of war work. First they built barges for the Coast Guard and the army, and then they won a contract to build four small tug boats for the army. All were wooden, seventy-one tons, a bit under seventy-three feet long by eighteen feet wide, with 240-horsepower diesel engines. They were designated STs, governmentese for small tug: ST-457, ST-458, ST-459 and ST-460.[307] An average of fifty workers was on the payroll as the boats took shape. It was a proud day for everyone when nine-year-old Jo Ann Anderson of Rosedale, wearing a red plaid skirt and a red jacket, broke a bottle of champagne across the bow and ST-457 slid down the ways on September 16, 1943.[308]

The war could change lives in unexpected ways. In the Gig Harbor home of Peter and Christine Land, one day there was a knock at the door. It was a law officer, battling back tears, telling his friend Peter to pack quickly and come with him. The internment of Japanese-Americans during the war is well known. Less well known is the internment of several thousand Germans and Italians. Peter Land was one of those interned. All the explanation offered to his puzzled and frightened young daughter, Rosemary, was, "Daddy has to go away for a while."

He was gone for about a year, and then returned and tried to pick up his life as best he could. He took a job laying sewer pipe for the new housing being built for war workers in Bremerton. He bought bonds to support the war effort and tried to live quietly. The parents never spoke of what had happened with their daughter, not even when Peter died in 1957. The missing year of his life remains a mystery to her still.[309]

Bert Uddenberg saw business dwindle at his Ford dealership, as American industry's conversion to wartime production ended the manufacture of new cars. He fell back on his family roots and focused his considerable energy on his Peninsula Dairy Store, which included an ice cream counter and soda fountain. His daughters Lola, Jeanette, and Shirley worked in the store some of the time. Bert Junior, who was eleven years old in 1943, helped out by stocking shelves on weekends, washing dishes for the soda fountain, pumping gas, and climbing up on hoods to wash car windows.

Jeanette and Lola later enlisted in the Navy WAVES (Women Accepted for Volunteer Emergency Service). Jeanette became an Ensign and was assigned to the Norfolk Naval Shipyard in Portsmouth, Virginia, as an assistant to the supply officer. Pharmacist's Mate Lola Uddenberg saw service at the San Diego Naval Hospital, where she helped deliver the babies that just kept coming into the world, war or no war.

Letters, news, and mementos kept flowing in from the fighting front. In September 1944 the *Gateway* reported that Pete Alvestad of Gig Harbor had received a Purple Heart sent by his son, Ben, a paratrooper sergeant serving in Europe. (Purple Hearts are medals issued for wounds suffered in the line of duty.) The medal marked Ben's second wound, but the paper said he was on the road to recovery.[310]

At the Thirty-fourth General Hospital at Blandford Camp in England, where doctors tried to repair the wreckage of war, Private Frank Peterson of Gig Harbor served as a cook.[311] On February 21, 1945, the U.S. Navy escort carrier *Bismark Sea* was sunk by Japanese aerial attack off Iwo Jima. In April the *Gateway* announced that among the nearly four hundred survivors was Seaman First Class L. C. Johnson, whose address was Route 1, Forest Beach, Gig Harbor.[312]

As the war neared its end, Kathleen Watson found herself in Germany, traveling with General George Patton's hard-charging Third Army. She had come to continental Europe with her Red Cross crew after D-Day, and had followed the Red Ball Express supply truck convoys across France. She was at Viechlahr when the war in Europe ended on V-E Day, May 8, 1945. Before returning home in 1946, she saw Paris, Cannes, Rome, the Vatican, Milan, bits of Switzerland, and a host of German cities. In what must have been a poignant moment, she paid a visit to the ancient city of York in the north of England, and met five of the sisters her father had left when he emigrated to America decades before.

Peninsula men and women were in the war to the very end. At Okinawa, the last big battle of the war, in June 1945 Private Dale D. Lauridsen of Gig Harbor received the Combat Infantryman's badge, awarded for coolness and aggressiveness under fire. Until he was inducted into the army in October 1944, Dale had been helping his father, Nelo Lauridsen, on the family farm.[313]

Soldiers could be called to all sorts of duty, as Marine Platoon Sergeant Fred A. Wood disclosed in an April 17, 1945 letter to his parents back in Rosedale. "My experiences of this past weekend started Friday noon, they suddenly canceled all our classes and told us to shine our gear and press our clothes such as they had never been before, also to pack a few articles to last for a couple of days away from camp. That was all the information we received until that night when the word was finally passed that our O. C. class, the 4th, now the senior outfit, also the one with most overseas men, were going to be the Marine honor guard for President Roosevelt's funeral."

Wood and his men marched in the procession through Washington, D.C., and then were taken to Hyde Park, New York for the burial. Wood stood about a hundred feet from the grave, and the politicians, ambassadors, generals, and admirals passed within about six feet of his spot. There went General George Marshal, Admiral King, President Truman, Vice President Henry Wallace, the cabinet, the Supreme Court, Ambassador Anthony Eden of Great Britain, and a host of others. "I could go on naming celebrities to fill pages," he mused. "I doubt if any of us will ever again see so many at such close range."[314]

When it was all counted up, it was believed that 356 peninsula men and women served in the armed forces. All had put dreams on hold, had endured hardships, and had accepted the risk of death in service to their country. Thirteen paid freedom's ultimate price:

Air Force First Lieutenant Harold Mitts – Reported lost with fifteen others over Japanese-occupied Kiska Island in Alaska's Aleutian Island chain in October 1942.[315]

Army Paratrooper Private Kenneth W. Kirkendoll – Killed with twelve others in the crash of a C-47 transport plane during war training exercises near Camp McCall, North Carolina in September 1944.[316]

George Nelson

Douglas Mortenson

Air Force Sergeant Lyle S. Jones – Enlisted after graduation from Gig Harbor High School in 1939. Reported missing in action on a bomber raid from England at the age of twenty-four.[317]

Robert Niemann

Army Private John M. Swenson – Born in Crescent Valley, graduated from Gig Harbor High School, entered military service in February 1943. He was killed in Luxembourg on Christmas Eve 1944.

Air Force Lieutenant Raymond Edwards – Born in Gig Harbor and graduated from Gig Harbor High School, he was reported missing over Italy on his second air mission, December 20, 1944.[318]

Air Force Sergeant Willard Chessman – A resident of Longbranch, with a sister in Gig Harbor, he survived repeated missions as a tail gunner of a B-17 over Europe, only to die at the hands of a hit and run driver on a Texas Air Base. He died on February 3, 1945 at the age of twenty-two.

Sergeant Carl Pearson – The son of Mr. and Mrs. Clifford N. Pearson of Warren, he died in Germany on March 31, 1945.

Private Herman Niemann – A nineteen-year-old resident of Vaughn on the Longbranch Peninsula, he died on patrol duty at Hamilton Field, California in June 1943, when the submachine gun he was carrying accidentally discharged. The body was shipped to Tacoma for burial.[319]

Air Force Corporal Arnold Boers - A former Rosedale resident who afterward moved to Seattle, Boers was killed on January 18, 1945, on a mission to parachute supplies to American and Chinese troops fighting the Japanese in the Burma Mountains. He was twenty-three years old.

Sylvester Metzinger

Wars have a way of shaking people loose from their roots and sending them in new directions. The Civil War had sent young men west, eventually leading some of them as far afield as Gig Harbor and the peninsula. A popular song from World War I carried both a promise and a warning in the verse, "How ya gonna keep 'em down on the farm after they've seen Paree?"

World War II had put more than sixteen million Americans into uniform, moving many of them around the globe. Millions of civilians had migrated to fill the burgeoning needs of wartime industrial production. Millions of women had worked outside their homes for the first time in their lives. As Gig Harbor residents returned to civilian life and peaceful pursuits, some inevitably chose to follow new dreams in fields far removed from the little peninsula on Puget Sound.

Yet if World War II took some citizens away, it ultimately brought many more. The population grew in the aftermath of war. Locals waited impatiently for work to begin on the new bridge, and started to ponder more seriously the question of cityhood.

World War II servicemen's memorial, erected in 1942, still stands at Harbor Ridge Intermediate School, the site of the old Union High School. Photo by Linda McCowen

Chapter 10

Cityhood and a Homecoming

Two ancient elements, fire and water, conspired to push Gig Harbor toward cityhood. The fire started in Ralph Johnson's garage at the head of the bay and roared relentlessly up the waterfront. Before the morning of January 4, 1945 was over, flames had consumed the George F. Keeney building, the Home Cafe, the storeroom of Finholm's Market, and the Finholm's apartment as well. A bucket brigade made up mostly high school boys was as valiant as it was futile, battling the blaze with water from the bay while calls for help went out to the wider world.

"An attempt was made to secure help from Tacoma," the *Gateway* recorded ruefully, "but there was the usual excuse that equipment could not be taken from the city limits." Only the arrival of two Coast Guard firefighters saved Betty's Beauty Shop and brought the fire to an end.[320]

The loss was not altogether permanent. By the next month, crews were at work on a new fifty-by-seventy-foot garage for Ralph Johnson, a new cement block building for Finholm, and a bigger Home Cafe, complete with an electric kitchen, eleven restaurant bar stools, five booths, a basement where the Lion's Club would hold its meetings, and a dining room overlooking the bay.[321]

This was by no means the town's first fire, and it was far from the last, but something new began to rise out of the ashes. It gave new urgency to ideas that were already taking form. Gig Harbor had no organized fire protection, no sewer system, and no police force of its own. People living here enjoyed few of the services available in the big city across The Narrows. It was time to begin thinking about incorporating into a real city. A dependable water supply became another pressing need. When a long dry spell caused a number of backyard wells to run dry, the concept of a community water tower looked increasingly attractive.

The few community services the harbor did have were mostly homegrown efforts. Milan Mikich, a World War I veteran, a purchasing agent for native greenery,[322] and a voracious reader, joined the Pierce County Library Board and secured permission to organize a Gig Harbor branch library early in 1946. The community had been accumulating a stock of books for years, but Mikich's move made it official. Tucked into a little waterfront building known as Finholm's shed, the library was operated for six hours every Wednesday by Lucy Goodman and Laura Smythe. John Sweeney, who lived next door, ran an electric line over so the library could have electricity at no charge. The Spadoni brothers kept their bills unusually low for the fuel to heat the new library. There were two hundred books on hand the day the library opened, and fifty-eight of them went out that day. By the next year, a bookmobile was extending service to eleven stops around the peninsula.[323]

Incorporation had its foes. Chief among them was C. E. Shaw, who was back in the sign painting business after his days as a rooster-racing entrepreneur. Shaw saw the proposal to incorporate as nothing more than a scheme to wrest more tax dollars out of the local populace. He put his considerable talents as a cartoonist to work in the fight to halt the drive. "Why should we spoil a wonderful place to live by voting more taxes, laws rules regulations restrictions and petty graft

Lucy Goodman and Laura Smythe opened the Pierce County Library in John Finholm's shed at the head of the bay in 1946, thanks to the efforts of Milan Mikich, local greenery purchasing agent, avid reader, and poet. Photo by Frank Owen Shaw

that follow in order to put sewerage [*sic*] and water plugs along the business section?" he cried.

The question of incorporation was put to a vote of the people for the first time in September 1945. It lost by thirteen votes. Supporters said it was because fishermen who would have voted *yes* were away and could not vote. They resolved to try again. Shaw and Judge H. R. "Dick" Thurston fought it out week after week in the pages of *The Peninsula Gateway*, Shaw invoking the specter of endless taxes, and Thurston pointing to the promised land of services and benefits.

Higher taxes or not, voters passed the proposal on June 29, 1946. Gig Harbor was on its way to official status as a fourth-class town, later climbing to cityhood in 1981.[324] The vote was not a walkaway. In Precinct One the measure failed fifty-one to fifty-nine, but Precinct Two put it over the top with a hefty ninety to fifty-six in favor.

Town officials were elected at the same time. There was no pre-determined slate of candidates. Voters were simply given a blank ballot and told to write in one name of their choice for mayor, and five for city council. A few folks had made it known that they were interested in serving. At least two women, Mary Secor and Ann Moore, threw their hats into the ring. They were among the ninety-two individuals who garnered votes, but politics was still a man's world in the Gig Harbor of 1946.

WAITING FOR HIM TO STICK OUT HIS NECK

C.E. Shaw, local promoter and sign painter, objected to the incorporation of Gig Harbor in 1946, as shown in his pen and ink drawing.

Dr. Harold Ryan, who had once gazed across The Narrows from Point Defiance and dreamed of owning a white cottage overlooking the water, and who had practiced dentistry in Gig Harbor for half of his forty-six years, was elected mayor with ninety-one votes. For town council the voters dug deep into the peninsula's heritage and came up with the names Keith Uddenberg, Tony Stanich, C.O. Austin, Emmett Ross, and John Finholm.

Keith Uddenberg was a grocer, like his grandfather, but he operated on a grander scale than old Axel could ever have imagined. At their height, Keith's stores employed hundreds of people across Washington and stood as the largest privately held supermarket chain in the state. He was also the head of the local Chamber of Commerce. In March 1947 he would open a new concrete fifty-by-one-hundred-foot Shurfine Grocery store in Gig Harbor. Reflecting changing times, the new store would be surrounded by what the *Gateway* called "roomy parking space," and would operate on a cash basis, rather than credit.[325]

The fishing community was represented by Emmett Ross and Antone (Tony) Stanich. Emmett was the grandson of John Ross, who had come to Gig Harbor from the Adriatic island of Permuda in 1888. Emmett belonged to the Eagles, and so did Tony Stanich. Tony came from a fishing family, but was primarily known for the grocery store that he and his brother John had run for better than a score of years. The Stanich Grocery, near the corner of Harborview and Novak, ca-

Keith Uddenberg opened his new Thriftway Grocery on Harborview Drive, with Gig Harbor Pharmacy next door, in 1947. Photo by Frank Owen Shaw

tered largely to fishermen, carrying items suited to Slavonian palates such as Crown of Savoy olive oil, Madonna Tomato Paste, and Albarosa sardines in olive oil.[326] It was the last of the buy-on-credit, pay-at-the-end-of-fishing-season grocery stores.

John Finholm was born just up the shoreline a few miles, at Olalla, in 1909 and had operated a grocery store in Gig Harbor since 1931. Like fellow councilmen Austin and Uddenberg, he was a member of the Lion's Club.

For treasurer, Leander Finholm won with forty-two votes in a multi-candidate race. Technically, he was the newest of the lot. Born in Larsmo, Finland, in 1871, he had been on Puget Sound since 1893, but had come to live in Gig Harbor only six years earlier. He was manager and principal stockholder of the Island Empire Telephone Company. Treasurer was not an easy job in Gig Harbor. Revenues were not as plentiful as C. E. Shaw had feared, and it was nine years before Gig Harbor finally produced a balanced budget.

For C. O. Austin, election to the town council turned out to be something of a last hurrah. He had been running his sawmill near the mouth of Donkey Creek since 1909. Lately, he had been refusing to let anyone else run the saws, declaring that they were dangerous and he did not want to be responsible for injuries. He was all too right about the danger. Five days short of Christmas 1946, he was alone in the mill, working on a carriage for transporting logs, when he was somehow dragged into a circular saw.[327]

The center of town continued to be at the head of the bay until the post office moved in 1954. Finholm's Market undergoes renovations, Sweeney Block is at left

By the time he was found and an ambulance could arrive, he was dead. On the day of his funeral, Mayor Ryan joined Robert Alvestad, Nels Tveter, Gus Schusinger, Louis Fymouth, and Bert Uddenberg as a pallbearer. He issued a proclamation, calling on all businesses in Gig Harbor to close for two hours that afternoon in Austin's memory.

The mill lay idle for a few months until John H. Galbraith purchased it from Austin's estate and began planning to expand and employ twenty to forty workers. He was already the biggest employer in Gig Harbor, as the owner of the Peninsula Cafe, Galbraith Motor Company, and Gig Harbor Hardware and Grocery. Galbraith had operated sawmills in Eatonville and Fairfax in the foothills around Mount Rainier. He had been mayor of Eatonville for twenty-seven years before moving to Rosedale and building a house he named Questover in 1940.

There was no town hall as yet. The council met sometimes in the venerable Grand Army of the Republic Hall, sometimes in Judge Thurston's workshop behind his electric shop in the shadow of the Peninsula Hotel building, near the corner of Pioneer and Harborview.

C.O. Austin ran his mill from 1909 until his untimely death in 1946, shortly after being elected to the new city council.

(l-r) Mayor Harold Ryan, Antone Stanich, Judge J.R. Thurston, Marshal Chet Jones, Keith Uddenberg, and Fred Perkins show off the town's first police car, 1948.

Slowly, the apparatus necessary to run a small city slipped into gear. In June 1948 Bert Uddenberg's Ford dealership delivered Gig Harbor's first official police vehicle, a brand new Ford V-8 panel delivery van that served both as a patrol car and paddy wagon. There was not yet a jail. When someone needed to be locked up, Gig Harbor officials transported him to Port Orchard in Kitsap County, which charged $1.50 a day for the wrongdoer's keep.[328]

Chet Jones, who was appointed marshal for Gig Harbor in 1948, found plenty of work. The city was thankfully short on violent crimes, but his duties extended to reading water meters and collecting fees, chasing down stray dogs, filling potholes in the streets, and using his patrol car as an ambulance.

The town council did not forget its commitment to a dependable water supply. By the summer of 1949, the town had a 250,000 gallon storage tank and a 265 foot well pumping 360 gallons of water a minute in initial tests. The town had three hundred families living inside its boundaries, and it was estimated that the waterworks could supply more than six times that number. As a reminder of the changing landscape, drillers found rounded rocks at one hundred feet below ground, which was taken to be evidence of a long-buried river bed.[329]

By the late 1940s the peninsula was reasonably self-sufficient, so far as goods and services were concerned. Need ready-mixed concrete? Call the Hemley Brothers at 3231. War surplus? There was

Workmen dig up No. Harborview Drive in front of Ralph Johnson's Garage for the installation of a town water system, 1949. Photo by Frank Owen Shaw

plenty of that available, and Andersen's Bargain House on Judson Avenue had aluminum folding cots for $5.75 and mess kits for a quarter. Welding and blacksmithing? Call Ken Peterson's Weldit Shop at 2124. He could fix washing machines and lawn mowers, build, repair, or rent trailers and perform many another feat of iron mongery.

Haircut? Ambrose Moore had been in business at the head of the bay since 1924. Milk? It could be had in any of several grocery stories, but for delivery there was the Pomo Doro Dairy, owned and run by the siblings Bernard, Victor, and Adelaide Degassa. They had forty head of Jersey and Guernsey cows at their command.

Plumbing? Henry N. Olson's Gig Harbor Plumbing and Heating Company specialized in hot water and steam heating systems. Dressmaking? Call Betty Shuey or Hazel Dabroe at 2115. They were open 10 A.M. to 6 P.M., closed on Monday. Funeral arrangements? Call Perkins Funeral Home at 2310. F. M. Perkins, Master Mason and past president of the Lion's Club, had been burying his departed neighbors since 1928.

Electric appliances? There were several places to go, including Pryear Electric where Otto Pryear, in the new concrete Finholm building opposite the post office, offered a full line of appliances, paint, wallpaper, and phonograph records.[330] On December 24, 1948 he ran a big ad in *The Peninsula Gateway* for something new:

Before You Buy
A Television Set...
be sure to
See and Hear
Stromberg-Carlson
The "Cadillac" of the Radio & Television Industry
At
Pryear Electric
Open House
Television Demonstrations
Wednesday thru Sunday Nights
7:30 to 10:00 P. M.[331]

With that, Gig Harbor had its first advertisement for a television. Within two weeks, Pryear's competition, in the form of Gig Harbor's John D. Ross of Sepic Electric Company, was advertising demonstrations of the RCA Victor "Sightseer" television, complete with matching table, purchasable for just twenty-five percent down and fifteen months to pay.[332]

The rest of the peninsula did not wither away and die because a small part of it had incorporated into a town. The country grocery stores often became the standard bearers of rural communities. Across the road from the Rosedale School, John and Vera Eide were making plans to expand their store, which sold a full line of groceries, including Meadowsweet ice cream, and which pumped Standard gasoline into the tanks of the district's growing fleet of automobiles.[333]

In Arletta, Oscar Dulin and Royal Haslam operated a cash store with what the *Gateway* called, "Red & White foods of all kinds, also a line of meats." Haslam was a newcomer from Baker, Oregon, but Dulin had been on the peninsula since 1899.[334]

Wollochet Bay had the E. W. Anderson Grocery, which boasted groceries, meats, fishing tackle, and prepared medicines. At nearby Picnic Point, The Forsythe General Merchandise Store laid claim to being the oldest business house on the peninsula.[335]

With its growing population, the peninsula could now support another high school, which opened in 1947 with the unsurprising name

Vera Eide tends the counter of her Rosedale store, a fixture in the area until the 1990s.

of Peninsula High School. Through remodeling and relocations, Peninsula High and Gig Harbor High would continue to flourish. Their football teams still clash in a highly competitive annual match known as the Fish Bowl.

1950 was a memorable year on several scores. January saw the blizzard of the century. Over a fourteen-hour period on January 13, ten inches of snow and eight-degree temperatures blew in on fierce winds. Mail, ferry service, and pretty much everything else ground to a halt. Things were especially rough at Horsehead Bay. Angry waves there tore at bulkheads and icy winds tore at everything else. The lights went out at 11:10 on the morning of the thirteenth, and stayed out for three days.

Sam Osten, sitting in the corner of his living room, saw an old growth Douglas fir crash through his roof, its limbs missing him by less than a foot on either side. He tried to go to his neighbor, Jim Corkery, but found the main road blocked by fallen trees. George O'Keenan was a little luckier. A tree hit his roof, too, but only displaced a few shingles. The Bergstroms and Woodmans also found trees on their roofs. Cleone Soule and his wife missed the show, having left when their pipes froze. Kathryn Ness found eight trees down on the short drive between her home and the highway.

The bay at Gig Harbor froze over for the first time since the winter of 1923-24, and 1904 before that. Walkers and skaters ventured

The frozen harbor in February, 1950 provided a playground for skating and sledding. Photo by Frank Owen Shaw

out, finding the ice a foot thick at the head of the bay and five inches thick at the center. The harbor mouth remained unfrozen, but the footing was safe as far out as Bud Conan's Union Oil dock. Fishermen, with their boats frozen in port, found it more worrisome than beautiful. Andrew Skansie and some of the others went out and tried to break up the ice around their boats, hoping for warmer weather.[336] The cold snap finally ended on February 3, with a light snow that turned to rain.

Baseball fans in Gig Harbor remembered 1950 as the year the town team went undefeated against all rivals in regular play. It was the biggest thing baseball fans had seen on the harbor since left-handed pitcher Nick Novak led the Gig Harbor Ferries to victory over the Teamsters with seventeen strikeouts in 1924. That was the same game where Nick's brother Frank had four hits in the 9-5 win.

More than anything else, 1950 would be remembered as the year the new bridge opened. Once World War II ended, everyone knew it was only a matter of time before another bridge spanned The Narrows. This one would be wider, taller, and much more expensive. Engineers had studied the dramatic death of the first bridge and believed they had discovered the reasons for the collapse. First, the bridge was too narrow in proportion to its length. Galloping Gertie's roadway had been only 26 feet wide. The new roadway would be almost fifty feet across. It would hold two lanes of traffic in each direction, instead

The second Narrows Bridge opened on October 14, 1950. Photo by Frank Owen Shaw

of one. The sidewalks would be narrower this time, but this bridge was not intended to be a pedestrian bridge.

Perhaps more importantly, the first engineers had overlooked the importance of aerodynamics. Galloping Gertie had been built with closed girders, through which the winds could not pass. The new bridge would have open girders. Grillwork in the roadbed between the on-coming lanes would further dissipate contrary winds. Strategically placed hydraulic jacks would absorb shocks and counter the oscillation that had ripped the old bridge apart. Sturdy Gertie has stood unfazed through several earthquakes and the gales of more than half a century.

Governor Langlie opened the new bridge on October 14, 1950, and $11,541 in tolls was collected that first day. Traffic continued to far exceed expectations. Early plans had called for tolls to be charged until 1977 to pay off the $14,000,000 construction costs. As it turned out, tolls were discontinued in October 1964, at which time the costs had been recovered with enough left over to fund maintenance for years to come. Planners had thought daily traffic might reach 5,800 vehicles by 1977. In reality, the average was a whopping 28,897 by 1974. The little peninsula's days of isolation were clearly at an end.[337]

There were not any racing roosters to greet visitors in October

1950, but C. E. Shaw's supply of ideas was far from exhausted. In 1951 he launched a contest to find the most perfectly rounded rock. Grinding glaciers, pounding surf, and flowing streams had all conspired to seed the soil and sands of Puget Sound with thousands of candidates. The standards were com-

Miss Round Rock. Photo by Frank Owen Shaw

plex and exacting, and the competition was fierce. Area businesses exhibited the contestants as interest mounted. In September 1951, judges decided that a rock on display at the Gig Harbor Hardware Company had beaten its closest competitor by a margin of fifteen-one-thousandths of an inch. William Ruhle of Tacoma claimed the top prize of one hundred dollars.

Gig Harbor was a community that wanted its population to grow. In 1955 a number of peninsula area businesses banded together to sponsor a promotional film. The narrator was at pains to point out this area was nothing fancy, just "comfortable, friendly, uncrowded. … a worry-free place to raise kids." There in the grainy black-and-white images was Peninsula High School, enrollment 340, served by buses which transported ninety percent of the students every day. The film showed the high school band and the drill team. There was the baseball field, built by area residents with their own bulldozers, rakes, and shovels in what they called "Operation Turf." The team pitcher, and king of the junior prom that year, was Gary Moore, who threw seven no-hitters in his high school career. He looked like a major league prospect until an old football injury began to undermine his arm later in college.

Viewers saw a few seconds of old Clarence "Nick" Burnham, and heard him recommend that they ask Miss Lucy Goodman about the

Lucy Goodman in her kindergarten class, located on North Harborview Drive.

old days, and add that she had been his teacher. Miss Lucy told the camera about her memories of the roadless harbor, of rowboats, trees to the water's edge, and treks with fifty-pound flour sacks through the bear haunted woods. "I've seen the harbor grow from almost nothing to the present time," she said, "and I think it has a bright future."

Miss Lucy was a fixture of Gig Harbor, as permanent as the bay. If anyone saw a 1933 blue coupe creeping along at fifteen miles per hour, carefully straddling the center line of the road, they knew it was she, going to or from another day of teaching her private kindergarten in north Gig Harbor.

Miss Lucy had never married. She lived with her niece, Verna Wheeler, and year after year Vera urged "Aunt Lou" to retire. But how could she retire with yet another generation of parents wanting to start their children off with the fundamentals? In 1958, when Dr. Karl Peterson asked if he could enroll his daughter, the white-haired teacher replied, "Well Karl, there's some question about my continuing with it. That stove pipe must be replaced, and there are other things in need of repair. I don't think I can get them in order."

Karl asked to borrow the key, and a few days later Miss Lucy opened the old schoolhouse to find the walls painted, new curtains hung, a new stovepipe in place, and the old wood stove polished to a high sheen. Even the 1840[338] pump organ was working again after years of

Lucy Goodman stands in the doorway of her kindergarten, between the Sweeney house and the library.

rest.[339] When people asked her about retirement, she gave her stock answer, "I just can't find a rocking chair that will fit me."[340]

That same year, as Miss Lucy quietly observed her eighty-ninth birthday, a reporter asked her if she employed modern methods. She fixed him with those blue eyes and said with a smile, "I just teach them." Her fee was the same as it had always been, a dollar a week per child. Later generations might have thought of this as a day care, but to Miss Lucy and her pupils it was school, and most of her students entered the public school able to read and count. To teach basic mathematics, she devised a game that carried some meaning in a fishing town. She set out a basket of paper fish, with a problem on one side, such as *four plus three*. The first student to answer *seven* got to keep the fish. Competition to make the best day's catch was keen.[341]

In 1960 Miss Lucy joined a reunion of Goodman family members from far corners of the nation for a photograph in front of the brick Gig Harbor Intermediate School. The school had just been renamed Goodman School, in honor of the family – and the teacher – who had given so much to the life of the community. In 1962 the failure of her driving test finally convinced Miss Lucy to close out a teaching career that had lasted an astonishing seventy-six years, generally considered to be the longest in U.S. history.

With a steady flow of traffic passing by the town, a few entrepreneurs in the 1950s began looking for ways to make those cars stop and spend their money. One of the first businesses to cater more to the tourists than the locals was Skandia Gaard, near the top of Peacock

Scandia Gaard opened in 1958 on the Peacock family homestead, showcasing Scandinavian arts and crafts in its museum and gift shop. Photo by Frank Owen Shaw

Hill. In 1956, when Olaf Thortensen and Wilbur Johnson were trekking up and down the West Coast looking for a place to establish a Scandinavian museum, they chanced upon Gig Harbor. From up on the hill, The Narrows looked like a Norwegian fjord, and Crescent Valley resembled the kind of dale that Thortensen remembered from his native Norway. As luck would have it, a perfect property was for sale. The home that Civil War veteran W. L. Peacock had built in 1889 was still there. For the last quarter century it had belonged to Ed Fay, who raised chickens on the property.

The partners used some of the old multipane chicken house windows to make display cases for their Scandinavian antiques. The old barn became a *Norsk Chalet* filled with old world antiques, local shells, and Indian relics. The brooder house became a *Svenska Stugan*, or Swedish cottage. Another chicken house became a fireplace room, furnished as a Norwegian living space from another era. The Gig Harbor Art League lent a hand by fashioning decorative plywood Scandinavian figures for the outside of the barn. It was a reminder of the kind of Scandinavia many of the families in Cromwell and Crescent Valley had left behind a few generations back.

Skandia Gaard began to bring a growing stream of curious folks over from Tacoma and farther afield to see what it was all about.[342] In another link with the harbor's past, some of C.E. Shaw's old Roosterville shelters for his racing roosters were brought up the hill, restored, and repainted in their original colors. By 1961 the venture had added a gift shop, public restrooms, and weekly folk-dance program. The dancers were mostly Scandinavian, but Milan and Jane Mikich offered lessons in the dances of Milan's native Yugoslavia.[343]

Boat building at Gig Harbor took a new turn in 1958. The Douglas Fir Plywood Association, headquartered in Tacoma, had put out a call for designs for a plywood sailboat suitable for both racing and cruising. It had to "provide sleeping accommodations for a crew of four; be capable of being built by reasonably skilled amateurs; provide auxiliary power by an outboard motor that could be easily removed and stowed and out-perform other sailboats in its class."

Ben Seaborn, a naval architect of Seattle, brought Gig Harbor's Ed Hoppen a model fashioned from bits of cardboard and asked him, "Think you can build that out of plywood?" After a year of tinkering and designing in his shipyard, Hoppen launched hull number one, christened *Thunderbird,* in November 1958. It was just under twenty-six feet long, and more than lived up to all specifications, including speed. A town accustomed to seeing working boats hit the water now got used to the launching of pleasure craft.

Hoppen eventually turned out sixteen Thunderbirds in his shipyard, and he sold plans for two dollars to anyone who wanted to try the project at home. Plenty of plywood and two thousand hours of work in a home garage could make any "reasonably skilled amateur" a sailboat owner. At least 1,200 are known to have been built worldwide. They proved durable, as well. Hull number one is still seaworthy and came back to Gig Harbor in 2002 as a donation to the historical society from Ann and Guy Hoppen, Ed's son.[344]

More folks were recognizing the recreational potential of the peninsula. With the advent of faster outboard motors, water skiing started to become a popular pastime. Horsehead Bay was a favorite spot, and Gig Harbor itself still had room in the 1950s for a boat and skier to hit full throttle. There had been a sportsmen's club on the peninsula for years, but in 1957 Artondale became home to a golf course. With the

The first Thunderbird sailboat is launched in November, 1958 at Eddon Boat Company in Gig Harbor. Ed Hoppen, the boat's co-designer and builder stands in the cockpit. Photo by Harbine Monroe

coming of the new, some of the old had to vanish. The 120-by-40-foot mansard roofed barn and the 40-by-80-foot loafing shed that George Ferguson had built around the turn of the century vanished to make way for the golfers' well-manicured greens.[345]

Businesses came and went on the peninsula, faces changing as the years passed. A few folks went out and made names for themselves in the world. Who could forget C.E. Shaw, who had gone on national radio in New York with racing roosters? It was hard to predict sometimes just what might catch the public's fancy. A Rosedale girl named Sadie Hoy married a man from Tacoma named Karos, and went away to gain national fame as a reader of coffee grounds, making what *The Peninsula Gateway* described as "many startling predictions."[346]

Young Carl Moller enjoyed a fleeting moment of fame in the spring of 1937, when the nationally syndicated *Ripley's Believe It or Not* told its readers, "Schoolboy Carl Moller requires 3 hours 10 minutes to get to school each day. He has never been late in two years."[347] That was all Ripley's had to say. They failed to mention that he lived at Sunrise Beach just up the north shore from Gig Harbor.

It is not always easy to spot the one person who will grow up to be famous. Like so many others, Luther Jerstad did not start out in Gig Harbor. He was born in Brooton, Minnesota, in 1936, and his life almost ended right there. It would have been hard to foresee his destiny when he came into the world weighing just three pounds and one ounce. He spent his first days in one of his father's shoe boxes, which served as an incubator, propped on bricks with a couple of forty-watt bulbs underneath it for warmth.[348]

Luther, who went by the name of Lute, came to Gig Harbor with his parents when he was in the sixth grade. In those days, his parents would have attracted more attention in the little community. They were both teachers. Alf Jerstad taught typing and bookkeeping at Peninsula High School for fifteen years. His wife, Frida, taught geometry, algebra, and general math at the same school.

It was only in high school that Lute began to make his name. He was a natural born athlete. He was not big – when he was full grown he stood five feet and five inches tall – but he was fast and determined. He lettered in football, baseball, and basketball at Peninsula High. Later, at Pacific Lutheran University, Lute's 1958 basketball teammates voted him Most Inspiring.

At Peninsula Lutheran Church, the Knapp brothers, Byron, Calvin and Forest, introduced Lute to the sport of mountain climbing. Their father had climbed Mount Rainier years before, and the Knapp boys knew their way around most of the local peaks. They started him out on Mount St. Helens, a 9,677-foot dormant volcano in southwestern Washington. Lute took to climbing naturally, sometimes leading the way, and they got up and down the mountain with time left to drive to the ocean.[349]

Lute began climbing every chance he got, sometimes with the Knapps, sometimes with the legendary climbing twins Lou and Jim Whittaker of Redmond, near Seattle. He climbed Mount Adams, Rainier, Olympus, and most of the other significant peaks in the area. Later, Lute worked seasonally with the guide service on Mount Rainier and climbed Washington's highest peak at least thirty-five times.[350] The guides were a hardy lot, but even here Lute stood out. One day at the summit, he reached into his backpack and pulled out, of all things, a watermelon to share with his companions. In 1961 he was co-leader of an expedition to the mountains of Canada's Yukon Territory. In 1962 he climbed Alaska's 20,000-foot Mount McKinley.

Lute Jerstad on the climb to Mt. Everest, 1963. Photo courtesy of Pacific Lutheran University

These were credentials enough in 1963 to win him a spot on the first all-American expedition to Mount Everest. There were roughly 186 million Americans in 1963, and not one of them had ever been to the top of Earth's highest mountain. In May of that year, a handful of Americans finally made it to the top of Everest, and it happened that one of them was from a little place called Gig Harbor.

Lute had been married since 1957 to Paula Blair, whose father had been the bookkeeper of the peninsula's Island Telephone and Telegraph Company. They had a five-year-old son named Karl and a daughter named Janna, who was born in April 1963 while her father was in Nepal preparing for the climb. The Everest expedition he joined was considered the greatest mountain climbing effort America had ever mounted, and five of its members reached the summit.

Lute was there on May 22, capturing the first motion picture images ever shot at the top of the world. On the way down, there was a brush with disaster. Darkness overtook them, and Jerstad and two companions had to bivouac at the 28,000 foot level without a tent, stove, or sleeping bag. No humans had ever spent an unprotected night at such heights and survived. Lute's companions lost most of their toes to frostbite. Lute himself was more fortunate, but he never regained full feeling in his fingers and toes.

The expedition caught the imagination of America, and excitement reached a fever pitch in the Northwest, which had contributed three members to the venture. The Mayor of Gig Harbor, Lute's family, the press, and dozens of cheering admirers were on hand to greet him when his plane touched down at SeaTac airport. There was a press conference and a motorcade in Seattle, where confetti showered down from the windows above. In Tacoma, a police motorcade escorted the Jerstad car through red lights, finally leaving him late at night in front of the toll booth at Narrows Bridge, where he could not pass over to Gig Harbor until he paid his bridge toll. Even celebrity had its limits.

On June 26, 1963, the biggest crowd Gig Harbor had ever seen watched Lute parade in triumph through the city. The procession began at 6:30 that evening on Judson Street, just up from the water-front, overlooking the harbor entrance where Sam Jerisich and his companions had come rowing in just shy of a hundred years before.

The convertible bearing Lute and his wife turned west on Harbor-view Drive. They passed the old Novak Hotel, which had not been a hotel since The Narrows Bridge made it too easy for visitors to get back to Tacoma. Close beside the building was the huge old Skansie boat building shed. Mitchell Skansie had died in 1939, and the business had declined after the war, but the shed was still sturdy and ready for whatever use might come its way. Across the street, the old brick Skansie house now belonged to Olive and Dick Fuqua. Olive had assisted John Insel as a mail carrier, and later had her own route on the Longbranch Peninsula. Six years earlier, Dick Fuqua had partnered with Milt Roby to restore taxi service to the area.

The motorcade passed Pioneer Way, and there stood the GAR Hall, now in its seventh decade, a reminder of the days when Miles Hunt, Joseph Goodman, and the other old Union Army vets had gathered to recall the days of 1861-65. The building had passed through many incarnations since then: an Episcopal church, a town hall, a polling place, a state patrol office, and a country store for the Peninsula Orthopedic Guild. A little farther up Pioneer on the left loomed the steeple of the old Memorial Presbyterian Church. The Presbyterians had moved out the year before, in favor of a big new church higher up the hill, and the building stood forlornly in search of a new tenant.

On the other side of Harborview, close to the water, stood the old Dorotich home, a survivor from the 1880s when Joe Dorotich wed Caroline Jerisich and built a house to raise their first child in. Like the Makovich home and others, it had stayed in the family across the generations.

Well-wishers came out to watch and wave from their front lawns and their workplaces. Paul Alvestad was there. In his youth he had delivered newspapers across Depression-era Gig Harbor. Now he was the postmaster. Lute's wife had dropped by the post office often during the climb and kept him informed of its progress.[351] Tony and Addie

Stanich and their daughter Irene watched from in front of their grocery. A few houses down, on the other side of the street, the Malich family crowded onto their front steps, watching the Peninsula High School Band in their green uniforms and white buck shoes. It was short notice for a band on summer break, but Lute was one of their own. Just about all of them had taken classes from his parents. They gave it their best, blaring away at *Hi Neighbor*, among other tunes.

The Fourth Division band from Fort Lewis had come over to lend a hand, and so had the Afifi Arab Patrol. They were Shriners who never missed a parade. The color guard was furnished by the Herman Uddenberg Post of the Veterans of Foreign Wars, named for the Gig Harbor boy who died in the First World War. There were four fire engines in the parade, a far cry from only a generation earlier, when high school students fought a waterfront fire with buckets of seawater. There was an ambulance in the parade, and a string of law enforcement vehicles – another reminder of how far the little town had come in sixteen years of incorporation. Some dogs, catching the excitement, chased the parade down Harborview Drive.

Some folks did miss the parade. One was Gretchen Wilbert, who had come to Wollochet Bay with her husband in 1954. She knew about the parade, but she had her hands full with three preteen children. In 2004 she would still have her hands full in her fourth term as mayor of Gig Harbor.[352] C. E. Shaw, the old promoter and rooster racer, was in declining health and may have missed the parade, but his daughter Jane was there, standing in front of Uddenberg's Ford dealership as the motorcade passed.

The parade ended at the yacht basin opposite Finholm's Market. At 7:30 there was a reception in the Fellowship Hall of the Peninsula Lutheran Church and a banquet sponsored by the Lion's Club. It looked like a big day to Rosemary Ross, granddaughter of the Albert and Sara Yates who had helped settle Rosedale long ago. It still looked big when she reflected back decades later, after an eventful life and years of service on the Gig Harbor City Council. It also looked big to young Doug Knapp, helping his scout troop direct traffic in the church parking lot. Little did he know he would one day write a book about this and scores of other events in the history of the Gig Harbor Peninsula Lutherans.

Gig Harbor Mayor George Gilbert was at the reception to present Lute with a key to the city. So was the Mayor of Tacoma, in case the young mountain climber had need for a second oversized key. This was still a small enough community for some of the folks to recognize one another across the room. There was Proc Peacock and his wife Alta. Proc had survived a Halloween stunt gone tragically wrong, and he had not let a little thing like a glass eye stand in the way of a successful real estate career. Alta came from Longbranch on the Key Peninsula. There was Bud DeWalt and his wife Adele. Bud had lived all but six years of his life on Wollochet Bay and had served in New Guinea in World War II. Adele was the daughter of Scandinavians Melcer and Bertha Larson, who had farmed and raised poultry at Sunny Bay. She had learned math in the class taught by Lute's mother.[353] Lute's father, Alf, nearing the end of his teaching career, came to the podium and said, "I want to thank you one and all. I know a lot of prayers were said for this expedition. I think they were answered."[354]

There was a three minute ovation when Lute entered the hall. Gig Harbor was proud of the local boy who had made good. He had not had an easy time, not on Everest, and not at the start of his life, but Lute had done all right, and done better than all right, whatever might lie ahead. So, all things considered, had the little town and the peninsula where it lay.

226

Making a living

Nick Novakovich stands on the porch of his meat market on Harborview Drive.

The Mar-Jay Drive-In, on the approach to the Narrows Bridge, was dismantled and rebuilt as the Span Drive-In. The third Narrows Bridge caused the building to be razed to make room for tollbooths.

St. Peter Brothers Groceries & Feed on Harborview Drive in 1906. It later became the Stanich Grocery store.

The Peninsula Gateway office, October 26, 1947. The building was originally part of the second Gig Harbor school. Photo by Frank Owen Shaw

Frank Owen Shaw captures the nightlife in Gig Harbor showing the Roxy Theater and the pool hall, December 9, 1949.

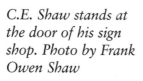

C.E. Shaw stands at the door of his sign shop. Photo by Frank Owen Shaw

Dr. Harold Ryan's dentist office and Judge H.R. Thurston's Pioneer Electric Co. after a winter snowstorm, 1930s.

People's Wharf, Haury's Boathouse, and the Ferry Tavern, February 3, 1950. Photo by Frank Owen Shaw

Bert Uddenberg opened this Ford dealership in 1934 at the corner of Stinson and Harborview Drive.

W.E. White Real Estate Agency in Rosedale, circa 1900. W.E. White is second from right.

The W.E. White store in Wauna, 1906

The "Beehive" stove served the Warren community on Hales Passage in 1910.

North Harborview Drive in 1915 showing the Burnham store, Kendall Hall to the right, and boys playing on the road.

Glein Boat Co. in 1946, later known as Eddon Boat Co., Blue Heron, and eventually Northwest Boatyard.

Karl Sehmel in his converted Model T truck leaves for southern California with Christmas trees in 1920.

Grand opening of Shively's Appliance Store, 1947, on North Harborview Drive in the Sweeney Block.

Epilogue

The Only Thing Certain is Change

On Friday, November 22, 1963, co-chairs Jerry Uddenberg and Donna Nelson were overseeing preparations for the Peninsula High School Senior Ball. Student volunteers were busy decorating when Jerry stepped forward and announced that President John Kennedy had been shot in Dallas, Texas. The ball was cancelled, and the decorations were taken down and burned.[355] Another generation, like the Pearl Harbor generation before them, would now remember forever what they were doing when they heard life-changing news. It was another of the pivotal points where the world and the way people viewed it changed suddenly and forever.

The year 1964 was a time for looking backward and a time for looking forward. It was the year that Lucy Goodman died at the age of ninety-five. It was a time to consider a seventy-six-year teaching career and a life that stretched back to the days when the peninsula was raw and untamed. When she and her family arrived in 1883, there was still an Indian village on Donkey Creek, and the only way to reach the outside world was by rowboat. When she died, there was a great steel bridge to the mainland and an airport on the lower end of the peninsula. Mary Jane Turner, a Gig Harbor legend in her own right, conducted the funeral service, and Miss Lucy was taken up Crescent Valley to Gig Harbor Cemetery to join the other pioneers.

In November 1963, Senator Henry M. Jackson was on hand for the dedication of the Tacoma Industrial Airport,[356] which occupied a wide expanse of the ground above Point Fosdick. Where Emmett Hunt had labored through a long day and sometimes a longer night to bring the mail across from Steilacoom, a plane could now rise and reach Portland or the Midwest in a matter of hours.

This was also the moment when Gig Harbor looked backward and forward at the same time. It began quietly on November 6, 1963, with a meeting of three peninsula women. Gail Reed, Jewel Holsinger, and Esther Snowden assembled with the goal of organizing a study group for Peninsula women. Each of the three was assigned to recruit three or four prospective members for a general meeting. Their study interests included history, geology, industry, transportation, and other topics. Perhaps because their first guest speaker was Bruce LeRoy, Director of the Washington State Historical Society, the growing group began to focus on the history of the Gig Harbor Peninsula. They began researching the history of the fishing industry, the cemeteries, the churches, the schools, and the Mosquito Fleet. On June 3, 1970, the group incorporated as the Peninsula Historical Society.[357]

Once there was an organization to receive them, donations began to appear. In 1974 Verna Wheeler presented a hand bell, and perfectly illustrated the value of a historical society. A few more years, a change of hands or two, and it might have been just another of the thousands of anonymous bells cluttering the antique stores and mantles of America. Verna was there to explain, and the society was there to document, that this was not just A bell, it was THE bell. It was the very one that Verna's mother, Anna Goodman Wheeler, and her aunt, Lucy Goodman, had used to summon children into the schoolhouse in the long-vanished days when the student body of all Gig Harbor totaled ten students. Anyone who saw the bell, anyone who touched

The Gig Harbor Peninsula Historical Society was formed as the Peninsula Historical Society in 1964. The society sold popcorn during the Harbor Holidays celebration in 1973.

it, anyone who heard its ringing peals, was connected with the early dawn of the peninsula's history.

More artifacts flooded in. Indian baskets fashioned by Annie Squally of Wollochet Bay, antique fishing gear, a 1920s gas pump, early kitchen tools, and sundry other artifacts that told the story of the area's development found a permanent home. Here were photos, commissioned in the 1880s by a proud Alfred Burnham, documenting the development of the first sawmill and other industries on the shore of Gig Harbor. They had passed into the hands of Frank Shaw, the son of Rooster Racing C. E. Shaw. Frank was a fine photographer in his own right, and he recognized the value of the first images ever made of Gig Harbor. He saved them from time and decay, presenting them to a society with the means and the determination to preserve them into the vast uncertain future.

The historical society led a vagabond existence for its first few years. It found display space in the basement of the new Gig Harbor Town Hall for a time in the 1970s, later taking up quarters in former churches and other homes. In 1998, when it had found more spacious museum quarters on a hill above Donkey Creek, the historical society was presented with one more challenge and opportunity.

Kathleen Watson, whose family had come to the peninsula in 1916, died on September 8, 1998. She had led a successful life, and at the end she wanted to give something back to the community where she had spent her early years. She left a bequest, generous and unexpected, to write histories of the Walla Walla and Gig Harbor localities where her family had lived. A man from Tacoma was commissioned to do the writing. Many in the community aided greatly in the research and the telling of the story. All who worked on it hope you enjoyed the story.

The population of Gig Harbor was listed as 6,456 in the 2000 census. The peninsula area as a whole was estimated at about 50,000. The median age was 44.6, and the population was 94.17% white. Minority presences are slowly growing. The census showed a total of 99 (1.53%) Asians and 72 (1.11%) Blacks.

With growth, the peninsula is experiencing the best and worst of urban life. Thai, Italian, Mexican, and other cuisines can be found here. A multiplex theater shows movies, and several live stages display the area's outstanding talent. Summer theater takes place in what was once the Peacock house, and was more recently the Scandia Gaard. The Encore Theater, close beside Highway 16, recently mounted a daring production of *Cabaret*. With the good comes the bad. A meth lab was recently discovered in one of the city's older homes, and a rash of burglaries struck area businesses. At the same time, the peninsula's rural setting was emphasized by the recent collision of a car and a bear.

What does the future hold for the peninsula? One sure lesson of history is that change is at least as certain as death and taxes. I've tried to convey in these pages how it must have looked at different moments in the past. No one can tell you how it will look in years to come. I can only tell you what I saw in the summer of 2004. For a start, the new Narrows Bridge is beginning to take shape just south of the current one. So far, it boasts only a foundation, but giant cranes are in place to move things along. The stretch of Highway 16 near the bridge is being widened to handle the added traffic flow. Inevitably this has cut into some stretches that once were wild. A few weeks ago, there were three dead possums along the stretch of highway between the bridge and the Gig Harbor City Center turnoff. Last week there were none. Things must be settling down.

Let's take a walk, for starters, around the harbor. Down near the harbor mouth a property went on sale recently for upwards of three million dollars. It includes a beautiful new home with a sweeping view of the water and Mount Rainier, along with an older beach cottage and a net shed. It is a choice spot, but the price would probably astonish Peter Skansie, the original owner of the cottage and net shed. The agent handling the sale is Tova Uddenberg, descended from pioneer merchant Axel Uddenberg.

A little farther along the western shore we come to the net shed where Randy Babich and his crew are readying the *Paragon* for another voyage to Alaska. The big flag on his dock flies at half mast for the recent death of former President Reagan as he discusses the current state of the fishing industry. A descendant of both Sam Jerisich and Spiro Babich, Randy studied dentistry at the University of Washington until the call of the sea became too strong. The salmon runs in Alaska have been enormous in recent years, but the price paid to fishermen is often lower than in his grandparents' day. To help make fishing profitable, he and his wife started a salmon caviar business and he also uses long lines barbed with fishhooks to snare dogfish, which the English favor for fish and chips.[358]

Toward the inner harbor, the Tides Tavern stands on pilings over the water. Long ago, when wheezing steamboats of the Puget Sound Mosquito Fleet stopped at Gig Harbor on their runs, it was Uddenberg's West Side Grocery. At one point after Prohibition ended, it was converted into the Ferry Tavern. More recently it was Three Finger Jack's. Now, as "the Tides," it has gone smoke free and food has replaced beer as the main attraction. Pictures and notes on the wall suggest that its regulars and visitors have ventured far. On one wall is an autographed color photo of Canadian astronaut Chris Hadfield, with a note pronouncing the Tides the "Perfect spot after a long trip." Another photo shows Colonel James Bales and Sergeant Mike Bales "near the Kuwait border," a reminder that area men and women are still answering their country's call to service.

The new long and sleek Frank Russell Foundation building was recently completed next door. Like the old settler said about the mountain, it's beautiful, but it sure does block the view. To their credit, the Frank Russell architects created railings and a walkway so people can go around back and view the harbor to their hearts' content.

The red brick Harbor Inn Restaurant is another place to view the bay, out its big back windows. From here the harbor is still narrow enough to resemble a wide and very slow river. Long ago, the Harbor Inn was the Novak Hotel, which survived time, two fires, and the Great Depression. In its many incarnations the building has been a hotel, bath house, pool hall, grocery, barber shop, and tavern. Since

1975 the Drohan family has operated it as a restaurant.[359] The shoreline all along the harbor sits in a deep bowl surrounded by hills. A cross on the wall of the restaurant is a silent memorial to a waitress killed in 1989 when an out-of-control truck careened down the hill on Pioneer Way and smashed into the front of the building.

Across the street is Spiro's Pizza and a host of other shops in what was once the Peninsula Hotel. One of the old porcelain claw-footed bathtubs remains in place in an upstairs room. On the corner stands a combination of shops called Neptune's Court. The owner is Rose Tarabochia, who has been known to greet new acquaintances only half-jokingly with, "I'm Rose Tarabochia. I own Gig Harbor." Her son Nick Jr. recently sold his boat, the *Kathy H.*, to pursue new dreams after 32 years of fishing. If the call of the sea should prove too strong yet again, he retains ownership of the gill-netter *Christine Jane.*

Up the hill just a bit on the other side of Pioneer Way is Tarabochia Street. The homes there have a uniform slightly different look from the rest of the town. Over on the east side of Tacoma there was a development called Salishan, where government housing was built during World War II to house the flood of families shifted by troop movements and industrial war work. By 1954, some of the houses had gone surplus, and the Tarabochias got the idea of barging some of

The buildings that once housed the Peninsula Hotel, electric company, and bank are still in use in 2004.

Corner of Pioneer Way and Harborview Drive, 2004

236

them over to Gig Harbor and setting them down on prepared foundations. The houses were up and ready for occupancy by the end of 1955, with a starting rent of $42.50 per month. I wonder now how many of the folks living on Tarabochia Street know that their homes once floated around Point Defiance and in through the entrance to Gig Harbor.

A little farther down Harborview, an inviting red brick bed and breakfast called The Rose is the latest incarnation of the home where Mitchell Skansie watched his boats take shape across the street, and where Olive Fuqua watched Lute Jerstad's parade pass by in 1963. Among the many Gig Harbor people who went above and beyond the call of duty to help this book along are the present owners, Mort and Nancy Altman. They not only answered my questions, they also showed me the house, down to the ancient furnace in the basement and the window where ferry tickets went back on sale after Galloping Gertie made her memorable tumble.

A bronze statue of one of the early commercial fishermen stands at Jerisich Dock, recently expanded with the acquisition of the Skansie property next door. Near the statue is a memorial to the Gig Harbor fishermen lost at sea: John Ancich Jr., Gordon Armstrong, Joseph Cloud, Visco Karmelich, Robert Lysell, Henry Moller Jr., Scott Tyree, and Jerry Bushard. Casual strollers must wonder who these men were and what happened. I know now, because Lee Makovich wrote of it last year in *The Fishermen's News*,[360] and because Randy Babich keeps the yellowed clipping from a 1940 Seattle newspaper framed and mounted on the wall of his net shed.

Jerisich Dock with memorial to those Gig Harbor fishermen lost at sea, 2004

The men were lost from the *Varsity*, a seventy-foot combination seiner built in Tacoma and owned by Gig Harbor men Mike Katich, George Plancich, and Joe Cloud. Bound home from the sardine fishing grounds of California in February 1940, she smashed onto a reef in the night and began breaking apart in the surging seas. Shortwave distress calls crackled out from the stricken boat. Among those who struggled to stay in contact with the *Varsity* was young Peter Babich, working the radio set on the *Crusader*, moored in Gig Harbor. To compound the crisis, the *Varsity*'s skipper on this voyage was a Californian unfamiliar with the Northwest coast. He reported his position as south of Washington's Tatoosh Island. In reality, he and his crewmen were off the coast of Canada's Vancouver Island. By the time it was sorted out and help arrived, it was too late for three of the crewmen. Joe Cloud left a wife and three young children. He and Visco (Vince) Karmelich live as names on plates screwed onto a bronze plaque in Gig Harbor now. The other two lost on the *Varsity* were from outside the peninsula, and had to be memorialized elsewhere. Even a casual visitor is likely to notice that there are predrilled holes and room for more names on this memorial.

Farther around the harbor, approaching Donkey Creek, the last big stand of wooded land on the western shore has recently been sold and is being readied for development. Beside it, The Beach Basket, an eclectic gift shop, has operated for a generation in a building that was once part of Austin's mill. Its vertical logs remind observers of the construction style that once showcased the mill's products. A few paces

View of the head of the bay from Clay Hill, 2004

farther on, an old home has become The Bistro, a favorite breakfast spot as work on this book inched along. "Do you know who lived here when it was a house?" I asked a young waitress. She had no idea, but an older woman behind the counter said it had belonged to C. E. Trombley, the long-time editor of *The Peninsula Gateway*. He would be surprised to see a parking lot in his front yard, but he might enjoy the biscuits and gravy and the tempting desserts. Some family members, including a granddaughter or great-granddaughter, came by to look it over not long ago, according to the woman behind the counter.

Up Burnham Drive the Hy-Iu-Hee-Hee Inn still serves up cold beer and a game of pool. This is a new incarnation for the Inn, since the first one, where Alan (Doc) Watson and his friends once gathered, was torn down when Highway 16 plowed up the spine of the peninsula. One piece of the old bar survives. On a dimly lighted wall, a dark slab of cedar board bears inscriptions set down sometime in the 1940s or 50s in artistic fashion by C.E. Shaw. On it live the words of many Gig Harbor stalwarts otherwise long silenced by time.

Yet farther around the bay, Finholm's Market is still there. Though ownership has changed, the name is the same. A mural on the front wall depicts one of the old time Mosquito Fleet steamers passing in front of the Olympic Mountains. Stare at it long enough, and you can darn near see the water ripple. A nearby viewing tower built by the local Lion's Club offers a superb view of the harbor from the top of eighty-five wooden steps. It, too, was named for the Finholms. Across the street, Anthony's Home Port is the latest incarnation of what was

Finholm's Market and the old post office along North Harborview Drive, 2004

once the Shorline Restaurant. Boats approaching from the back still see the big Shorline sign.

Highway 16 divides the peninsula in two, at the same time that it unites it with the wider world. On its shoulders, businesses and shopping centers in numbers Axel Uddenberg and the other early merchants could never have imagined. Up Borgen Boulevard toward the north end of the peninsula sits a huge new retail development which began in 2001 with Target and Albertsons, and now includes many more specialty stores. There are evergreens all around, but the homes are sure to follow.

One piece of greenery that seems sure to be saved is an eighty-some acre portion of the old Sehmel farm in the Rosedale area. Descendants of the old German settler are watching as Homestead Park takes shape.

The farms, poultry, and cattle of the peninsula have largely vanished, though some of the fields linger. The pastures now are more likely to hold a horse or two, switching their tails at flies in the summer heat. Some of the old farmhouses remain, refurbished by descendants or by newcomers anxious to enjoy something close to country life. Some of the new homes are jaw-droppingly beautiful. Money has come to the peninsula in a major way, and these homes reflect it. Some of the more spectacular ones are appearing now among the evergreens and madronas of Gig Harbor's eastern shore.

Vera Eide's grocery store is still up in Rosedale, though the name over the door is now Templeton's. The pump out front that once sold Standard gasoline has been replaced with a modern one selling Chevron. Last time I passed by this summer, the price was $2.02 and nine-tenths. Inside, the clock on the wall facing the door bears a little card reading "Eide's Time." Vera never believed in daylight savings time, and she kept her clock on standard time all year, adding the card to help deflect the customers who felt compelled to tell her it was an hour off. "We don't touch it," said a clerk this summer. It's right half the year anyway. Rosedale School has vanished from across the street, but a baseball field has stayed.

How do you know when to stop writing? There are multiple answers to choose from. The most satisfying one would be, "When everything possible has been found, and the story cannot be told more elegantly than it already is." That one never happens. The sensible answer would be, "When the publisher and the editorial committee order a halt so the book can be published at long last." That one is closest to the truth.

But the most self-revealing answer is that in the early phase of this project, I cast about for a word to describe the Gig Harbor Peninsula. The best I could come up with was "lumpy," which the editorial committee wisely rejected. Now, after four years of staring at maps, I can suggest that the peninsula, viewed from the side, resembles the front end of a large dog, with muscular forearms and cocked ears, gazing intently at a well-gnawed bone. The muscular forearm is Point Fosdick. The cocked ears are Horsehead Bay and Raft Island. The well-gnawed bone is Fox Island.

You don't see it? Try looking at a map every week for the next four years. When things like that start happening, I know I have been gazing too long at this particular inkblot, time to step back and give it a rest. Thank you, Gig Harbor, Rosedale, Warren, Cromwell, Wollochet Bay, Horsehead Bay, Raft Island, Lay Inlet, Rosedale, Arletta, Artondale, Sunrise Beach, and other people and places on this definitely-not-lumpy-shaped peninsula. It's been an education and a privilege.

The sand spit at the head of the bay entering Gig Harbor during the 1999 LeMans sailboat race. The lighthouse is on the right.

Present day Gig Harbor images by Linda McCowen

Providing an education

Rosedale School, 1905

Wollochet School, circa 1910

Wauna School, circa 1910

Crescent Valley School, built in 1913. The fire escape for the second floor was a slide at the side of the building. The structure was sold in 1949 to the John Paul Jones Masonic Lodge. The top floor was lowered to ground level and the cupola was removed. Photo by Frank Owen Shaw

*Elgin School,
circa 1905*

*Cromwell School,
circa 1910*

*Arletta School, built
by the Works Progress
Administration in
1938. The building
became the Hales Pass
Community Center.*

*Lincoln School on
Dorotich Street in west
Gig Harbor, 1950s.*

The students of Midway School, 1914. The school has been preserved by the Doyle and Murphy families. In 2004, Alice Murphy Doyle donated the building to the Gig Harbor Peninsula Historical Society for restoration and preservation.

Lucy Goodman with students – (l-r) Lyndall Messer, Lillian Vernhardson, Mabel Scott, Alice Uddenberg, Minnie Gellerman in June, 1912

Peninsula High School in Purdy, 1947

Lifestyles

*Memorial Day
services on People's
Wharf, 1890*

*Herman Claussen
plays the Victrola
entertaining people
at Camp HaHa,
1905. Herman's
daughter Elsie sits
on the right.*

*A leisurely afternoon
picking berries*

The Gig Harbor Ferries, 1924. The team played against community teams in the surrounding area.

Touch football at Lincoln School, September 21, 1937

Gig Harbor's baseball team, 1948. Team players were sponsored by town businesses.

C.E. Shaw's sign promoting Gig Harbor's Centennial Celebration, 1947, delayed six years due to WWII.

Shirley Finholm, Jeanene Thomas, and Ellen Waali pose in front of a C.E. Shaw billboard advertising Gig Harbor merchants in 1950, with the opening of the second Narrows Bridge. Photo by Frank Owen Shaw

Miss Huckleberry Geraldine Johnson, October 20, 1948. Photo by Frank Owen Shaw

William Wilkinson, standing next to his horse and hay wagon on his Rosedale Street farm

Hauling bales of hay from Berg's Landing to the Hageness farm

Lillie Hunt Patrick in her Gig Harbor kitchen

Lars Peterson family gathering hay, 1940 – (l-r) Eunice, Klarion, Marvin (driver), Orlando (on running board), David, and Loes with their 1928 Chevrolet

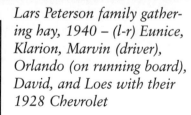

Amanda Carlson (l) at her Crescent Valley home

John Dulin, owner of the Arletta store, with sons Oscar and Ernest delivering cordwood

Charlie Eyrish hauling a load of wood in Rosedale, 1915

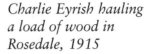

Young Annie Squally

Herman Claussen shows off his berries at his Sunrise Beach farm

Amateur Garden Club members pose for the opening of their new clubhouse, 1938. The building is still standing on Harborview Drive.

Appendix A

Skansie-built boats from the ledger kept by Mitchell Skansie:

1912

Boat *Oceania*, 65 feet long, 15 feet wide, 8 feet deep, 50 H. P. Standard engine built for Joe and Mitchell Skansie. Sold to Atlin Construction Co. of Vancouver B.C. Price $6,400.

Boat *Mermaid*, 60 feet long, 40 H. P., built for Lee Makovich. Price $4,500.

Boat *Confidence*, built by Martinolich under our direction and finished by us. 60 feet long, 40 H. P. Standard built for Anton Borovich. Price $5,000.

1913

President built for Andrew Babich, 30 H.P. Frisco Standard, Price $3,600.

Boat *Monach*, 50 feet long, 20 H. P. F. S., built for Nick Costello. Price $3,000.

Boat *St. Joseph*, 50 feet long, 20 H. P. F. S., built for Peter Ancich. Price $3,500.

Boat *Frisco*, 50 feet long, 20 H. P. F. S., built for Nick Plancich. Price $3,500.

Boat *Oceana*, 55 feet long, 30 H. P. T. C. F. S., Built for Joe & M. Skansie. Price $3,800.

1914

Boat *Governor*, 55 feet long, 40 H. P. F. S., built for Andrew Skansie. Price $4,500.

Boat *City of Clinton*, 50 feet long, 20 H. P. F. S., built for John Burke. Price $3,400.

Boat *Johnny E.*, 50 feet long, 30 H. P. T. C. F. S. Imperial engine. Built for Peter Evirch.

Boat *Editor*, 50 feet long, 30 H. P. T. C. F. S., built for Nick Costello. Price $3,800.

Boat *Katherine*, 57 feet long, 40 H. P. F. S., built for Peter Skansie. Price $4,500.

1915

Boat *Shushartie*, 58 feet long, 40 H. P. F. S., built for Britishese. Price $4,400.

Boat *Louisiana*, 60 feet long, 40 H. P. F. S., built for Paul Dorotich. Price $5,000.

Boat *Tozartoos*, 60 feet long, 40 H. P. F. S., Built for Joe & M. Skansie. Price $4,900.

Boat *Commander*, 60 feet long, 40 H. P. F. S., built for John Vlahovich. Price $4,800.

Boat *President II*, 60 ft. long, 50 H. P. F. S., built for Andrew Babich. Price $6,000.

Boat *Montana*, 50 feet long, 30 H. P. T. C. F. S., built for Victor Kaluper. Price $3,000.

Boat *Gradac*, 60 feet long, 50 H. P. F. S., built for John Karjon. Price $6,000.

1916

Boat *Mariner*, 58 feet long, 40 H. P. F. S., 1916 built for John Skansie. Price $4,000.

Boat *Marietta G.*, 58 feet long, 40 H. P. F. S., built for Dominic Juluich. Price $4,000.

Boat *Ikaros*, 60 feet long, 40 H. P. F. S. Price $5,000.

Boat *Active*, 60 feet long, 40 H. P. Imperial, built for Joe & Mitchell Skansie. Price $5,500.

Boat *Uriel*, 55 feet long, 40 H. P. F. S., built for Roko Privinich. Price $4,800.

1917

Boat *Quilcene*, 67 feet long, 80 H. P. F. S., built for Glacier Fish Co. Price $9,000.

Boat *Homer*, 60 feet long, no engine. Built for James Spencer. Price $3,000.

Boat *Renfrew* – 60 feet long, 45 H. P. Imperial. Built for Lummi Bay. Price $5,000.

Boat *Young America*, 60 feet long, 40 H. P. F. S., built for John Naterlin. Price $5,000.

Boat *Clysdale*, 65 feet long, 55 H. P. Imperial, built for Pyramid Packing Co. Price $9,500.

Boat *Airdale*, 65 feet long, 50 H. P. F. S., built for, but unsold to Cooper River Pack Co. Price $10,500.

Boat *Superior*, 65 feet long, 50 H. P. F. S., built for Spiro Babich. Price $6,100.

Boat *Spokane*, 60 feet long. 45 H. P. Imperial, built for Andrew Skansie. Price $5,500.

Boat *Independence*, 60 feet long, 45 H. P. Imperial, built for Peter Skansie. Price $5,500.

Boat *Supreme*, 62 feet long, 45 H. P. Imperial, built for Andrew Babich. Price $6,000.

Boat *Prily*, 62 feet long, 40 H. P. F. S., built for Kukara. Price $5,500.

Boat *America First*, 61 feet long, 40 H. P. F. S., built for Kuljis. Price $5,500.

Boat *Daisy*, 56 feet long, 40 H. P. F. S., built for Naterlin. Price $5,200.

Boat *Louise III*, 30 H. P. F. S., built for Lucas Carr. Price $3,400.

1918

Boat *Burnett*, 65 feet long, 50 H. P. F. S., built for Burnett Inlet Packing Co. Price $11,000.

Boat *Emancipator*, 65 feet long, 50 H. P. F. S., built for Paul Puratich. Price $10,200.

Boat *General Pershing*, 65 feet long, 50 H. P. F. S. Built for Andrew Xitco. Price $10,300.

Boat *Alameda*, 65 feet long, 50 H. P. F. S., built for Carmen Stambuk. Price $10,500.

Boat *Latouche*, 62 feet long, 50 H. P. F. S., built for T. Deolahovich & Rabasa. Price $10,020.

Boat *Liberty Bell*, 65 feet long, 65 H. P. F. S., built for Luca Ross. Price $13,500.

1919

Boat *Buddy*, 75 feet long, 80 H. P. Union, built for Alaska Packing & Fisheries Co. Price $26,000.

Boat *Protector*, 65 feet long, 65 H. P. F. S., built for George Rosin. Price $13,165.

Boat *Vigilant*, 62 feet long, 50 H. P. F. S., built for John Naterlin. Price $11,350.

Boat *Humanity*, 68 feet long, 85 H. P., built for Justo Pesutich. Price $14,650.

Boat *Detroit*, 65 feet, 30 H. P., built for Andrew Skansie. Price $1,500.

Boat *Brookdale*, 50 H. P., built for Joe & Mitchell Skansie, built at cost. Price $13,750.

1919-1920

Boat, 53 foot, 55 H. P. Price $10,500.

Boat *Companion*, 65-60 engine, built for Nick & Joe Skansie.

Boat *Dream Land*, Built for Karner, Price $11,000.

Boat *Anton*, 63 feet long, 50 H. P. Standard.

Boat *St. Andrew*, 63 feet long, 50 H. P.

Boat *Welcome*, 50 H. P. F. S., built for John Stanich.

Boat *Babar*, 50 H. P. F. S., built for Nick Simms

Boat *On Time*, 60 P. C. O., built for Andrew Gilich.

Boat *Oceanic*, 60 H. P. C. O., built for Paul Serna and Tony Ancich.

Boat *Vernon*, 50 H. P. F. S., built for Andrew Skansi.

Boat *Star*, 50 H. P. F. S., built for John Bakovich.

Boat *Eight Brothers*, 60 H. P. F. S., built for Tony Mosich.

1920 – 1921

Ferry *Elk*, 100 H.P.C.O., built for Mitchell & Joe Skansie.

Ferry *City of Steilacoom*, 200 C. O., built for for Joe & Mitchell Skansie.

1924

Boat, *Golden West*, 80 H. P. F. S., built for Spiro Babich.

Boat, *Mt. Tacoma*, 50 H. P. F. S., built for Andrew Gilich.

1925

Boat *Vanguard*, 80 Enterprise D. O., built for Spiro Babich.

Boat *Shenandoah*, 65 Atlas Imperial, built for Pasco Dorotich, launched 28 May 1925.

Ferry *Wollochet*, 150 H. P. C. O., built for Skansie Ferry Co., launched 26 January 1925.

Boat *Greyling*, built for Andrew Berry and Tony Mladineo.

Boat *Majestic*, built for John and Jack Bujacich.

The entries in the ledger end here, but the boat building continued, even after Mitchell Skansie retired.

Notes

Chapter One: *Twa-Wal-Kut* Becomes Gig Harbor

1. A fathom is six feet.
2. Kathy Troost, (University of Washington Geologist), interview by author, Seattle, Wa., 14 January 2001.
3. Lucy Gurand, Deposition for claimants, taken at Puyallup Indian Reservation, Wa., 23 March 1927. (Lucy Gurand, also known as Lucy Blagham, was 85 at the time of her testimony. She indicated that the inhabitants of Gig Harbor often spent part of the year at Quartermaster Harbor on Vashon Island.)
4. Marian Smith, *The Puyallup-Nisqually,* Columbia University Contributions to Anthropology (New York: Columbia University Press, 1940): p. 11.
5. James Wickersham, *Nusqually [sic] Mythology: Studies of the Washington Indians*, Overland Monthly (October 1898), pp. 345-351.
6. Archibald Menzies, "Menzies' Journal of Vancouver's Voyage," *Archive of British Columbia, Memoir No. V* (1923): p. 34.
7. Murray Morgan, *Puget's Sound: A Narrative of Early Tacoma and the Southern Sound (*Seattle: University of Washington Press, 1979): pp. 6-14.
8. Bob Crandall, *Rosedale* (privately published, 1990): p. 3-4. (Crandall quotes the recollections of Mrs. W. E. White, prepared for a long-ago Old Settler's Day picnic. She refers to a pair of Hudson's Bay Company men named Jones and Winchester. No such names appear in Fort Nisqually's surviving employee roster.)
9. Morgan, pp. 44-55.
10. Confusion often arises regarding the roughly fifteen-mile difference between Fort Nisqually's historic and current locations. The historic setting was well south of Steilacoom near the present site of DuPont and Northwest Landing. In the 1930s, what remained of Fort Nisqually was moved and reconstructed in Tacoma's Point Defiance Park, well north of Steilacoom.
11. "Kotor: Virtual Tour of the Old City," http://www.idk.cg.yu/tour/ eframeset.htm, created by Danilo Mirkovich, viewed 10 January 2001.

Chapter Two: The Coming of the Slavonians

12. The exact designation is lot one of section six, township 21 north, of range two east of the Willamette Meridian.
13. On a February 17, 2002 visit to the Artondale Cemetery, the grave was slightly moss-covered but easily readable. An entry in *Gig Harbor Peninsula Area Cemeteries, Pierce County, State of Washington*, published by Tacoma-Pierce County Genealogical Society, 1982, gives the date of death as November 15, 1895.

14. Arthur R. Kruckeberg, *The Natural History of Puget Sound Country* (Seattle: University of Washington Press, 1991): pp. 88-89.

15. "Rare Fish is Caught by Gig Harbor Man," *Tacoma Daily Ledger*, 3 August 1913, p. 4.

16. "New Enterprise," *Washington Standard*, 8 April 1871, p. 2.

17. Thomas F. Gedosch, "A Note on the Dogfish Oil Industry of Washington Territory," *Pacific Northwest Quarterly*, April 1968, pp. 100-102.

18. *Washington Weekly Standard*, 29 April 1871, p. 3.

19. History of Gig Harbor, compiled for the Federal Writer's Project, 1937, manuscript in possession of Washington State Historical Society.

20. Branko Mita Cloakovic, *Yugoslav Migrations to America*, R and E Research Associates (San Francisco, 1973): p. 23.

21. "Generations later, woman traces Gig Harbor roots," *The Peninsula Gateway*, 8 July 1980, p. 6.

22. "Married Fifty Years!," *Tacoma News Tribune*, 6 February 1932.

23. *Annual Report of the Commissioner of Indian Affairs to the Secretary of the Interior for the Year 1879* (Washington, D.C.: Government Printing Office, 1879): p. 148.

24. David Squally, Subscribed and Sworn, 26 June 1917. The exactness of his birth date, unusual for a Native American of that time period, might possibly be explained by the fact that 1 May 1849 is the date of a brief but bloody clash at Fort Nisqually which left several natives and an American settler named Leander Wallace lying dead by the fort gate. It was an event with extensive consequences for southern Puget Sound history. If David Squally truly was born on that day, he was probably reminded of its significance at intervals throughout his life.

Chapter Three: A Growing Sense of Community

25. Gary Fuller Reese, *Origins of Pierce County Place Names* (Tacoma: R&M Press, 1989): p. 16.

26. Lucile McDonald, *Early Gig Harbor Steamboats* (Gig Harbor: Mostly Books, 1984): p. 8.

27. McDonald, p. 10.

28. McDonald, p. 14. The diary entry is dated January 17.

29. *The Joseph Goodman family*, unpublished six-page typescript in the collection of the Gig Harbor Peninsula Historical Society.

30. "Still Another Sawmill," *Tacoma Daily Ledger*, 25 March 1888.

31. *Olympia Washington Standard*, 5 April 1889.

32. Mary Ann Petrich and Barbara Roje, *The Yugoslav in Washington State*, Washington State Historical Society, 1984.

33. Land Title Co. of Pierce County, *Index of Recorded Plats in Pierce County, Washington* (1966): p. 38.

34. Crandall, p. 2. The recollections of the post office meeting are from a paper read by Mrs. W. E. White on Old Settler's Day at the Peninsula Fair.

35. Guy Reed Ramsey, *Postmarked Washington: Pierce County* (Tacoma: Washington State Historical Society, 1981): p. 36.

36. Larry A. Carlson, *Presbies on the Hill: The Unlikely Presbyterians of Gig Harbor, Washington 1887-1994* (privately published, 1994): p. 33.

37. Carlson, p. 35.

38. Carlson, p. 40.

39. "William J. Duley Heard From," *The Mankato [Minnesota] Review*, 18 August 1896.

Chapter Four: New Names, New Churches, and a Gold Rush

40. "Bought Up Gig Harbor," *Tacoma Daily Ledger*, 14 June 1890, p. 3.

41. "Gig Harbor Items," *Tacoma Daily Ledger*, 11 March 1893, p. 2.

42. "Steamer Messenger for Henderson Bay," (paid ad) *Allyn Times*, 30 January 1890, p.1. This was the last year of operation for the 91-foot steamer with her melodious two-tone whistle.

43. *The Nicholas Castelan Family,* two-page manuscript in the collection of the Gig Harbor Peninsula Historical Society. Daughter Pauline Castelan is quoted as saying, "I remember the donkey engine that stayed in the middle of it [the creek], pulling logs out of the woods, under the bridge, and into the bay."

44. Crandall, p. 75.

45. Crandall, pp. 176-177.

46. Crandall, pp. 30, 119.

47. Audrey J. Brady, *The Legacy of M. B. Hunt*, unpublished manuscript in the collection of the Gig Harbor Peninsula Historical Society, p. 3.

48. *Gig Harbor Peninsula Area Cemeteries, Pierce County, State of Washington*, Tacoma-Pierce County Genealogical Society (1982), p. 28.

49. "Logger revisits mighty fir tree he felled," *The Peninsula Gateway*, 28 March 1984, p. 8C.

50. "Point Fosdick Nearly Bare," *Tacoma Daily Ledger*, 7 January 1934, p. B6.

51. "The Fall of a Cedar," *Tacoma Daily Ledger*, 3 October 1889, p. 5.

52. "Killed in a Mill," *Tacoma Daily Ledger*, 4 October 1890, p. 3.

53. "Some Bits of History," *West Coast and Puget Sound Lumberman*, April 1898. This publication went through a series of name changes over the years, always keeping *Lumberman* as part of its title. Surviving issues were consulted at Tacoma Public Library and Washington State Historical Society.

54. *West Coast Lumberman*, December 1891, p. 4.

55. *Puget Sound Lumberman*, January 1893, p. 9.

56. *Washington, West Coast and Puget Sound Lumberman*, November 1899, p. 54.

57. "Output of Shingles and Stock on Hand in Washington 1892," *Puget Sound Lumberman*, January 1893, p. 16.

58. "A New Industry at Gig Harbor," *Tacoma Daily Ledger*, 9 September 1893, p. 5.

59. *Puget Sound Lumberman*, February 1894, p. 16.

60. "The Shingle Market," *Puget Sound Lumberman*, April 1893, p. 17.

61. *West Coast and Puget Sound Lumberman*, March 1896, p. 156.

62. Estelle Rust, Diary 1890-1891, in the collection of the Gig Harbor Peninsula Historical Society.

63. Gladys Para, "Dr. Rust's $2,500 judgment award was reduced to $500," *The Peninsula Gateway*, 22 January 1986, p. 2C.

64. Carlson, p. 51.

65. Carlson, p. 55.

66. "Gig Harbor Items," *Tacoma Daily Ledger*, 11 March 1893.

67. Erle Howell, *Methodism in the Northwest*, Pacific Northwest Conference Historical Society, p. 433.

68. "Ethel Margaret Mannen (formerly Burnham) oral interview, given August and September 1996 at the age of 97. Recorded and transcribed by a volunteer. Converted to HTML by Michael G. Gordon (grandson). Accessed May 2002, http://www.orneveien.org/slekt/gordon/1899emb/intview.htm.

69. Mannen interview.

70. "Restless doctor found niche as commercial promoter," *Albert Lea [MN] Tribune*, 10 August 1995, p. 2.

71. "Honor Memory of Gig Harbor Founder," *Tacoma Daily Ledger*, 16 July 1933, p. B5.

72. Jack R. Evans, *Little History of Gig Harbor, Washington* (Seattle: SCW Publications, 1988): p. 2.

73. "Gold Found at Gig Harbor," *Tacoma Daily Ledger*, 17 July 1897, p. 6. In this account the discovery of the gold is credited to "a Mr. Peacock."

74. "The Gold Craze Spreading," *Tacoma Daily Ledger*, 19 July 1897, p. 5.

75. Rowena L. Alcorn and Gordon D. Alcorn, "Old Days Recalled by Puget Sound Shipper Active in Making Steamboat History," *Tacoma News Tribune,* 23 October 1960.

76. The Grand Army of the Republic was an organization of Union veterans of the Civil War.

77. Duane Schultz, *Over the Earth I Come; the Great Sioux Uprising of 1862* (New York: St. Martin's Press, 1992): p. 4.

78. "William J. Duley Heard From," *Mankato [Minnesota] Review*, 18 August 1896.

Chapter Five: Hello and Goodbye in a New Century

79. "Steamer Crest is Destroyed by Fire," *Tacoma Daily Ledger*, 25 September 1900.
80. "Murderer Captured," *Tacoma Daily Ledger*, 18 June 1901, p. 1.
81. "Peninsula Pioneers," Gig Harbor Peninsula Historical Society website, accessed 7 August 2004, http://www.gigharbormuseum.org/onlinexh-B.html.
82. Mabel Shyleen Ellis, *Pioneer Days at Gig Harbor, Washington*, 1938, two-page typescript in the possession of the Gig Harbor Peninsula Historical Society.
83. Corduroy refers to a system of paving sections of road with logs or board laid lengthwise across the roadbed. It was widely used to make muddy stretches passable in the days of dirt roads.
84. Elaine Zimmerman (Mabel Shyleen's daughter), interviewed by Chris Erlich, Gig Harbor, Wa., 15 January 2002. Also, letter written by Elaine Zimmerman, 20 January 2002, in collection of the Gig Harbor Peninsula Historical Society.
85. "Pioneer Gets His Claim," *Tacoma Daily Ledger*, 21 October 1898, p. 8.
86. Diary of Mabel Shyleen, 1903-05, in the collection of the Gig Harbor Peninsula Historical Society.
87. Peter Skansie, *Autobiographical Sketch*, Gig Harbor Peninsula Historical Society.
88. William P. Bonney, *Pierce County History, Volume III*, p. 737.
89. Lee Makovich, "Quality and durability in a past era," *The Peninsula Gateway*, special supplement, 30 January 2002, p. 4.
90. Adella Holmaas, "Harry Malony, Gig Harbor Pioneer Built Beautiful Skiffs, Launches," *Tacoma News Tribune*, 2 August 1964, p. C-18.

Chapter Six: Merchants and Preachers and a Floating Butcher

91. Gladys Para, "Austin's sawmill provided employment to many in area," *The Peninsula Gateway*, 12 February 1986, p. 3C.
92. "Gig Harbor Stirs Up Latent Forces," *Tacoma Daily Ledger*, 12 May 1912, p. 47.
93. *Along the Waterfront*, compiled and written by students of Goodman Middle School, Gig Harbor, 1974-75, p. 22.
94. Crandall, p. 15.
95. "Gig Harbor Notes," *The Forum*, Tacoma, 28 May 1910, p. 2.
96. "Burley Couple to Celebrate," local newspaper, 1 July 1939.
97. William Farrand Prosser, *History of the Puget Sound Country* (New York: Lewis Publishing Company, 1903), Vol. I, pp. 474-76. The Cromwells had quite the historical pedigree, extending far back into England and early America. One of their line, through a long-ago marriage, was

Andrew Ely, a minuteman at Lexington on the day the American Revolution became a shooting war.

98. "Gig Harbor Stirs Up Latent Forces," *Tacoma Daily Ledger*, 12 May 1912, p. 47

99. Shyleen diary, p. 185.

100. Helen Maloney, *Artondale 1907-1915* (privately published), p. 10.

101. Gladys Para, "Old-fashioned general store had different owners, unique histories," *The Peninsula Gateway*, 25 March 1987.

102. Gladys Para, "Old-fashioned general store had different owners, unique histories," *The Peninsula Gateway*, 25 March 1987.

103. Crandall, pp. 61-66.

104. "Old Timers Recall Heyday of Shipping on Sound," undated newsclipping in the Gig Harbor Peninsula Historical Society collection.

105. Hazel Heckman, *Island in the Sound* (Seattle: University of Washington Press, 1987): p. 131.

106. "Wollochet Bay named during Wilkes expedition of 1841," *The Peninsula Gateway*, 13 October 1982.

107. Marcia Willoughby Tucker, *Day Island: a glimpse of the past* (Rhododendron Press, 1997): p. 23.

108. "R. W. Uhlman, Wollochet, Dies at 92," *Tacoma News Tribune*, 18 December 1956, p. 27.

109. "Pioneers Celebrate Saturday," *Tacoma Daily Ledger*, 1 May 1936.

110. "Gig Harbor Stirs Up Latent Forces," *Tacoma Daily Ledger*, 12 May 1912, p. 47.

111. Stephen, J. Forslund, *The Swedes in Tacoma and the Puget Sound Country, 1852-1976* (privately published, 1976): p. 62. All accounts agree that there were six Uddenberg children, but different sources give different names. It appears that Arthur may also have gone by the name Herman.

112. Maloney, p. 5.

113. "Missing Tacoma Woman was Shot and Then Clubbed," *Tacoma Daily Ledger*, 11 April 1910, p. 1.

114. "Formal Charge Against Wezler Filed in Court," *Tacoma Daily Ledger*, 12 April 1910, p.1.

115. Wezler Makes Confession," *Tacoma Sunday Ledger*, 24 April 1910, p. 1.

116. Martha Hoy Bernhartsen, *History of the Rosedale Union Church, 1882 to 1969* (privately published, 1969): pp. 3-5.

117. Douglas S. Knapp, *A History of Peninsula Lutheran Church, 1904-1979* (Clinton-Hull Printing Company, Ltd., 1985): pp. 4-12.

118. Carlson, p. 57.

119. Carlson, pp. 54-62.

120. *A Brief History of Methodism in Gig Harbor* (privately printed by the Gig Harbor Methodist Church).

121. Gladys Para, "A decade after Kitty Hawk Stromer buzzed harbor in seaplane," *The Peninsula Gateway*, 8 April 1987 p. 9B. For a more complete account of Stromer's career, see Marcia Willoughby Tucker, *Day Island: a glimpse of the past* [Rhododendron Press, 1997]: p. 23.
122. *Along the Waterfront*, compiled and written by students of Goodman Middle School, Gig Harbor, 1974-75, p. 25.
123. Gladys Para, "Old-fashioned general store had different owners, unique histories," *The Peninsula Gateway*, 25 March 1987.
124. Crandall, pp. 6, 181.
125. Silas W. Hampton, *History of Gig Harbor*, 1937, compiled as part of the Washington State Guide, sponsored by the Federal Writer's Project, in the collection of the Washington State Historical Society, Tacoma, Wa.
126. Gladys Para, "Local ferry became more curse than blessing," *The Peninsula Gateway*, 30 May 1984, p. 8C.
127. Crandall, p. 115.
128. Clarence Bagley, *History of Pierce County*, Vol. 3, p. 750.

Chapter Seven: Roaring into a Depression

129. "Gig Harbor Editor Dies," *Tacoma News Tribune*, 3 October 1953, p. 1.
130. Kathleen Watson (compiler), *The Watson Family of Gig Harbor* (self-published, 1990): vol. IV.
131. "Death Takes Oldest Woman Pioneer," *The Peninsula Gateway*, 20 October 1933, p. 1.
132. Mike Jerisich interview by tape recording, Gig Harbor, Wa., July 1989, in the collection of the Gig Harbor Peninsula Historical Society.
133. Crandall, p. 63.
134. Andy Buffington, *The History of Raft Island* (privately published booklet, 1998): p. 6.
135. Buffington, pp. 18-19.
136. Mrs. Hubert Secor, *Hubert Secor's Bus Business*, typescript in the collection of the Gig Harbor Peninsula Historical Society.
137. *The Peninsula Gateway*, 11 June 1986.
138. Later known as Central Washington University.
139. Gussie Schaffer, "From the Heart Messages," *The Peninsula Gateway*, 13 February 1991, p. C1.
140. Lea Anne Bantsari, "Miss Lucy Goodman – A woman who defined teaching during the early years," *The Peninsula Gateway*, 26 April 1989.
141. Joseph Goodman diary 1916-1931, in the collection of the Gig Harbor Peninsula Historical Society.
142. E.P. Chalcraft, *Seattle Post Intelligencer*, September 1958.
143. "Joseph Goodman, Patriarch of Gig Harbor and Civil War Vet, Tells of his 48 Years in Washington," *Tacoma News Tribune*, 14 May 1929.

144. Alta Peacock interview by author, Gig Harbor, Wa., 9 August 2004.

145. *The Peninsula Gateway*, 22 March 1946, p. 4.

146. Gladys Para, "Empress Theatre entertained with movies and vaudeville," *The Peninsula Gateway*, 19 March 1986, p. 3C.

147. Gladys Para, "Bank business was short lived, but building has long history," *The Peninsula Gateway*, 27 May 1987, p. 2B.

148. "Local Drug Store Raided," *The Peninsula Gateway*, 31 January 1930, p. 1.

149. "Seize Still at Cromwell," *The Peninsula Gateway*, 1 January 1932, p. 1.

150. Rose Tarabochia interview on tape recorder, Gig Harbor, Wa., 13 September 2000, in the collection of the Gig Harbor Peninsula Historical Society.

151. "Mainly About People," *The Peninsula Gateway*, 16 April 1948, p. 1.

152. "Hollycroft Gardens, Inc.," *The Peninsula Gateway*, 4 July 1947, p. 1.

153. Gladys Para, "Soundview holly came from Peyran's stock," *The Peninsula Gateway*, 14 January 1987, p. 7B.

154. "Finholm's Market: A Peninsula tradition," *The Peninsula Gateway*, January 1995, special feature.

155. Lynn Iverson, "Local history passes with trio of pioneers," *The Peninsula Gateway*, 27 November 1996, p. 3A.

156. "Woman Justice for Gig Harbor Served 8 Years in Post Office," *Tacoma Sunday Ledger*, 11 February 1923.

157. William P. Bonney, *History of Pierce County*, Volume III, pp. 647-8.

158. Carlson, p. 139.

159. "Dares Fire and Water!," undated Tacoma newspaper clipping in the collection of the Gig Harbor Peninsula Historical Society.

160. Gladys Para, "Skipper Elsie Claussen had many talents," *The Peninsula Gateway*, 17 June 1987.

161. Skansie Manuscript Collection, Mss II B110A, Washington State Historical Society Museum.

162. Lee Makovich, "Sailing with Spiro," *The Peninsula Gateway*, special supplement, 24 January 1996, page 7+.

163. Evans, p. 11.

164. Randy Babich (grandson of Spiro and son of Peter Babich) interview by author, Gig Harbor, Wa., 25 February 2001.

165. Babich interview, p. 10.

166. "Gig Harbor Fishermen Now in Port," *Tacoma Daily Ledger*, 17 November 1929, page D9.

167. Watson manuscript.

168. "Business Houses are Destroyed," *Tacoma Daily Ledger*, 12 January 1930, p. 1. Also "Tacoma Fireboat's Speedy Work Helps Save Business Section of Suburb," *Tacoma News Tribune*, 13 January 1930, p. 1.

169. "Gig Harbor Suffers a Bad Fire Monday Morning," *The Peninsula Gateway*, 19 November 1937, p. 1.

170. Paul Alvestad interview by author, Gig Harbor, Wa., 13 March 2004.

171. His given name was Clarence, but he was universally known as Nick by this time.
172. Diary of Nick Burnham, 1930-31 and 1942-44, in the collection of the Gig Harbor Peninsula Historical Society.
173. "Huckleberry Battle Rages," *Tacoma Daily Ledger*, 12 October 1933.
174. Alvestad interview.
175. *The Peninsula Gateway*, 3 June 1938, p. 8.
176. "Rosedale News," *The Peninsula Gateway*, 19 November 1937, p. 1.
177. *The Peninsula Gateway*, 12 February 1938, p. 1.
178. "Crescent Valley," *The Peninsula Gateway*, 21 January 1938, p. 1.
179. "Gig Harbor Sportsmen are Active Group," *The Peninsula Gateway*, 15 April 1938, p. 8.
180. "Federated Clubs Elect," *The Peninsula Gateway*, 21 January 1938, p. 1.
181. "Lodge Bulletins," *The Masonic Journal*, Tacoma, Wa., Vol. VI No. 11, February 1927, p. 21.
182. Paul W. Harvey, *Not Made with Hands: The Centennial History of Grand Lodge Masonry in Washington and Alaska, 1858-1958* (Tacoma: Masons of Washington, 1958): p. 247.
183. "National Event Observed Here," *The Peninsula Gateway*, 27 May 1938, p. 1.
184. "Air Mail Celebration Success," *The Peninsula Gateway*, 20 May 1938, p. 1.
185. "First Place For Gig Harbor Man," *The Peninsula Gateway*, 3 June 1938, , p. 8.
186. "Pig Takes to Water on Harbor," *Tacoma Daily Ledger*, 19 April 1934, p. 1.
187. Bart Ripp, "Gig Harbor rooster races something to crow about," *Tacoma News Tribune*, 11 March 1998, p. B10.

Chapter Eight: The Short Life of Galloping Gertie

188. "After Many Years," *Tacoma Times*, 12 September 1939.
189. "Major Bowes Believed Originator of Proposals to Bridge Narrows," *Tacoma News Tribune*, September 15, 1963. An artist's rendering of a bridge spanning The Narrows attributed to Bowes in this article seems actually to have been one prepared for a 9 April 1929 *Tacoma Daily Ledger* front-page feature.
190. E. T. Short, "After Many Years," *Tacoma Times*, 1 April 1937.
191. "To Bridge the Narrows," *The Peninsula Gateway*, 28 December 1923.
192. "Famous Engineer Tacoma Visitor," *Tacoma News Tribune*, 7 September 1927.
193. "Finds Narrows Span Feasible," *Tacoma Daily Ledger*, 27 November 1927.
194. "Soundings to Be Made in Narrows," *Tacoma Daily Ledger*, 23 November 1928.

195. "Dr. Steinman, Famous Bridge Designer and Builder to Tell Tacomans Tuesday Night About Span Project," *Tacoma News Tribune*, 5 March 1929.

196. "Narrows Span is City's Big Project," *Tacoma Daily Ledger*, 5 April 1929, p.1.

197. Morgan and Morgan, p. 117.

198. Public-No. 261-73rd Congress [H. R. 9530], An Act Granting the consent of Congress to the county of Pierce, a legal subdivision of the State of Washington to construct, maintain, and operate a toll bridge across Puget Sound, State of Washington, at or near a point commonly known as "The Narrows." Approved 28 May 1934.

199. Morgan and Morgan, p. 116.

200. "Bridge Price Too Low," *Tacoma Times* editorial, 8 November 1940.

201. "Gertie's Rise to Fame," *The Peninsula Gateway*, 17 February 2001.

202. "Narrows Bridge Slogans," *The Peninsula Gateway*, 12 February 1938, p. 1.

203. "The Narrows Bridge," *The Peninsula Gateway*, 25 February 1938, p. 1.

204. "Narrows Tides Are Problem for Engineers," *Tacoma News Tribune*, 9 March 1939.

205. "Narrows Tides Are Problem for Engineers," *Tacoma News Tribune*, 9 March 1939. On p. 97 of his book, *Bridging the Narrows*, Joe Gotchy supplies an alternate weight of 550 tons and possibly 56 anchors.

206. "Tacoma Narrows Bridge Progress Report," *The Peninsula Gateway*, 17 November 1939, p. 1.

207. "You Can Stroll Across Narrows Now!," *Tacoma News Tribune*, 17 December 1939.

208. "Progress of Bridge Construction," *The Peninsula Gateway*, 22 March 1940, p. 1.

209. "Man Who Fell From Bridge Will Recover," *Tacoma Times*, 30 July 1940. Also, "Painter Recalls his Fall from Narrows Span, *Tacoma News Tribune*, 9 November 1940.

210. Joe Gotchy, *Bridging the Narrows* (Gig Harbor: Peninsula Historical Society, 1990): p. 43.

211. "Sodium Light Units Are Efficient," *Tacoma Times*, 1 July 1940.

212. *Tacoma News Tribune*, 30 April 1940.

213. "Span Opened Last July 1," *Tacoma Times*, 8 November 1940, p. 1.

214. "Narrows Bridge Tolls," *The Peninsula Gateway*, 17 November 1939, p. 1.

215. "Gertie's Rise to Fame," *The Peninsula Gateway*, 17 February 2001.

216. "Fleetfoot Wins Rooster Derby, Races Big Event," *The Peninsula Gateway*, 5 July 1940, p. 1.

217. "A Few Highlights of the Celebration," *The Peninsula Gateway*, 5 July 1940, p. 1.

218. "Gig Harbor Band Active in Bridge Celebration," *The Peninsula Gateway*, 5 July 1940, p. 1.

219. " 'Narrows Bridge March' For Local Celebration," *The Peninsula Gateway*, 28 June 1940, p. 1.
220. "Camera Club Prize Winners With Bridge Pictures," *The Peninsula Gateway*, 5 July 1940, p. 1.
221. "2,053 Cars Cross Bridge First Day," *Tacoma Times*, 8 November 1940.
222. Gladys Para, "Narrows Bridge Collapsed 44 Years Ago This Month," *The Peninsula Gateway*, 21 November 1984.
223. "The Sidewalk Situation," *The Peninsula Gateway*, 22 March 1940.
224. "Accident Emphasizes Need of Stop Light," *The Peninsula Gateway*, 27 September 1940.
225. "Bad Corner Scene of Another Accident," *The Peninsula Gateway*, 4 October 1940, p. 1.
226. "Passenger Autos' Toll Cut 5 Cents," *Tacoma Times*, 1 November 1940.
227. "Bounce Gave Bridge Some Nicknames," *Tacoma News Tribune*, 8 November 1940.
228. "'Shock Absorbers' Will Eliminate Wind 'Bounce'," *Tacoma Times*, 1 July 1940, p. 17.
229. "Cables Will Curb Bridge's Bouncing," *Tacoma News Tribune*, 5 September 1940.
230. B. W. Brintnall, "Wind Collapses Center of Bridge," *Tacoma News Tribune*, 8 November 1940, p. 2.
231. "Signboard Slogan Loses Value When Big Bridge Falls," *Tacoma News Tribune*, 8 November 1940.
232. Alvestad interview.
233. Carlson, pp. 116-117.
234. "Span Mystery Man Had Big Thrill for Dime," *Tacoma News Tribune*, 8 November 1940.
235. "Galloping Gertie gallery opened," *Tacoma News Tribune*, 10 July 1977.
236. Frances (Borgen) Carlson interview by author, Gig Harbor, Wa., 15 August 2004.
237. "Last Man Over Span," *Tacoma News Tribune*, 8 November 1940.
238. "Narrows Bridge Wrecked by Storm," *The Peninsula Gateway*, 8 November 1940, p. 1. Further details are in "Truck Falls Into Water," *Tacoma News Tribune*, 7 November 1940.
239. "'Phobia' saved newsman's life," *Tacoma News Tribune*, 7 November 1975.
240. "Span Mystery Man Had Big Thrill for Dime," *Tacoma News Tribune*, 8 November 1940.
241. "Lensman recalls Gertie's gallop," *Tacoma News Tribune*, 7 November 1975.
242. Mike Ferguson, "Just About People: Gertie's collapse scared him silly," *Tacoma News Tribune*, February 1976.
243. Bruce Johnson, "Tacoma Tradewinds: Skansie yard spawned sturdy ferry service," *Tacoma News Tribune,* 19 December 1976, p. F9.

244. "Shuttle Service on Ferry Line," *Tacoma Times*, 8 November 1940.
245. Carlson, p. 116.

Chapter Nine: The Peninsula Goes to War

246. "Weather Statistics," *Tacoma News Tribune*, 8 December 1941.
247. Martha Jean (Insel) Robeson interview by author, Gig Harbor, Wa., 19 February 2001.
248. Peter Land, Application for a Certificate of Arrival, No 88-26-5, August 26, 1936. A copy in the possession of his daughter, Rosemary (Land) Ross.
249. Makovich interview.
250. Shirley Uddenberg Knapp interview by author, Gig Harbor, Wa., 26 February 2001.
251. Bert Uddenberg, Jr. interview by author, Gig Harbor, Wa., 18 February 2001.
252. Bud DeWalt interview by author, Wollochet Bay, Wa., 16 August 2004.
253. Don Sehmel interview by author, Gig Harbor, Wa., 5 May 2004.
254. Alvestad interview.
255. Joe Hoots interview by author, Gig Harbor, Wa., 26 April 2001.
256. John Ancich interview by author, Gig Harbor, Wa., 5 March 2001.
257. "Legion Dance," *The Peninsula Gateway*, 12 December 1941, p. 1.
258. "Harbor High Defeats Silverdale," *The Peninsula Gateway*, 30 January 1942, p. 1.
259. "Blackout Bulletins Available for Poultrymen," *The Peninsula Gateway*, 28 January 1942, p. 1.
260. "Petroleum Briquettes Again Available for Poultrymen," *The Peninsula Gateway*, 13 July 1945, p. 1.
261. "Washington Poultrymen Have Fine Outlook in '42," *The Peninsula Gateway*, 10 April 1942, p. 1.
262. "Last Rooster Races For The Duration," *The Peninsula Gateway*, 26 June 1942, p. 1.
263. "Local Aircraft Warning Station has New Plane Detector Device," *The Peninsula Gateway*, 23 January 1942, p. 1.
264. Report from the Seattle Fighter Wing, Office of Ground Observer Officer, Seattle, Wa., 4 February 1944.
265. Robeson interview.
266. "First Aid Class," *The Peninsula Gateway,* 19 December 1941, p. 1.
267. Ronald H. Bailey, *The Home Front: U.S.A.*, World War II series (Time Life Books, 1978): p. 105.
268. *The Peninsula Gateway*, 25 September 1942. The casualty stations included the Rosedale Community Hall and the Arletta schoolhouse.
269. "Lincoln School Has Air Raid Drill," *The Peninsula Gateway*, 19 December 1941, p. 1.

270. "Defense Meeting set for Tonight," *The Peninsula Gateway*,
30 January 1942, p. 1.
271. "$1,371.80 Raised for Red Cross," *The Peninsula Gateway*, 23 January 1942,
p. 1.
272. "Messenger Boys Wanted," *The Peninsula Gateway*, 7 August 1942, p. 1.
273. "Citizens urged to make Christmas Seal Returns," *The Peninsula Gateway*,
19 December 1941, p. 1
274. Robeson interview.
275. Makovich interview.
276. "Salvage To-day," *The Peninsula Gateway*, 17 April 1942, p. 1.
277. "Peninsula Makes Good," *The Peninsula Gateway*, 10 July 1942, p. 1.
278. "A Peninsula Casualty," *The Peninsula Gateway*, 19 December 1941, p. 1.
279. DeWalt interview.
280. "First Steps Taken for Guerilla Band," *The Peninsula Gateway*, 1 May 1942,
p. 1.
281. "Huge Growth In Traffic On Ferry System," *The Peninsula Gateway*,
13 March 1942, p. 1.
282. Robeson interview. Further details are from Bart Ripp, "The Day No one
Saw The President," *Tacoma News Tribune*, 11 October 1994.
283. Local News," *The Peninsula Gateway*, 11 September 1942, p. 1.
284. Robeson interview.
285. Watson, *The Watson Family of Gig Harbor*.
286. "News About Our Service Men," *The Peninsula Gateway*, 25 March 1944,
p. 1.
287. "A Message From Foxholes of France," *The Peninsula Gateway*,
28 July 1944, p. 1.
288. "Another Letter from Fox Holes of Europe," *The Peninsula Gateway*,
20 October 1944, p. 1.
289. "Citation: Silver Star," *The Peninsula Gateway*, 1 June 1945, p. 1.
290. "Tire Rationing Boards Now Operating," *The Peninsula Gateway*,
9 January 1942, p. 1.
291. Martha Jean Insel Robeson, personal recollections, 2002.
292. Ronald H. Bailey, *The Home Front: U.S.A.*, World War II series (Time Life
Books, 1978): p. 112.
293. Knapp interview.
294. "Finholm's Market and Grocery: The Village Grocer (With Apologies to
Longfellow)," *The Peninsula Gateway*, 27 August 1943.
295. "Victory Gardens," *The Peninsula Gateway*, 27 February 1942, p. 1.
296. Bailey, p. 108.
297. *The Peninsula Gateway*, 7 May 1943.
298. "Arletta School Jeep Drive," *The Peninsula Gateway*, 21 May 1943.
299. "Summing up of War Bond Drive," *The Peninsula Gateway*,
1 September 1944, p. 1.

300. Carlson, p. 123.

301. "News About Our Service Men," *The Peninsula Gateway*, 13 October 1944, p. 1. The accident itself was reported under "Accident Kills Gig Harbor 'Man," 29 September 1944, p.1.

302. "To Editor Gateway," *The Peninsula Gateway*, 15 May 1942, p. 1.

303. "Nick Ancich Passes," *The Peninsula Gateway*, 22 January 1943, p.1.

304. "Salmon sink Tarabochia's Phyllis T.," *The Peninsula Gateway*, 16 November 1983, p. 2C.

305. *Pacific Fisherman*, May 31, 1943.

306. Makovich interview. Also Ancich interview.

307. Gordon Newell, editor, *H. W. McCurdy Marine History of the Pacific Northwest* (Superior Publishing Company, 1966): p. 502.

308. "Army Diesel Tug Launched Here," *The Peninsula Gateway*, 24 September 1943, p.1.

309. Rosemary Land Ross interview by author, Gig Harbor, Wa., 2003. See also Peter William Land obituaries in *Tacoma News Tribune*, 23 July 1957, p. 25.

310. "Gig Harbor Boy Receives Decorations," *The Peninsula Gateway*, 1 September 1944, p. 1.

311. "News About Our Service Men," *The Peninsula Gateway*, 7 August 1945, p. 1.

312. "Peninsula Boy Among Survivors," *The Peninsula Gateway*, 18 April 1945, p. 1.

313. "Gig Harbor Boy Okinawa Veteran," *The Peninsula Gateway*, 13 July 1945, p. 1.

314. "A Letter of Interest from Servicemen," *The Peninsula Gateway*, 27 April 1945, p. 1.

315. *Tacoma News Tribune*, 9 October 1942.

316. "Tacoman dies in Plane Crash," *The Peninsula Gateway*, 29 September 1944, p. 1.

317. "Gig Harbor Flier Reported Missing," *The Peninsula Gateway*, 13 January 1944, p. 1.

318. "Lt. Raymond Edwards Reported Missing," *The Peninsula Gateway*, 12 January 1945, p. 1. A follow-up in the 16 March issue reported confirmation of his death and stated that he was returning from a bombing mission over Austria.

319. "Pvt. Herman C. Niemann Accidently Killed," *The Peninsula Gateway*, 25 June 1943, p. 1.

Chapter Ten: Cityhood and a Homecoming

320. " Head of Bay Hit by Fire," *The Peninsula Gateway*, 5 January 1945, p. 1.

321. "Extensive Rebuilding at Head of Bay*," The Peninsula Gateway*, 23 February 1945, p. 1.

322. "Milan Mikich," *The Peninsula Gateway*, 4 July 1947, p. 8.

323. Gladys Para, "Pierce County's First Rural Library Opened in Gig Harbor," *The Peninsula Gateway*, 8 January 1966, p. 3C.

324. "Suddenly Gig Harbor is a 'City'," *The Peninsula Gateway*, 28 January 1981, p. 3.

325. "Keith Uddenberg Store Opening," *The Peninsula Gateway*, 7 March 1947, p. 1.

326. 1942 receipt from D. F. DeBernardi & Co., Cheese, Olive Oil & Provisions of San Francisco, in the collection of the Gig Harbor Peninsula Historical Society. The store operated from 1924 to 1971.

327. "C.O. Austin Passes," *The Peninsula Gateway*, 27 December 1946, p. 1.

328. "Town Marshal Chet Jones Did It All," *The Peninsula Gateway*, 23 April 1986, p. 3C.

329. "New City Well Has Ample Flow," *The Peninsula Gateway*, 3 June 1949, p. 1.

330. "Pryear Electric," *The Peninsula Gateway*, 4 July 1947, p. 4.

331. "Before You Buy A Television Set...," *The Peninsula Gateway*, 24 December 1948, p. 4.

332. "New Idea in RCA Victor Television," *The Peninsula Gateway*, 7 January 1949, p. 3.

333. "Mainly About People," *The Peninsula Gateway*, 9 July 1948, p. 1. Also "Eide's of Rosedale," *The Peninsula Gateway*, 4 July 1947, p. 6.

334. "Arletta Cash Store," *The Peninsula Gateway*, 4 July 1947, p. 10.

335. "E. W. Anderson Grocery," and "Forsythe Store," *The Peninsula Gateway*, 4 July 1947, p. 10.

336. Gladys Para, "Fierce Storm froze harbor in 1950," *The Peninsula Gateway*, 2 August 1989.

337. Terry Grant, *Bridge to the Wilderness*, Gig Harbor Peninsula Historical Society & Museum, 2000.

338. Tony Hazarian, "Sweet notes of 'Miss Lucy' come alive at museum," *The Peninsula Gateway*, 25 October 1995, p. 3B.

339. Adella Holmaas, "Gig Harbor Woman, 89, Is Teaching 73rd Year," *Tacoma News Tribune*, 21 September 1958, p. A4.

340. "She's Been a Teacher for 74 Years," 1959 article in Gig Harbor Peninsula Historical Society collection.

341. E. P. Chalcraft, *Seattle Post Intelligencer*, 23 September 1958.

342. Adella Holmaas, "Partners Convert Old Farm Into Private Museum," *Tacoma News Tribune*, 8 June 1958.

343. Elizabeth Evans Wright, "Gig Harbor's Slice of Scandinavia," *Seattle Times Sunday Magazine*, 18 June 1961, p. 10.

344. Chris Erlich, "*Sailing History Comes to Museum with Donation of Thunderbird #1*," Media Release, 14 December 2002.

345. *The Peninsula Gateway*, 22 February 1957.
346. "Former Rosedale Girl, National Famous Coffee Ground Reader," *The Peninsula Gateway*, 6 February 1948, p. 3.
347. *"Ripley's Believe It or Not,"* published in newspapers nationwide, 28 April 1937.
348. "Climber had humble start," *Tacoma News Tribune*, 27 June 1963, p. 1.
349. Forest Knapp interview by author, Gig Harbor, Wa., 9 December 2002.
350. James Ramsey Uhlman, *Americans on Everest*, p. 301.
351. Alvestad interview.
352. Gretchen Wilbert interview by author, Gig Harbor, Wa., 16 August 2004.
353. Adele Larson DeWalt interview by author, Wollochet Bay, Wa., 16 August 2004.
354. Don Hannula, "Gig Harbor 'Flips' For Jerstad," *Tacoma News Tribune*, 27 June 1963, pp. A1-A2.

Epilogue: The Only Thing Certain Is Change

355. Kwaahes: Peninsula High School Yearbook, 1963, p.18.
356. "New Peninsula Airport Dedication Saturday," *The Peninsula Gateway*, 31 October 1963, p. 1.
357. Barbara Pearson, Notes from Society's Scrapbooks and Minute Books, 1990 (manuscript in the collection of the Gig Harbor Peninsula Historical Society).
358. Randy Babich interview by author, Gig Harbor, Wa., 12 June 2004.
359. Harbor Inn Restaurant website http://www.harborinn.com/about.html, accessed 13 August 2004.
360. Lee Makovich, "The Varsity Remembered," *The Fishermen's News*, June 2003, pp. 14-16.

Index

A

B

Presbyterian Church
   Turner, Mary Jane 139

R

S

W

Y

Photo Index

Reprints of most photos are available for purchase. Call the society at 253/858-6722.

Page / Photo description`	GHPHS Catalog #	Source
(Chapter 1)		
16 / Native American family makes camp	NA-005	Bonnie Anderson
17 / Puget Sound Indian with tall ships	NA-007	
19 / Lt. Charles Wilkes		
22 / Early fishermen at mouth of harbor	BFSH-024	Frank Shaw*
23 / Early Gig Harbor	HV-112	Edna Wyatt
23 / Early Gig Harbor sand spit	HV-109	
(Chapter 2)		
27 / Sam Jerisich	PF-090	
29 / Sam Jerisich family	PF-091	Mike Jerisich
30 / Purse seining	BFSH-146	Vincent Planich
31 / Gill netter	BFSH-144	Vincent Planich
35 / Nick and Clementine Novakovich	PF-155	
36 / F. Novak and L. Kimball	PF-152	R.C. Mojean
36 / Josephine and John Novak	PF-695	N. Markovich, Sr.
38 / Annie Squally weaving basket	IND-652(S)	Dick Uhlman
(Chapter 3)		
41 / Miles Hunt family	PF-056	J. Lyle-Roberton
45 / Joseph Goodman	PF-810	Verna Wheeler
46 / Joseph Goodman family	PF-239	Verna Wheeler
49 / Dr. Alfred Mark Burnham	PF-015	
49 / Dr. A. M. Burnham and family	RES-089	
51 / Joseph Dorotich family	PF-156	
52 / Joseph Dorotich home at Millville	134(S)	Marie Gustafson
54 / Young's Landing	RES-036	
55 / Fennimore Young family, Courtesy of Chapel Hill Presbyterian Church		
(Chapter 4)		
56 / Gig Harbor, head of the bay	HV-026	
57 / *Messenger*	BSTM-055	Ed Goldman
59 / Ben Lay's Rosedale store by dock, Courtesy of Tacoma Public Library		
60 / Chrissy Yates	PF-787	Bob Crandall
60 / Yates and Lands await steamboat	PF-368	Rosemary Ross
61 / Lay Inlet, Courtesy of Tacoma Public Library		
63 / Steam Donkey	LG-002	Richard Rowley
63 / Removing logs by rail	LG-003	Richard Rowley
64 / Gig Harbor Sawmill Co.	BUS-258	
64 / Tall ships at Gig Harbor Sawmill Co.	BSAIL-002	Bujacich
65 / Prentice Shingle Mill	BUS-041	Frank Shaw*

67 / Rust and Johnston families PF-130
68 / Dr. Thomas J. Weekes, Courtesy of Chapel Hill Presbyterian Church
69 / Methodist Episcopal Church CH-009 Frank Shaw*
71 / *Victor*, Hunt steamboat BSTM-112 J. Lyle-Robertson
72 / Floyd Hunt PF-056 J. Lyle-Robertson
73 / Grand Army of the Republic Hall GH-173(S) Shirk-DeBolt

(Chapter 5)
75 / *Crest* loading produce BSTM-009 Mary Ambrose
77 / John and Lydia Carlson family picnic CH-052 Judy Gillette
78 / Charles Sehmel family at home RES-179 Don Sehmel
79 / Erik and Marta Sandin family PF-321 M.J. Packard
79 / Sandin family, Hunt Road bridge BDR-079 M.J. Packard
80 / Samuelson family picking berries FRM-030 N. S. McCormick
81 / Nils and Mary Shyleen home RES-178 E. Zimmerman
81 / Mabel Shyleen PF-180
82 / John and Lydia Carlson home RES-118 Mary Ambrose
85 / Goodman family picnic, Crescent Lake CE-092 Verna Wheeler
87 / Mabel Shyleen Ellis wedding photo PWED-002
89 / Peter Skansie PF-199
90 / Peter, Mitchell, Joe, Andrew Skansie PF-973 Uhlman, Ewing
90 / *Oceania* BFSH-024 Uhlman, Ewing
91 / *Defiance* ready for launch HV-205 Thelma Campbell
91 / Robert Crawford BB-023 Howard Green
92 / Conrad Anderson BFSH-046
92 / *Shenandoah* after launch, Courtesy of Washington State Historical Society, Tacoma

(Photo Section-Harvesting the sea)
93 / Fishing in trough on June 6, 1911 BFSH-046
93 / *Eagle* 1905 BFSH-052 Ebba Uddenberg
93 / *Aeroplane* and *Fairplay* 1906 BFSH-172 Uhlman, Ewing
94 / Peter Skansie on oar-powered boat BFSH-132 Hans Sauness
94 / Oar-powered fishing boat BFSH-184
94 / Christy Skarponi BC-023 Christy Skarponi
94 / *Avalon* and *Genius* BFSH-065 Don Gilich
95 / *Corregidor* BFSH-202 Castelan
95 / *Editor* BFSH-074 Pauline Stanich
95 / *George A* BFSH-028 Tarabochia
95 / *Glory of the Seas* BFSH-109 Minnie Malich
95 / Five fishing vessels BFSH-054 Helga Ross
96 / *Majestic* BFSH-019(S) Bujacich
96 / *Majestic* pulls up net full of fish BFSH-020(S) Bujacich
96 / J. Bujacich and *Majestic* crew BC-015 Bujacich
96 / T. Skrivanich and M. Bussanich, *Elector* BFSH-034
96 / *Victory* BFSH-063 Don Gilich
97 / Emmett Ross mends net BC-013 Helga Ross
97 / *Welcome*, Courtesy of the Jerkovich family

280

97 / *Spokane* crew   C-002
97 / Launch of *Pacific Raider*   CE-094

(Chapter 6)

99 / C.O. Austin Mill	BUS-016	Shaw Collection
100 / C.O. Austin Mill crew	BUS-052	F. & M. Erickson
100 / Rosedale Slough	BDR-041	
101 / Berries unloaded from *Crest*	BDR-032	Verna Wheeler
102 / Elias Muri family	PF-111	Earl Erickson
103 / *Crest* at Picnic Point	BSTM-019	
104 / Jacobson home, Crescent Valley	RUR-SC 126	
105 / Strout store	BUS-006	Shirley Dearth
105 / Novak's store	BUS-008	Dick Uhlman
106 / *Butcher*	BUS-370	Dick Uhlman
107 / Axel Uddenberg	PF-275	
107 / Axel Uddenberg store	BUS-003	
108 / Axel Uddenberg grocery wagon	BUS-008	
110 / Rosedale Union Church	CH-023	
110 / Cromwell Lutheran Church	Crmwl10(S)	McCormick
111 / Memorial Presbyterian Church	CH-011	J. Lyle-Roberton
112 / Presbyterian Ladies Aid Society	CH-001	Smith Snyder
113 / St. Nicholas Catholic Church	CH-025	Clara McCabe
114 / Methodist Ladies Aid Society	CH-010	
114 / Gustav Stromer with seaplane	TRANS-021	J. Lyle-Roberton
115 / Hunt family in automobile	PF-061	J. Lyle-Roberton
116 / First Gig Harbor ferry	BFER-002	R. C. Mojean
117 / Peace Day Celebration	CE-109	Eloise Siegner
118 / Herman Uddenberg	BUS-051	Mary Secor

(Chapter 7)

119 / E. and C.E. Trombley, *Peninsula Gateway*	E-01(N)	Shaw Collection
120 / John Watson, *History of Pierce County, Wash.*		
120 / Aimée Lowe, *History of Pierce County, Wash.*		
121 / Lowe homestead at Pt. Evans	RES-080	Kathleen Watson
122 / Watson neighborhood housewarming	CE-091	Kathleen Watson
123 / John Watson, PERCLAWAM, Union High School		
123 / Kathleen Watson, PERCLAWAM, Union High School		
123 / Kathleen Watson, senior play, PERCLAWAM, Union High School		
123 / Kathleen Watson, tennis champions, PERCLAWAM, Union High School		
123 / Alan Watson, PERCLAWAM, Union High School		
124 / Mayor Harold Ryan	PF-794	Dr. Harold Ryan
125 / A. Jerisich, J. Skansie, J. VanWaters	NAMER-002	Dick Uhlman
125 / Rachel Burnham	PF-076	Frank Shaw*
130 / Gig Harbor Stage	TRANS-024	Lola Kooley
132 / Lucy Goodman and class	SCH-043	
133 / Union High School	SCH-003	
134 / Peninsula Hotel, Sunset Pool Hall	S&B-028	

135 / Novak Hotel, service station, shoe repair   BUS-027
135 / First National Bank   BUS-031
137 / Philip Peyran's Hollycroft farm   FRM-008
137 / Finholm's Market   BUS-389   Ron Finholm
138 / Theresa Sweeney   PF-216
138 / Theresa Sweeney house   BUS-009   Leo Sweeney
139 / Sweeney Block   S&B-017   Dr. Harold Ryan
140 / Mary Jane Turner   CH-022
141 / Elsie Claussen   BSTM-045
145 / John Watson, senior play, *PERCLAWAM*, Union High School
148 / Horseshoe Lake   REC-018   Gustafson
149 / Fortnightly Club   ORG-022
150 / First air mail   CE-046   Bob Merry
152 / Clarence and Vie Shaw   PF-171   Shaw Collection
153 / Roosterettes start Rooster Races   CE-181   Shaw Collection

(Photo Section-Plying the waters)
155 / *Sentinel*   BSTM-069
155 / *Elsie C III* loading passengers   BSTM-044   M. Summerhays
155 / *Atalanta* and crew   BSTM-008   Packard, Mojean
155 / Well-dressed passengers   BSTM-015   Grace Woodruff
155 / Boarding steamer from rowboat   BSTM-079
156 / *Emrose*   BSTM-038
156 / *City of Tacoma, Defiance, Skansonia*   F-84 (N)   Shaw Collection
156 / *Wollochet*   BFER-017   Laura Rose
156 / *Gloria*   BFER-010   Leona Larson
157 / *Bay Island* at Arletta Dock   BSTM-021   Grace Woodruff
157 / *Arcadia*   BSTM-036
157 / *Burro*   BSTM-024
157 / *Florence K*, Courtesy of Tacoma Public Library

(Chapter 8)
163 / Caisson for First Narrows Bridge   NB-2157   Goldman
165 / Cable for bridge   89-34-51   Goldman
167 / First Narrows Bridge opens   NB-013   Goldman
171 / First Narrows Bridge twisting   NB-041   Joe Gotchy
174 / First Narrows Bridge falls   NB-232   James Bell
176 / Workers on wreakage, first bridge   NB-051   Goldman

(Chapter 9)
195 / Victory Garden   B-03(N)   Shaw Collection
203 / World War II memorial, Courtesy of Linda McCowen

(Chapter 10)
205 / Pierce County Library   G-61(N)   Shaw Collection
207 / Thriftway and pharmacy   S&B-005   Shaw Collection
208 / Finholm Market   FIC

282

* Photographs from Dr. A.M. Burnham home, preserved and donated to society by Frank Owen Shaw